CW00751670

INTO THE ARENA

THE CARE SERIES

Into the Arena

Why Christians should be involved in politics

PAUL MILLER

SERIES EDITOR
THE REVD DR NIGEL M DE S CAMERON

KINGSWAY PUBLICATIONS
EASTBOURNE

Unless otherwise indicated, biblical quotations are from the
New International Version © 1973, 1978, 1984
by The International Bible Society.

Front Cover photo: Tony Stone Photolibrary—London

ISBN 0 85476 282 5

Printed in Great Britain for
KINGSWAY PUBLICATIONS LTD
1 St Anne's Road, Eastbourne, E Sussex BN21 3UN by
Richard Clay Ltd, Bungay, Suffolk
Typeset by Nuprint Ltd, Harpenden, Herts

Introduction to the Series

All around us, Christians are waking up to their responsibility to *care*—for one another, and for all their neighbours in God's world. The old 'social gospel' has been discredited. It tried to rewrite the message and mission of the church as a social and political programme. Many evangelical Christians responded by retreating into a pietism which denied, in effect, that the gospel had social and political implications at all. But more and more they are being called back to their historic role as the heirs of Wilberforce and Shaftesbury. With a fresh confidence in its biblical mandate, the evangelical conscience has reawakened from its fearful slumbers.

Around twenty years ago, two historic developments marked the beginnings of this decisive move towards the recovery of our evangelical heritage. One was the establishment by the Evangelical Alliance of TEAR Fund, to channel evangelical care to needy people overseas. The other was the setting up of the nationwide Festival of Light—now known as CARE (Christian Action, Research and Education)—to channel evangelical concern for the nation. CARE expressed Christian concern through both practical caring initiatives and public, political campaigning.

The roots of CARE's understanding of its mission lie in our stewardship of God's world (which stems from our creation) and our obligations of neighbour-love (underlined anew in Jesus Christ). We have no option but to care for others; and there are two ways in which we may do so—by practical caring for those round about us, and by campaigning for the defence and enhancement of the Christian values of the nation.

This *CARE series* spans these twin concerns. Some books address major public questions, which may be highly controversial. Others focus on practical issues of Christian caring. We pray that this series will help many Christians think through our obligation to be 'salt and light' in society, as loving neighbours and responsible stewards.

NIGEL M DE S CAMERON

Acknowledgments

The author thanks Nigel Cameron, Ian Prior and Herbert Schlossberg for giving themselves to read and critique the early versions of this book. In challenging my thinking on a number of issues they have forced me to strengthen weak points and abandon hopeless ones. For this I am grateful.

I would be remiss if I did not also thank my wife Mary who generously gave up time so I could write. She also gave, in equally generous measures, advice on the book's style and content— advice I often adopted...eventually!

Contents

I

The King and I

Jerry Falwell is more often found on a pulpit, whipping up the southern faithful, than within Oxford's hushed halls of learning. Yet there he was in March 1985, debating at the union society. One student spoke up and welcomed him as 'the Ian Paisley of the Sunbelt'. Falwell, used to this sort of thing, deadpanned, 'Who's he?' Undeterred, the ardent heckler shot back with, 'The ayatollah of Northern Ireland.'

On the other side of the Atlantic, another university man, A. Giametti, President of Yale University, rose magisterially to his own pulpit to warn the 1,267 members of Yale's incoming freshman class against Falwell and his Moral Majority. Denouncing them as 'peddlars of coercion' and as 'angry at change, rigid in... chauvinistic slogans', he did his fatherly best to protect the innocent and impressionable young minds in his charge from the corruption of this new barbarian menace.

While many may differ from the Giamettis of this world—journalist William F. Buckley, Jr (himself a Yale graduate) wrote, 'To be lectured against the perils of the Moral Majority on entering Yale is on the order of being lectured on the danger of bedbugs on entering a brothel'—Giametti's alarmist view seems to predominate among our media and educational élites.

Why all the fuss? The outraged shrieks and high blood pressure all stem from this one fact: that Falwell mixes religion with politics. Announcing that 'I believe in the separation of church and state but not in the separation of God and government,' he went on the offensive against what he regarded as 'the politicisation of immorality in our society'. In 1979 he founded a political organisation to give a voice to the unheard 'moral majority' in America. He acted on moral absolutes. Worse, he acted on unpopular moral absolutes.

Falwell in the 1980s had moved a long way from his position in 1965. Then he chastised clergy for their involvement in the civil rights issue, stating:

> Believing the Bible as I do, I would find it impossible to stop preaching the pure saving gospel of Jesus Christ, and begin doing anything else— including fighting communism, or participating in civil rights reforms.... Preachers are not called to be politicians but to be soul winners.[1]

Who is right: the Falwell of 1965 or the Falwell of 1985? Not even Christians are united as to the answer. Clamorous opposition to Falwell came not only from the camp of the secular humanists; it came from the church of Jesus Christ as well. Staunch fundamentalist Bob Jones (of Bob Jones University) went so far as to say that Jerry Falwell was the greatest instrument of Satan in America today![2] Clive Calver, head of the Evangelical Alliance of England and Wales, in an address to Christians filling the Albert Hall, London, in 1988, to stand against abortion, soothingly reassured his listeners that 'we are not starting another Moral Majority'.

Britain, trying to accommodate both an established church and a pluralistic society, is hardly clearer than America. The halls of power in Westminster hold an equally jaundiced view towards mixing politics with religion. When the Anglican report on inner cities, *Faith in the City*, was made public, Tory cabinet ministers erupted with indignant denunciations of mixing faith with politics. Clergy were told that they should stick to their province— heaven—and let the politicians get on with their particular patch—the earth; the then Prime Minister, Margaret Thatcher, led this particular charge in her usual spirited manner.

What do we, as Christians, think? What does the Bible say about all this? Is our faith dynamic when kept to the private sphere of personal morality but dangerous when allowed to intrude into the public sphere of legislation? Just what is the relationship of the gospel to government? Shouldn't Christians leave the business of government to the world while they get on with the real business of saving souls? After all, isn't government insignificant in the light of eternity? Isn't it useless for changing hearts and a dispiriting effort to organise chaos anyway? (Well summed up in a slip made by Chicago's Mayor Daley when, during the riots of the 1968 Democratic Convention, he told reporters, 'Gentlemen, get the thing straight once and for all. The policeman isn't there to create disorder, the policeman is there to preserve disorder.')

The dominion mandate

To begin to answer these questions let's first look at what has been called the 'cultural mandate' or the 'dominion mandate' of the Bible. Genesis 1:26 and 28 states:

> Then God said, 'Let us make man in our image, in our likeness, and let them rule over the fish of the sea and the birds of the air, over the livestock, over all the earth, and over all the creatures that move along the ground.'... God blessed them and said to them, 'Be fruitful and increase in number; fill the earth and subdue it. Rule over...every living creature....'

Here is the dominion mandate in the opening chapters of the Bible. Rule! Take dominion. Rule under me! Man and woman were made in the image of God. As God was a ruler (*the* ruler), so they were to be rulers. Genesis 1 highlights this as the very first consequence of man and woman's 'creatureship', of being made like God. 'Let us make man in our image...and let them rule.' So central was God's dominion mandate that it is the very first feature mentioned about man and woman after their creation. Rule with God. It's the King and I ruling over creation.

Notice that the sphere of man and woman's dominion was not the heavens but the earth. God's interest was evidently not solely in things spiritual but in things material. The 'fish...birds...livestock...the earth' are what were on his mind in this commissioning service. God's enthusiasms are not narrowed to prayer and praise but extend to potatoes and peas! Life before the Fall did not consist of one l-o-n-g Bible study.

I think it is obvious that God was not only giving man and woman a mandate in the fields of agriculture and animal husbandry—the two fields mentioned specifically here in Genesis. These were only illustrative of the entire created order which they were to explore and rule. Man and woman were not only to develop agriculture and horticulture but 'culture' full stop—the world of the arts and literature, the life of the mind. This is why the dominion mandate can also be called the 'cultural mandate'.

Psalm 115:16 says, 'The highest heavens belong to the Lord, but the earth he has given to man.' God has delegated his rulership to us. What we have here is not a God whose stretching cosmic responsibilities leave him reluctant to take on yet another world with its multiplying opportunities and its multiplying problems. God does not have a time management problem! No, rather God shares authority with us out of the goodness of his heart. Humanity is God's junior partner, not his dogsbody.

Psalm 103:19 states, 'The Lord has established his throne in heaven, and his kingdom rules over all.' Here we see that though God's throne (the symbol of absolute authority) is in heaven, his authority is not limited to this sphere. His rulership extends to everything, both in heaven and on earth—'over all' is the way the psalmist puts it. 'All' is a very comprehensive word. It is no accident that the psalmist used it. There is nothing, whether spiritual or material, outside the kingdom of God. God's kingdom was meant to rule not only over the church but over economics, education, science, the media, entertainment, government, and so on.

Ezekiel 36:2 records a revelation given to the prophet: 'This is what the Sovereign Lord says: The enemy said of you, "Aha! The ancient heights have become our possession." ' The enemy's plan, then, was to take possession of Israel's inheritance, and that is his same plan today. Whereas Christ said, 'The meek shall inherit the earth,' Satan boasts, 'The weak shall inherit nothing, pal! You take Wednesday nights and Sunday mornings and I'll take the rest. You take the church and I'll take the media, the schools and universities, the businesses.'

In an article in *The Guardian*, Geoffrey Taylor appealed to the Christian church in the following terms:

> No Darwinian struggle to survive explains why 'lower' animals carry on their struggle without cruelty while we almost glory in it at times. I sometimes wish the churches would give a bit more attention to this question and not be ashamed of the answers they come up with. After all, they ask us to believe in God, which most people tell the opinion pollsters they do. Why should we not equally believe in the devil, and a devil who is constantly trying to undermine the work of God?... Indeed, one of the advantages of a Judaeo-Christian view of creation... is that it explains evil better than any other hypothesis.[3]

Satan wants to divert believers from their inheritance. He wants to torpedo the efforts of well-meaning unbelievers so that strife and darkness prevail at every level of society. Can't we see everywhere his malevolent influence working hand in hand with human sin? Consider the following.

The family. This institution set up by God as an avenue of blessing between men and women, and between children and adults, is often just the opposite. In the mid-1980s in England and Wales, two-thirds of all murders were by a husband of his wife or vice versa. About 25 per cent of all violent crimes reported to the police were assaults on wives!

Education. Two of London's school districts, Haringey and Ealing, were instructed in 1986 by their local councillors to root out 'heterosexist propaganda'.[4] Schoolchildren were to be impartially presented with a full selection of sexual lifestyles before deciding whether to follow the norm or not. Is this healthy education or training in perversion? Why not try the same 'open-minded' approach with sado-masochistic sex? At a certain point 'impartiality' becomes cowardly indecisiveness. In Haringey and Ealing that point was passed long ago.

At Harper Elementary School in Evansville, Indiana, the principal barred Christian workers from meeting together before classes even though other teachers and aids were allowed to gather and talk about politics and sports. One school board member's reasoning was that children might see the teachers with a Bible and religious materials, and 'We don't want the children exposed to them.'[5]

Expose them to homosexuality but protect them from the Bible! If it sounds topsy-turvy it's because it is.

Media. 'If it's bad news, print it' reigns as the operative principle of our organs of communication. While possessing tremendous potential to enlighten and elevate, the media have equal potential to degrade and mislead.

For instance, the media were influential in driving Christianity, of the fundamentalist variety, into America's cultural backwater early on in our present century. Media events such as the Scopes 'Monkey Trial' in 1925—over the issue of evolution—were snapped up as key opportunities to further the 'progressive' agenda. Instead of fairly and objectively reporting the intelligent arguments on both sides, the evolutionists were depicted as the forces of light, progress and intelligence, nobly battling Christian bigots and obscurantists.

H.L. Mencken's coverage was typical. A brilliant journalist, notorious for his scathing sarcasm, Mencken hated fundamentalism and puritanism (which he identified as 'the haunting fear that someone, somewhere, may be happy'[6]). Even the death, one week after the trial, of William Jennings Bryan, the fundamentalist defending Tennessee's anti-evolutionary law, did not slow Mencken's acid pen. Acid cannot afford to be delicate.

In Mencken's anti-eulogy to Bryan—thrice defeated Democratic presidential candidate and former Secretary of State—he wrote that it was appropriate that Bryan had spent his last days in a 'one-horse Tennessee village' because Bryan loved all country people, including the 'gaping primates of the upland valleys', and delighted in 'greasy victuals of the farmhouse kitchen, country smells' and 'the tune of cocks crowing on the dunghill'. Bryan had made the grade of a country saint. 'His place in Tennessee hagiography is secure. If the village barber saved any of his hair, then it is curing gall-stones down there today.'[7]

If God was not made to look stupid, his followers were.

Government. The twentieth century, too, often seems to be the record of governments bringing not peace and order but war and chaos. World War I saw the flower of the youth of Britain and Europe extinguished. Fathers never came home; laughing eyes turned cold with the finality of death. A mere twenty-one years later the brooding resentments left from the first war flashed up into another worldwide conflagration which snuffed out more multiplied millions.

Now I believe taking up arms is quite justified under certain conditions, but one does not need to be a pacifist to know that such slaughter as our 'enlightened' century has seen is as evil as it is tragic.

Governments have not only warred against foreign nations, they have warred against their own people. In 1988 an official Soviet newspaper, *Nedelya*, admitted for the first time that during the Stalin era as many as fifty million were killed or condemned to the labour camps from which they never emerged. The figures do not include the twenty million Russians who died due to World War II.[8]

Should Christians throw up their hands in despair, saying, 'What do you expect? Sin and Satan are everywhere. Things won't get any better till Jesus returns to rescue us from this mess'?

Never! Jesus did not end his ministry in defeat and despair. He rose in triumph! He has provided a remedy for sin and a bulwark against Satan that is effective in this age as well as in the age to come. This world will never be heaven but it needn't be hell either.

When Christ rose he left behind his church to take his victory to the world. We are to take his kingdom into every nook and cranny; into every sphere of the world—media, government, and so on. It is said that nature abhors a vacuum; well, so does the supernatural. If good vacates the sphere of government then evil will move in. It was Adolf Hitler who said to a gathering of pastors 'interfering' with government policies, 'I will protect the German people. You take care of the church. You pastors should worry about getting people to heaven and leave this world to me.'[9]

All the world

John 17:14–19 records Jesus' words: 'They are not of the world.... My prayer is not that you take them out of the world.... I have sent them into the world.' Jesus' strategy was not one of withdrawal from the world but of *penetration* into all the world. His word to his disciples was 'Go.' They were not to wait for the world to come to them.

'Go into all the world,' said Jesus (Mk 16:15). 'All the world' was primarily geographical, but not only geographical. Mission enthusiasts have begun to point out in recent years that we have not fulfilled this command to go into 'all the world' simply by placing missionaries in every country and county of the world. Our focus must not only be on geographical units but on 'people groups' and cultural units. One geographical unit may contain ten different people groups. The missionaries may be reaching two or three of these cultural groups while completely missing the other seven to eight. 'All the world' evangelism is only satisfied when these neglected people groups are also penetrated with the gospel.

But 'all the world' is even more extensive than geographical and cultural; it is also occupational (to use the term loosely). The world is divided into a multiplicity of occupations which can be categorised into roughly seven areas: church, family, education, arts and entertainment, media, business, and government. These have been termed 'the mind-moulders' by Youth With A Mission founder Loren Cunningham, due to their crucial role in forming the beliefs, assumptions and values in every human society. They are the leaven in society for either good or evil. They originate values, form values and communicate values.

Have we really done our job of going into 'all the world' if we have not penetrated these areas with gospel values? I don't think so. I don't think so because of God's desire, as seen in the scriptures quoted above, to express his sovereignty over every aspect of life: over things spiritual, things material and things cultural.

Note that John the Baptist did not confine himself to preaching about the coming Messiah. He also concerned himself with the family and work lives of his listeners. He instructed tax collectors and soldiers how to conduct themselves in their professions (see Luke 3:10–14). He eventually got himself killed, not for preaching theology but for bringing home some choice truths about King Herod's family life (see Mark 6:18–19). God's kingdom extends over all of life.

The following diagram may help you see more clearly the job before us of reaching 'all the world' in the full sense of the word.

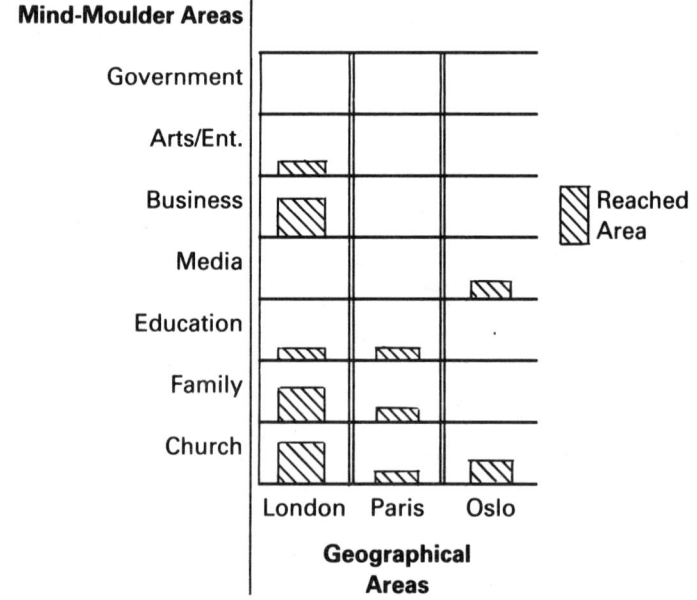

The horizontal axis represents the geographical spheres: the nations, the cities, the villages, the jungles. The church was sent out to reach 'all the world' in its most basic, literal, geographic sense. Missionaries were to cross oceans and trek over deserts in order to take the gospel into every corner of our world.

The vertical axis depicts the mind-moulder, cultural spheres present in each of the geographical areas. Mark 16:15 has not been fulfilled simply by the establishment of a church in any given geographical sphere. Once rooted in a place the good news must also penetrate into these mind-moulders, into the family, into business life, into educational practice. A society cannot really be considered 'already reached' until this has happened. Where this has not happened the chart is bare, depicting the shallow reach of the gospel in that particular locality.

Human life is not structured just into geographical units. It is also structured according to the mind-moulding units of jobs, vocations and clubs. We relate not only to our physical neighbour, we relate along job lines, vocational lines and through areas of common interest. This world of jobs, vocations and clubs is what we mean by the mind-moulders. Each of these mind-moulders has its own norms, its own values and thought-forms which must be salted with the gospel. We really have not finished our job until we have penetrated the mind-moulder squares on the chart along with the geographical squares.

Evangelism may be the first order of business but it's not the last.

The God-shrinkers

Christians convinced that Jesus is 'Lord of all or not Lord at all', convinced that they should therefore take the kingdom into every facet of life, will not find it easy to put these convictions to work. They face two major trends at work in our society which will slow them down. Possibly, they will stop them from ever getting started. These are the 'God-shrinkers', beliefs which would confine the God of the heavens and the earth to one slice of life. But he doesn't want one slice; he made the whole pie! One of these trends is at work in society in general, the other at work in the church. The first trend is secularisation; the second trend is pietism.

Secularisation has been defined as:

the process through which...successive sectors of society and culture have been freed from the decisive influence of religious ideas and institutions. In other words, secularization is the process by which we have neutralized the social and cultural significance of religion in the central areas of modern society, such as the worlds of science, technology, bureaucracy and so on, making religious ideas less meaningful and religious institutions more marginal.[10]

So secularisation works on two levels: on the level of institutions and on the level of ideas. The institution of the church, which was once the focal point of society, is replaced by other institutions. Whereas once the church was at the centre of education, welfare, the arts and government, its activities have been taken over by non-religious bodies.[11] The professional has replaced the priest. The church as an institution has stepped out, or been forced out, to the sidelines. No longer is it the key player in society it once was. It is seen as a frumpy onlooker doddering along on its last legs. Its tinkerings can be politely indulged without being seriously entertained.

On the level of ideas, secularisation relegates faith to the bin marked 'superstitions'. Faith is out and science is in. The test-tube mentality is king. 'Seeing is believing.' Rationality, in its narrowest sense, lords it over our Western cultures and shoots down anything that dares raise its head on the horizon. Technology, not divine intervention, is seen as the 'obvious' solution to the ills of mankind. This is secularisation at work.

If secularisation makes the church's institutions seem irrelevant, it makes its ideas seem outdated. In a secularised society, all this talk about God and sin, heaven and hell, sounds embarrassingly simple-minded ('Adam and Eve? You can't be serious?!'), hidebound and, well, just not 'modern'. And, of course, to be modern is good and to be old-fashioned is bad. Of course!

Secularisation is what makes modern life modern.[12] It is at the heart of modern man and modern society. Our modern era (1600 until today) is set apart from the past great eras of Western civilisation—the ancient pagan era (up until AD 300), and the medieval, church era (from AD 300 to 1600)—by just this aspect of secularisation. Paganism and Christianity were deadly enemies but they were united in this one thing: they took the supernatural seriously. The new paganism sympathises with the old paganism's morals, while jettisoning its gods as dark nonsense. It is a paganism that has been secularised and sanitised for one-dimensional minds.

Our world is secular, modern, and proud of it. In G.K. Chesterton's words:

> The 20th century is the only period in all human history where men brag of being modern. For though today is always today, and the moment is always modern, we are the only men in all history who fell back upon bragging about the mere fact that today is not yesterday.

Our civilisation has equated the mere passage of time with progress. It has forgotten that the passage of time also means encroaching infirmity and death.

It is this mindset which so powerfully grips all our modern, Westernised societies. Counter it by introducing God into the everyday practicalities of life and you will run straight into this great wall of prejudice, this unquestioned assumption of modernity. Those not ready for a fight had better not even step into the arena.

If we are to be world changers, if we ever expect to take the kingdom into 'all the world', then we will have to develop King David's trick of being hard of hearing yet sharp of eyesight. While the whole of the Hebrew army saw an impressive giant, Goliath, David saw an impressive God (1 Sam 17:47). While God's army heard Goliath's boastful challenge and quaked, for David it was a case of 'in one ear and out the other' (1 Sam 17:11ff).

Shall the world influence us or shall we influence the world? Do we believe, with the Bible, that 'his kingdom rules over all', or do we believe with the secularisers that 'his kingdom rules over the church hall—and that's all'? Believe God's word. Act on it. Believing precedes acting. If we do not really believe something, we won't actually act on it. Hence the high priority the devil puts on his lying ministry. No, we will never begin to introduce the kingdom into law, economics, the arts, and so on, if we don't believe God has any business being there.

But it is not just secularisation which persuades us that God has no place in the mind-moulders; it is also pietism within the church. Pietism began as a healthy reaction against dry formalism and a too abstract Christianity. It emphasised the personal devotional disciplines of prayer and Bible reading. But it too readily grew to opposing the spiritual (good) to the material (bad), the devotional (good) to the intellectual (bad). When pietism was wedded to the fervent evangelistic outlook of most evangelical churches, it res-

ulted in the 'lifeboat' view of Christian mission. Instead of seeing
the gospel as the salt which would work through all segments of
society, preserving that which was godly, the gospel was seen
simply as an emergency rescue mechanism to pull people out of,
and away from, a hopelessly decadent world. A pietist would make
no attempt to improve society. Typically, he would desert society
while trying to take as many people as possible with him.

Do not mistake me. We need to sense the urgency of the
'lifeboat mentality' in rescuing sinners from a decidedly wicked
world. The Bible holds no punches on this score. But the gospel is
greater than a lifeboat; it's an ocean liner. It's not merely bobbing
on a powerful ocean of sin; it's cruising along on those very same
raging waters, majestic and undaunted, making for its predeter-
mined destination.

Jesus did not say, 'Desert the world.' He said, 'Go into all the
world.' The pietistic emphasis on personal, devotional disciplines is
good as long as it is wed to the dominion mandate. Without
devotional disciplines Christian salt will be tasteless. Yuck! Without the dominion mandate Christian salt will be useless. Christian
salt bottled up in a shaker makes a good centre-piece, but table
decoration is not what Christ had in mind. Christian salt is to make
the world thirsty for God. It is meant to halt the rot of sin.

Millions of slaves must have rejoiced that William Wilberforce
was no pietist running from the world of politics. Early on in his
political career, Wilberforce underwent a conversion to Christianity. He questioned everything: himself, his God, his religion,
his destiny. He began to feel that if he would live for God he must
withdraw from the world. Confused, torn with conflicting emo-
tions, he sought spiritual counsel. He made his way secretly (the
fashionable world of 1785 regarded the evangelicals with contempt
and suspicion) to his boyhood hero, the sixty-year-old ex-sailor, ex-
slave trader, ex-lecher, John Newton, now a vicar and author of the
well-loved hymn 'Amazing Grace'. Newton—contrary to the general run of evangelicalism which shunned public life as worldly—
advised Wilberforce not to cut himself off from his present circles
or to withdraw from public life, writing to him, 'It is hoped and
believed that the Lord has raised you up for the good of His church
and for the good of the nation.'[13] How right he was he little knew.
Twenty-two years after this twilight interview, the slave trade was
abolished throughout the British empire, and that primarily due to

the determined labours of one man; one man who decided to take his Christian convictions into Parliament—William Wilberforce.

Vocation

I have two heroes in my life, each cut from very different cloth. One is C.S. Lewis, a shining light in the intellectual and literary world. He was learned, cultured, vastly interesting, gently eccentric (that is to say, quintessentially English), the producer of scores of captivating and enlightening essays which delight us still today. He was also devout and influential in the spiritual growth of innumerable individuals.

General William Booth and his Salvation Army were very different characters indeed. They were deliberately unlearned in the literature of the world, completely uninterested in the genteel arts, the rough and ready buccaneers of street evangelism, outspoken and wildly adventurous fools for Christ. If C.S. Lewis was the master of the light touch, they were masters of the gospel broadside. They caused such a stir that thousands of street 'roughs' formed bands of Skeleton Armies to physically halt their trumpeting parades and forthright evangelism. They shook England, the world and hell.

I admire both but whom should I emulate? C.S. Lewis entered the world of education. He spent much of his time with students, poring over medieval literature. He embodied the cultural mandate. The Salvation Army left all that to concentrate on direct evangelism. 'First things first' was their attitude. 'Who can give time to frivolity and culture when there is a war on? Every man into the breech!' They were the embodiment of the evangelistic mandate. The Great Commission was their one and only call. What is the model for us?

The concept of calling, or vocation, helps us here. We are involved in many different activities, all of which claim our time and commitment. We are involved in church activities, job responsibilities, personal growth goals, family and civic duties, and so on. At the centre, though, of all these activities is our calling, that ministry which God has called us to do which must not be sacrificed for anything else. No one involves himself exclusively in his area of calling. Our lives are broader than that. Nevertheless, many of these other involvements are optional. Our calling, however, is obligatory. It is non-negotiable. A Christian does not toss out his calling as he might his bridge night. It is at the core of life.

We cannot do everything. A sense of vocation will show us just what we should be doing. It will guide us as to exactly where we should be concentrating our efforts. The alternative is to run everywhere, trying to do a bit of this and a bit of that, and never really finish anything. If we hear a speaker describing the crying need for evangelism we'll start making plans for Bible school and the mission field—until we hear the next speaker, who emphasises that really the church's current, pressing priority is saving the unborn facing abortion. So off we run until we are faced with the next dynamic speaker's message on the church's call to the poor and downtrodden. We cannot do everything. Do not mechanically copy someone else's lifestyle: 'If I want him to remain alive until I return, what is that to you?' (Jn 21:22). Sort out with God which one of the mind-moulders you are called to. Then follow him no matter what.

Partnership

The church of Jesus Christ is an international, multi-ministry affair that needs both the C.S. Lewises and the General Booths. It needs those called to the church and those called to government. Only then will the kingdom come 'on earth as it is in heaven'. In heaven, the kingdom rules over every aspect of life, *especially* the government ('King' and 'kingdom' are governmental words). Heaven is the place where all is governed totally by the will of God.

The work of the kingdom is a partnership where each of us needs to play his different, God-ordained role. 'I planted the seed, Apollos watered it, but God made it grow.... For we are God's fellow workers' (1 Cor 3:6, 9). Some are called to pastor, some to the business world; some to be evangelists, some to be politicians; some to the front lines of foreign missions, some to support them from home. Paul was called to be a preacher, Daniel was called into the government of a pagan king.

In 1983 Youth With A Mission, an international mission dedicated to world evangelism, was given (!) a 173-foot long, 1,053 ton vessel. The gift was an amazing demonstration of how vocations can work differently, but together. The vessel was to be used as a mercy ship for the nations. With holds able to carry 80 tons of normal cargo, and with berths for sixty people, she was ideal for carrying supplies to smaller ports that her much bigger sister ship, the *Anastasis*, could not enter. The story behind this gift is as fascinating as it is instructive.

A Baptist electronics manufacturer, Keith Larkin, bought the *Petite Forte* to fulfil a twenty-year dream. It started as a dream to own a private yacht. As the years went by, God enlarged the vision and Keith and his family began to see that God wanted the ship for his own purpose. They would run it as a ministry—use it to expand the kingdom.

Keith manufactures telephone headsets for Bell and NASA. The Columbia space shuttle flights have used his equipment. Over the years he attended church on occasion and gave a little money to the poor. In 1977 God began to really get hold of Keith, his family and his business. Commitment to Christ began to grip every area of their lives. Their business, which was struggling, was committed 100 per cent to God's work. They had a compulsion to turn everything over to the support of world evangelism.

As a family—husband, wife and children—they decided that they would have few personal assets, that everything would go into a trust to support missions. They all agreed. They all worked hard in the company and God began to bless. Keith said, 'I never knew the joy of total commitment. It is fun to just follow God. My wife and three children are completely a part of this.'

Keith and his family finally saw the opportunity to fulfil this life-long dream of a ship for God in 1983 when they heard about the *Petite Forte*. You can imagine their excitement as they saw God provide for the purchase and initial sailing. Walking the decks for the first time as owner, Keith thanked God for this fulfilment of a promise and a dream.

As Keith spent his first night with his family on the vessel—his promise ship—sleep just would not come. He lay tossing on his bunk. Then God spoke: 'Keith, you are not a missionary. You're really an electronics businessman. I want you to tear this thing out of your heart and give it to Youth With A Mission. Let these professionals do the work—you go back and build electronics.' Keith simply says, 'I had to obey.'

God had a vital role for Keith Larkin but it was not to be as a front-line missionary. His role was to launch the *Petite Forte*, appropriately renamed the *Good Samaritan*, into world ministry. YWAM's role was to take it up and do the ministry. Because of his obedience, tens of thousands in the ports of the world will be presented with the two-handed gospel, one hand dispensing physical aid, the other hand the word of life.

Government is part of the world too

If all that I have been saying above is true, then the answer to the question with which we opened this chapter, the question as to whether Christians have any right to be involved in politics, should be obvious. Politics is part of the world that Christ came to redeem. It's his world. Of course he has a right to it. And so do his children.

But if we have settled this question, we still have not settled the thorniest question: Just how is Christ's rule meant to be expressed in the political realm? That Christ wants to rule over politics is settled, I trust. But *how* should Christians express this rule? We agree that God's word is relevant to the realm of politics; but just how is it relevant? Put it another way: that God has something to say is clear, but just *what* is he saying? That is far from being obvious. Should we be aiming for a theocracy? A tyranny of the just? Should we allow compromise with God's standards? Should we allow sinful laws to be legislated? Should we try to legislate morality? What exactly should we be aiming at?

The principle stands: 'He who aims at nothing hits it.' Merely getting stirred up about the dominion theme gets us nowhere. We need to get biblically informed. Only then can we get biblically involved.

I think the old Greek was probably right who said, 'History is philosophy teaching us by examples.' Now if it is also true that those who cannot remember the past are condemned to repeat it, then perhaps our best starting point is past history. Let's look back in history to see how the church has attempted to handle the relationship between the gospel and the government. Perhaps then we can begin to find some answers to questions that desperately need answering.

2

The Gospel and Government in History

Broadly speaking, the church has four different models of church/state interaction. We shall look at each of these models as adopted by the following Christian churches: Anabaptist, Roman Catholics and Reformed, Lutherans, and Baptists. The following line graph gives a pictorial overview of the historical setting of each of these positions, showing the date of entry and the time span involved.

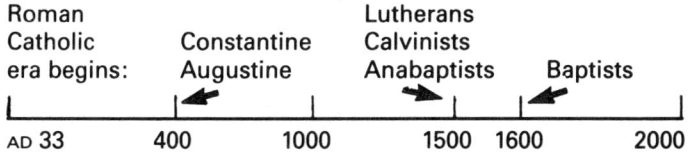

We will examine each position briefly.

Anabaptists

'Total withdrawal' just about sums up the Anabaptist position towards politics. During the sixteenth-century Reformation, while the mainline Protestants (the Lutherans and the Calvinists) were breaking away from the Roman Cathlics, an even more radical movement was born: the Antibaptists—the pioneers of much that the average evangelical believes today.

They infuriated the mainline Reformers by insisting that infant baptism did not save anybody. They taught that baptism was a sign of conversion, of repentance and faith; they held that, as an infant could not really respond to Jesus' call to 'Come and follow me', infant baptism was unbiblical. The Anabaptists also objected to the Reformers' concept of a 'state church' to which everybody belonged by birth and baptism. They contended that the church was entered only by a 'new birth', by those who accepted Christ's call to costly discipleship. These views were, in the Reformers' eyes, a threat to the spiritual reformation of society—a threat that had to be nullified.

Anabaptists threatened more than just the religious leaders, they also threatened the civil rulers with their view of church/state relations: they taught that no real Christian could in good conscience hold government office, take any kind of oath of allegiance or fight in the army. The Anabaptist Articles of Schleitheim (1527) called the magistrate's office 'carnal' and said that the magistrate's sword is to be rejected by Christians as 'outside the perfection of Christ'.[14] Anabaptist leader Peter Ridemann taught that 'No Christian is a ruler and no ruler is a Christian.'[15]

Anabaptists accepted that government was necessary for the physical restraint of evil and they believed that the government and the sword were both ordained by God. The rub, however, was in their preaching that these roles were appropriate only for the heathen.

They understood the Sermon on the Mount as God's comprehensive word on moral behaviour. They were also convinced that this sermon plainly proclaimed non-resistance to be the Christian's sole possible response to evil. This is why Anabaptists said that the use of force, even by a policeman, was sinful and 'outside the perfection of Christ'. This view, of course, effectively nullifies Christian involvement in government, for what is government if it has no sword behind it? It seems that the Anabaptists tried to govern the world as if it were the church; seeing that this was impossible, they decided it was better not to govern it at all. Withdrawal was better than compromise.

The Anabaptists taught that God never meant his people to waste efforts on restraining evil or reforming society. Instead, we should be converting society. The Christian was not to patch up the old society but devote himself to building God's new society, the church. Total withdrawal from the governing of society was their answer to the church/state dilemma.

Roman Catholic and Reformed

The exact opposite view was held by Calvinists (the Reformed churches) and Roman Catholics. Their view could be titled 'dominion means dominance'. It may seem strange to lump together the Roman and Reformed theologies but, for our purpose here, we can do so with ease—they substantially agreed with one another on political philosophy. Roman Catholic theologian John A. Coleman, SJ, has written: 'In general, Calvinist theories of church and state will be closer than other Protestant options to Thomistic Catholic positions.'[16]

The Roman Catholic position had been firmed up during that historical period known as the Middle Ages. The Middle Ages witnessed the see-sawing back and forth of power between the Catholic Popes and the civil rulers, with the Popes claiming the right to govern not just the church but civil society as well. This power battle went through three stages.[17] In the first period, from AD 700 to 1050, the Pope theoretically held supreme temporal lordship but, in fact, the emperor was supreme. Popes attempted to emulate the high-handed approach of the early Bishop of Milan, Ambrose (AD 373–397), who brought the Roman emperor Theodosius to his knees on several occasions. Paul Johnson tells us:

> During the reign of Theodosius, Christian mob attacks on synagogues became common.... In 388 the Jewish synagogue of Callinicum on the Euphrates was burnt down at the instigation of the local bishop. Theodosius decided to make this a test-case, and ordered it rebuilt at Christian expense. Ambrose hotly opposed the decision.... He wrote to Theodosius: 'Which is more important, the parade of discipline or the cause of religion? The maintenance of civil law is secondary to religious interest.' He preached a sermon on these lines in the emperor's presence, and Theodosius lamely withdrew his orders.[18]

During the early Middle Ages, such attempts to subdue the civil power to the power of the church usually failed. The rulers could afford to ignore the church and did so with pleasure.

During the second period of the Middle Ages (1050–1300), however, the church claimed and held temporal lordship. Popes claimed the right to be judged by no one, the right to depose emperors, the right to absolve subjects from allegiance to the civil rulers. They claimed that rulers should kiss the feet of Christ's representative here on earth—the Pope!

Pope Boniface VIII wrote in 1296:

> Both [swords] are in the power of the church, the spiritual sword and
> the material. But the latter is to be used for the church, the former by
> her; the former by the priest, the latter by kings and captains but at the
> will and by the permission of the priest. The one sword, therefore,
> should be under the other, and temporal authority subject to spir-
> itual.... If, therefore, the earthly power err, it shall be judged by the
> spiritual power.... But if the spiritual power err, it can only be judged
> by God, not by man.[19]

These papal claims were not wholly to be deplored, however.
They were a welcome counterbalance to the religious pretensions
of the secular rulers of the day. The papacy may have had mis-
placed secular pretensions; it is no less true that kings and
emperors had inflated religious pretensions. The confluence in one
office of both religious and secular authority is a sure-fire recipe for
oppression. Historian R.W. Southern comments on the 'sacred
character' of these early secular rulers that 'set them above bishops
and priests in the government of the Christian community'.[20] Prior
to the eleventh century, it was not the Pope but the emperor who
carried the title 'vicar of Christ'.[21] Kings and emperors controlled
much of the church: they owned much of the church's property,
they appointed bishops, called church councils and promulgated
church law.[22] One twelfth-century document, the *Norman Anony-
mous*, even claimed that 'both Christ's kingship and priesthood are
transferred directly to kings through the sacrament of coronation.
As vicar of Christ, the king...can perform sacra-
ments...communion...can forgive sins.'[23]

During this second period of the Middle Ages, the papacy began
afresh to resist secular rulers' religious pretensions. Pope Gregory
VII, in 1075,

> declared the political and legal supremacy of the papacy over the entire
> church and the independence of the clergy from secular control. Gre-
> gory also asserted the ultimate supremacy of the pope in secular mat-
> ters, including the authority to depose emperors and kings.[24]

Gregory was to be applauded for freeing the church from the rule
of secular kings. We only regret that he went well beyond that to
assert the church's rule over the state.

Archbishop Thomas à Becket echoed Pope Gregory's themes,

both good and bad, in his challenge to King Henry II of England in the 1160s. The dispute started in 1163 when King Henry began to deal with numerous cases of clerical theft and violent robbery. Since his coronation in 1157 there had been a reported 100 murders committed by clerks of the religious orders. Thomas à Becket denied the king the right to try these cases, saying:

> The clergy, by reason of their orders and distinctive office, have Christ alone as King. . . . And since they are not under secular kings, but under their own king, the King of Heaven, they should be ruled by their own law; and if they are transgressors they should be punished by their own law, which had its own means of coercion. . . . Christian kings ought to submit their administration to ecclesiastics, not impose it upon them. . . . Christian princes should be obedient to the dictates of the church, rather than prefer their own authority, and princes should bow their heads to bishops rather than judge them.[25]

Not surprisingly, the king's relationship with Becket grew increasingly strained. Eventually, one of Henry's knights killed Becket—and whether this was done at the clear command of the king or by the initiative of a knight intent on pleasing his lord is to this day unclear.

During the third period of the Middle Ages (1300–1520), the secular rulers established their ascendancy over the Pope; the church as an institution lost its political dominance over society; the Pope's ultimate weapon, excommunication, lost its sting.

While the reality of church power was lost, the Catholic Church never abandoned its theory of church dominance. Right up until the twentieth century the Catholic Church condemned freedom of religion. The modern, liberal, pluralistic state was damned as a heresy. Pope Pius XII said in 1939: 'That which does not correspond to the truth and the norm of morality has, objectively, no right either to existence or to propaganda or to action.'[26] Error had no right to exist.

Calvin held similar views. He felt that civil government, along with its secular purposes, was to be a tool of the church in furthering spiritual aims. He wrote:

> Holy Kings are greatly praised in Scripture because they restored the worship of God when it was corrupted or destroyed, or took care of religion that under them it might flourish pure and unblemished. . . .

This proves the folly of those who would neglect the concern for God and would give attention only to rendering justice among men.[27]

The law was there to help people be better Christians. Geneva, under Calvin's sway, passed laws in keeping with this philosophy. In 1558 the Geneva Council passed 'sumptuary laws' limiting the conspicuous consumption of food and displays of dress. Hair arrangements and types of adornment were carefully regulated. Banquets were not allowed to feature more than three courses or more than four dishes per course.[28]

In 1546, in an effort to control overeating and drinking, five *abbayes* were created to replace Geneva's taverns. Here

> the host was to allow no improper language, dice playing, dancing, or dishonest songs, nor was anyone allowed to enter after 9 p.m. Each person who ate or drank had to pray first; a French Bible was required on the premises so that anyone could read who wished, and conversation about the Word of God was to be encouraged.[29]

Not surprisingly, these *abbayes* lasted the grand total of one month. Public outcry brought the taverns back.

It would be unfair to imply that sumptuary laws were uniquely a product of Calvin's Reformed theology. Sumptuary laws were a historical commonplace: Catholic France had them on the books,[30] pre-Calvinist England used them,[31] and they were to be found in the pre-Christian era in Sparta and Rome.[32] We simply point out here that Calvin's theology did nothing to counteract this sort of thinking; indeed, it strengthened it.

The Puritans who emigrated to North America, as disciples of Calvin, continued to assign the government a key role in the promotion of piety. The New Haven Colony laws of 1653 stated:

> This Court thus framed, shall first with all care and diligence from time to time provide for the maintenance of the purity of Religion, and suppresse the contrary, according to their best Light, and directions from the word of God.[33]

Massachusetts' John Cotton wrote, in 1647, 'It is carnal and worldly and, indeed, an ungodly imagination to confine the magistrate's charge to the bodies and goods of the subject, and to exclude them from the care of their souls.'[34]

All this is not to say that the Massachusetts Puritans ever advocated theocracy in terms of church elders ruling the state. In fact, church elders were not eligible to serve as civil magistrates. Church and state were distinct. However, church control over politics was exercised through the ruling that only church members in good standing were to be given citizenship. If that is not a theocracy then it is the nearest you can get to it.

Lutherans

The Lutherans had quite a different understanding. Martin Luther had very clear views about the government's place and he was not at all shy about stating them. In fact—no retiring lily, he—Luther boldly proclaimed, 'I have written more splendidly and profitably of civil authority than any teacher has ever done (except perhaps St Augustine) since the times of the apostles.'[35] Perhaps we ought to pay heed, then!

Luther's view was that government was simply intended to bring order and maintain justice between people. It should stay away from legislating religious practices. Martin Luther was an Augustinian monk who threw off his monasticism along with his Catholicism. (Flannery O'Connor has wryly noted that the difference between Catholics and Protestants was that overzealous Catholics often disappeared into a monastic order and were never heard from again whereas Protestants were free to run around wreaking havoc.) Luther saw that withdrawal from the world was not the higher road to holiness. He still believed, like the Roman Catholic and Reformed theologians, in God's sovereignty over all creation, but he also believed that this kingdom rule was expressed through two distinct modes, two 'regiments' as he called them: the worldly, governmental kingdom and the spiritual kingdom.[36] Luther—at the early stage of his reformism, at least—felt that the most serious error of political thought in his time was the confusion of these two kingdoms.

He objected to the way the Anabaptists tried to govern the world as if it were the church. Anabaptists wanted society governed according to the gospel (specifically, the Sermon on the Mount) or not at all. Luther thought the law, not the gospel, the proper basis for civil government. The sword rather than turning the other cheek was God's operative principle in the political sphere.

Luther disagreed with the papacy on quite different grounds. He objected to the way the papacy used political instruments for

religious purposes. He objected to the crusades against the Turks
as blasphemous twistings of the very nature of the gospel. If the
government could not be based on the gospel's 'turning the other
cheek' principle, neither could the gospel be based on the sword or
furthered by the governmental force.

Luther, picking up on Christ's contrast between the kingdom of
God and the kingdom of the world, stressed that these two kingdoms had two completely different sets of goals and modes of
operation. He wrote:

> The first [class of men] belongs to the kingdom of God, the second to
> the kingdom of this world. Those belonging to the kingdom of
> God...are subject to Christ.... these people need no secular law or
> sword. All who are not Christians belong to the kingdom of the world
> and are under the law.... God has provided for non-Christians a
> different government outside the Christian estate and God's kingdom,
> and has subjected them to the sword, so that, even though they would
> do so, they cannot practise their wickedness....[37]

Christians operated under grace, the world under law. The state
was never meant to be a tool to minister Christ's grace and revelation. Christianity, the realm of grace, did not have to reign in the
government, the realm of law. It was because of his concept of two
kingdoms, each fairly autonomous, that Luther could say that if he
were presented with a choice between a ruler who was good but
imprudent and one that was bad but prudent, he would choose the
prudent but bad. Why? Because, Luther said, the good but imprudent ruler would throw everything into disorder whereas the prudent but bad ruler would have enough sense to restrain evil.

Luther disavowed, at the beginning of his ministry, the right of
the state to punish heretics. However, as the papacy's attempt to
crush the Reformation intensified, he increasingly relied on the
German princes for support. He thus gradually dropped his tolerant attitude and his opposition to the sword used on God's behalf.
His earlier teaching, however, was still there to be picked up by
other Christians more willing to carry it forward.

Baptists and Friends

A century after Luther, we witness the emergence of yet another
new set of believers with their own particular insights into Scripture: the Baptists. To them particularly can we trace the theological

underpinnings of our modern doctrine of the separation of church and state (not just the toleration of church beliefs by the state). They differed from the Anabaptists in that they believed Christians could and should fully participate in the life of the state. They differed from Luther in their consistent, unequivocal advocation of the individual's liberty of conscience. They felt that the evil of a man seeking to play God by forcing belief was a worse danger than the risk of theological error should man be allowed to freely find his own convictions.

Thomas Helwys, probably the founder of the first Baptist congregation in England, wrote, in 1611:

> For men's religion to God, is betwixt God and themselves; and the king shall not answere for it, neither may the king be judged betwene God and man. Let them be heretikes, Turcks, Jewes, or whatsoever it apperteynes not to the earthly power to punish them in the least measure.[38]

Baptists were eventually to introduce this theology of religious freedom into America's New World. Their way was prepared by the Pilgrims, another dissenting sect (they were Puritans who had formally separated from the Church of England), holding views similar to the Baptists'. John Robinson, their teacher in Holland before they sailed off to Plymouth Rock in Cape Cod, preached:

> The magistrate is not by virtue of his office to meddle with religion or matters of conscience...to force and compel men to this or that form of religion or doctrine; but to leave Christian religion free to every man's conscience and to handle only civil transgressions....[39]

The Pilgrims left behind a seventeenth-century England tense with the unresolved ideological conflict between sincere Christians who differed radically on the role of the state. Even Oliver Cromwell, who swept all before him on the field of battle, was unable to bring harmony on the field of warring religious opinions.

Cromwell, a devout seventeenth-century believer who had at one point dreamed of emigrating to the American New World with the aim of building a godly kingdom, championed the forces of those seeking greater political and religious freedom in England. He recruited devout soldiers to his side in the struggle against King Charles I. These were men who marched into battle singing the psalms. Spiritual zeal, however, did not ensure a smooth course.

Once victorious, Cromwell found himself embroiled in further controversy. Continually, he was called upon to referee between the Presbyterians, who believed in centralised control of religious beliefs through a national assembly, an assembly whose duty it was to impose uniformity of belief, and the Independents, who believed in a decentralised Calvinism in which spiritual authority rested with local assemblies. The Independents' view, with its implicit tolerance towards shades of opinion, was abhorrent to the Presbyterians. They wanted Cromwell to ensure religious uniformity in the army and they wanted him to do so by forcing his officers to take an oath in the form of a religious covenant. Cromwell would have none of it saying, 'I had rather that Mahometanism were permitted amongst us than that one of God's children should be persecuted.'[40]

So stiff did this disagreement become between the Presbyterians and Cromwell that on 4 June 1647 Cromwell was forced to flee London in order to thwart the Presbyterians' plan to arrest him upon his next appearing at the House of Commons.

These differences were imported into the New World. The Puritans of the Massachusetts Bay Colony believed, along with their Presbyterian brothers in England, in a centralised and governmentally controlled religious faith. They, too, had no time for tolerance. John Cotton wrote, 'Toleration made the world anti-Christian.'[41] Another New England divine, Nathaniel Ward, wrote that the only liberty owed to dissenters was the 'liberty to keep away from us'.[42]

With such convictions, it was only natural that the Massachusetts Bay Colony banished Baptists in 1644. Roger Williams—no Baptist, but a firm advocate of the view that civil rulers should not enforce the 'first table' of the Ten Commandments—also had to flee the colony, in 1636, when his teaching incurred the wrath of Boston's Puritan establishment.[43] He had taught that the 'first table' had to do with a man's personal relationship with God and was therefore no business of the civil government. Civil rulers should confine themselves to enforcing the 'second table' of the Ten Commandments, the table concerned with man's social relationships.

Roger Williams, out of his disillusionment with the Bay Colony, founded the colony of Rhode Island. Rhode Island was built on the principle of religious toleration. Granted, this principle of toleration did not extend so far as to grant either Jews or Roman

Catholics the privilege of citizenship, but it did protect these groups from more active forms of persecution. Williams defended this principle of toleration, saying, 'God requireth not any uniformity of Religion.... The civil sword may make a nation of hypocrites and anti-Christians, but not one true Christian.'[44] The Bay Colony could not have agreed less but learned to live with their irritating neighbour.

These views, so dearly held by Roger Williams and Baptists such as Thomas Helwys, were later championed by American politicians Thomas Jefferson and James Madison. The fringe became mainstream. Baptist ideas about the non-establishment of religion found their way into the First Amendment of America's Constitution. Thomas Jefferson, with his 'wall of separation between Church and State',[45] came riding into power partly as the result of the widespread backing of American Baptists. These Baptists wielded increasing political influence as, with the second Great Awakening (beginning in 1799), they joined the Methodists in becoming 'by far the largest among Protestant denominations'.[46] Religious freedom was here to stay.

So who is right? We have seen the Anabaptists, who stressed purity and who dismissed the civil realm as unworthy of a Christian. We have seen the Catholics and Calvinists, who took seriously God's sovereignty over all creation but, in taking it seriously, seemed to lose the graciousness which ought to mark God's rule. (It should be noted that numerous historically Catholic positions changed with Vatican II in the 1960s.) We have seen the Lutherans (initially) and the Baptists, who were strong on the liberty of man's conscience before God but who were weak on a scriptural rationale for the church's prophetic ministry to government: if liberty of conscience were all-important then what rationale was there for challenging and redirecting a government who misused their liberty of conscience?

Which view was the correct one? All, none or one of them? In our next chapter we will begin to respond to the four views advanced in this chapter.

3

Responses to Historical Models

Total withdrawal?

The Anabaptists were a vital, spiritual movement, strong on evangelism, church life and true discipleship, but weak on a biblical view of government. By teaching that the only proper response to civil government is non-participation, they denied government the benefit of Christian salt. In advocating a radical withdrawal from worldly activity, the Anabaptists were, in effect, setting up their own form of monasticism. It was a monasticism without monasteries; it was lifestyle monasticism. (Meanwhile, Luther was reacting against his monastic background and pressing his followers to get more involved with secular callings.)

The Anabaptists, in their lifestyle monasticism, completely ignored the dominion or cultural mandate as laid out in Chapter 1 of this book. We have seen that God has an interest in the world, an interest not only in its evangelisation but in its cultural development. The Anabaptists failed to embrace this interest.

The Anabaptists also failed to see that Christ's admonition to turn the other cheek was only one part of his teaching on the place of force and violence. If, as the Anabaptists taught, a Christian ought never to take up arms, and if violence of any sort was indeed 'outside the perfection of Christ', then Christ himself was 'outside the perfection of Christ'! The same Christ who taught us to turn the other cheek also turned out the money changers with what can only be honestly described as violence: swinging a whip, overturning tables, shoving out bewildered businessmen. No gentle appeals to 'please leave the premises at your earliest convenience' here.

The same Christ who meekly gave up his life, and forbade Peter to defend him, also preached sermons full of verbal violence. Just read his sermon in Matthew 23 with its multiplicity of 'Woe to yous', with its hardhitting accusation of hypocrisy, pride and greed, with its rampant name-calling ('son of hell', 'blind fools', 'blind guides'—a biting insult if ever there was one; what could be more useless than a blind guide?—'whitewashed tombs', 'snakes', 'brood of vipers'), all addressed personally and pointedly through Christ's remorseless use of 'You...you...you...'. In painting a vivid word picture—'You strain out a gnat but swallow a camel' (Mt 23:24)—Jesus was as barbed and wickedly funny as any contemporary political cartoonist.

And what could be more violent than hell—a place of eternal, never-ending punishment? Jesus never shrank from this subject; in fact, he talked about hell more than any other biblical preacher or prophet. Not only did Jesus talk about hell, he himself will be an agent of violence when he returns to earth the second time:

> With justice he judges and makes war.... The armies of heaven were
> following him, riding on white horses.... Out of his mouth comes a
> sharp sword with which to strike down the nations. 'He will rule them
> with an iron sceptre.' He treads the winepress of the fury of the wrath of
> God Almighty (Rev 19:11–15).

In the light of these scriptures it is difficult to accept the Anabaptist position that violence is sinful and outside Christ's perfection. God is the God of peace but he is unashamedly the God of war when he needs to be.

Opposition to Christians using the sword was one of the Anabaptists' chief objections to Christians' participation in politics. They rightly understood that worldly government was impossible without the sword, without the use of force; and this they took to be unChristian. But if this wholesale opposition to the sword is biblically unfounded then surely their opposition to political involvement is equally unfounded.

The Anabaptists made God irrelevant to government. They simply abandoned this entire area. As a consequence, they never produced social champions in the mould of Wilberforce or Shaftesbury. Their emphasis was counter-cultural rather than culture-reclaiming. (Surely this accounts in part for the revival of interest in the Anabaptist tradition in the 'counter-cultural' 1960s.)

God is clearly interested in the eternal good that can be accomplished through the church in its redemptive mission, but he is also interested in the temporal good that can be accomplished through government. After all, government was as much God's idea as was the church. Both institutions are God-ordained and both institutions were set up to 'do you good' (Rom 13:1). What God considers good, humanity should not consider good-for-nothing.

Although the Anabaptists were a shining example and a tremendous model of the evangelistic/discipleship mandate, they were no model of the dominion mandate. Indeed, they did not want to be.

Dominion means dominance?

The Anabaptist position was totally at odds with the Reformed and Catholic position, a position we have characterised as 'dominion means dominance'. Certainly, one cannot but agree with the Reformed/Catholic position that God is the Lord of all life—the public realm as well as the private; civil society as well as church societies. On the other hand, one cannot help but disagree with their understanding of how God's sovereignty is to be worked out. A system which legally compels belief and punishes unbelief does too much violence to the value God prizes so highly: freedom.

Now some may argue that I am simply a captive of our modern mindset, a mindset which worships at the feet of the tin god 'liberty'.[47] But I think we can see sound biblical reasons why a state-enforced faith is no biblical faith. It fundamentally contravenes the thrust of God's dealings with humanity. God's whole approach, both in creating human beings and redeeming them, puts a premium on the individual's freedom to choose.

At creation, God made man and woman free to act as they wished, and therefore free to sin. Implicit in man and woman being made in God's image was the right to (limited) sovereignty over themselves. They were not made as robots. God not only gave man and woman freedom, the ability freely to choose among differing options, he put them in a position where they were forced to exercise this freedom with purpose. He put before man and woman the forbidden tree of the knowledge of good and evil.

Notice that this tree was not hidden away in some obscure grove hundreds of miles away but that it was placed 'in the middle of the garden' (Gen 2:9). It was easily accessible. In fact, it was right next to the tree of life, also in the middle of the garden. Every time Adam and Eve went to eat from the tree of life they would be confronted with the other tree. The choice was continually set before them. This was no accident. God wanted them freely to choose obedience. That is why he pointed the tree out to Adam and Eve in the first place.

Notice, too, that God gave the devil ready access to the garden. There was no legion of angels guarding the garden gates with instructions to keep Satan out at all costs. God not only allowed humanity choice in the garden, he also allowed temptation there. The choice between alternatives was now more than just an abstract, mental exercise. With Satan on the scene the evil alternative was made to look attractive. God allowed all this because he wanted them to learn to cope with their freedom. They didn't.

Now some might say, 'Yes, yes. I believe in giving people freedom to sin as God did in the garden. But I also believe that, even as God immediately punished Adam and Eve's sin, so we should face sinners with the legal consequences of their sin and unbelief. We should punish all religious transgressions.' This approach does not really honour the freedom God has given us. This sort of freedom is no sort of freedom. What is the difference between it and non-freedom?

God, in fact, does not punish every act of unrighteousness. In this life, he does not consistently bring the consequences of sin upon the heads of the unrighteous. People sin and even prosper, to the great frustration of the psalmist who confessed, 'I envied the arrogant when I saw the prosperity of the wicked. They have no struggles; their bodies are healthy and strong' (Ps 73:3–4). The saints, in the light of God's propensity to let sin run its course unhampered, not infrequently complain, 'How long, Sovereign Lord...until you judge?' (Rev 6:10). God not only gives people freedom to sin, he also grants a certain freedom from the immediate consequences of these sins.

The element of freedom was essential not only at the creation of man and woman but also at their redemption. The very nature of redemption and conversion demands freedom. Conversion is turning from loving and trusting ourselves to loving and trusting Christ the Lord and Saviour. But love and trust cannot be forced; instead they are won. They are won as we see the nature of God in the face of Christ, the heart of God in the deeds of Christ. You cannot wrench words of love from a man's lips by putting a sword to his throat.

These bittersweet words, attributed to Napoleon as he paced his lonely, island exile ruminating on his rise and fall, express it well:

> Alexander, Caesar and Hannibal conquered the world but they had no friends.... Jesus founded his empire upon love, and at this hour millions would die for him.... He has won the hearts of men, a task a conqueror cannot do.

Paul the zealous Jew went about compelling circumcision through terror and force. Paul the zealous Christian had a different way. Paul the convert knew that conversion meant winning hearts, not conforming behaviour, that persuasion must replace persecution. Conversion meant 'faith expressing itself through love' (Gal 5:6). But love is killed by violence and terror.

In the Old Testament, God set up a people to represent him, the political entity Israel. Political entities of necessity concern themselves with outward actions rather than with the inner life of the spirit. That is why it makes sense for them to use the sword—a very effective instrument for modifying behaviour! This, however, does not make sense for God's New Testament vehicle, the church, whose concern is not primarily with actions but with the inner life of the spirit.

One cannot achieve spiritual aims through worldly means. The church forgot this when it tried to advance the gospel through force. If we do not stand firmly on the freedom element in God's dealings with humanity, persecution begins to look, if not attractive, then reasonable. It did to the fifth-century apologist of persecution, Augustine, Bishop of Hippo.

Augustine initially opposed persecution but, observing its effectiveness in halting the Donatist heresy, he changed his mind. He wrote approvingly to a Donatist friend that he had seen his home town, previously Donatist, 'brought over to the Catholic unity by fear of the imperial edicts'.[48] Persecution worked and that was argument enough for Augustine! So relentlessly efficient was Augustine's campaign against the Donatist heretics that in many cases they were driven to mass suicide.

Augustine justified persecution by pointing out that God himself had used coercion and a violent shake-up to push the Apostle Paul into Christianity. And what else did Luke 14:23 mean ('Co out... and compel people to come in', RSV) except that compulsion was an altogether acceptable means of spreading the faith?

With a ghastly reasonableness Augustine wrote about heresy, saying:

> The necessity of harshness is greater in the investigation, than in the infliction, of punishment.... it is generally necessary to use more rigour in making inquisition, so that when the crime has been brought to light, there may be scope for displaying clemency.[49]

How merciful! If we do not place a premium on freedom then this awful logic on heresy actually begins to sound plausible.

Thomas Aquinas, the great thirteenth-century theologian, certainly did consider the argument plausible. His logic ran like this:

> Heresy is a sin which merits not only excommunication but also death, for it is worse to corrupt the Faith which is the life of the soul than to issue counterfeit coins which minister to the secular life. Since counterfeiters are justly killed by princes as enemies to the common good, so heretics also deserve the same punishment.[50]

Calvin was of like mind. When defending Geneva's killing of the heretic Servetus, he wrote:

> One should forget all mankind when His glory is in question.... God does not even allow whole towns and populations to be spared, but will have the walls razed and the memory of the inhabitants destroyed and all things ruined as a sign of His utter detestation, lest the contagion spread.[51]

'Forgetting all mankind' comes uncomfortably close to forgetting one's humanity. In fact, that is precisely where it seems to have led.

No, the gospel which declares that 'it is for freedom that Christ has set us free' (Gal 5:1) deserves better than this. The freedom to choose for God or against God is basic to God's whole approach to humanity. If God gives us the freedom to sin, who are we to do otherwise? Of course, this freedom is not absolute. God limits it. But surely this freedom is wider than Augustine, Calvin and others allow.

In the words of John Courtney Murray, one of the key Catholic theologians behind Vatican II's reversal of the longstanding Catholic opposition to religious liberty, 'Religious pluralism is against the will of God. But it is the human condition.'[52] In other words, God does not want men and women to sin, but he does allow it should individuals choose it. He does not obliterate unbelievers who profess false doctrine. That is an important guideline in any state that wants to govern according to God's ways. And that is where both Calvinists and Catholics have failed in the past. This does not, of course, mean that Calvinist and Catholic rule was a complete failure; it just means that at this one point of religious liberty it had serious shortcomings.

Two kingdoms?

What about the position held by Baptists and the early Luther that Christians need to involve themselves in politics without tyrannising the body politic, without mandating citizens' religious faith? Here is the biblical position. (A totally unremarkable confession to make in today's climate yet true nonetheless.) It is the position which best confesses God's way of 'doing religion'—'be in the world but not of the world' (Jn 17:15–18)—and God's way of 'doing politics'—'Render...to Caesar the things that are Caesar's, and to God the things that are God's' (Mt 22:21, RSV). This two kingdoms view does not totally withdraw from political life as the Anabaptists would have us to do. Luther's two kingdoms concept, in contradistinction to the Anabaptists', widens the focus of discipleship from the order of redemption to the order of creation. All the world becomes a field for God's work. In addition, Luther's two kingdoms theology does not involve the police in purging bad doctrine, the position entailed in the 'dominion means dominance' theology.

It would not be right to leave the impression that Calvin did not also believe in two distinct kingdoms. He too insisted that 'Christ's spiritual Kingdom and the civil jurisdiction are things completely distinct.... it is a Jewish vanity to seek and enclose Christ's Kingdom within the elements of this world'.[53] My contention with Calvin is not over whether he believed in two distinct kingdoms but over how he believed they were to interrelate. This is the real issue here.

Luther's and Calvin's theologies had differing strengths and weaknesses. Luther's theology was good in that in its early stages it denied the civil government jurisdiction over the religious sphere. Another strength of Luther's theology was that it gave human reason a creditable place. Luther's followers were not prone to the erroneous downplaying of reason.

Luther had his glaring weaknesses as well. There is not only the matter of his retraction, in practical terms, of his stand on religious liberty; there is also his tendency to abandon the civil realm to the non-Christian. Luther was very strong on resisting rulers when they interfered with religious faith (the vertical dimension) but weak on resisting rulers when they practised civil tyranny (the horizontal dimension). He said:

> No matter how intolerably they tax, they [princes] are to be obeyed, and everything is to be borne for God's sake.... Therefore if the government takes your possessions, your life and limb, and whatever you have, say: I gladly give it to you. I recognize you as my masters.[54]

It was exactly on these issues of taxes, possessions, and life and limb that the great battles for liberty were to be fought later in England and America. On these issues Luther was on the wrong side. He was so concerned for order in his admittedly tumultuous century that he overstated his case. He battled for religious liberty and had no energy left to give to civil liberty.

Calvin was better on this point in that he at least granted civil magistrates the right to resist the prince when the prince engaged in tyranny; not just religious tyranny but civil tyranny. Magistrates, in fact, were instructed that they had a 'duty' to withstand rulers who 'dishonestly betray the freedom of the people, of which they know that they have been appointed protectors by God's ordinance'.[55] Calvin was not content to 'let well enough alone', to abandon the civil polity to sin while he got on with building the church.

Thus Calvin laid, at the very outset of Reformed thinking, a concern that not only the religious sphere be reformed by God's kingdom, but the civil sphere as well. Civil rulers could be called to account for their civil duties in the here and now, not just later in eternity. On the whole, Reformed thinking was less passive than the Lutheran approach. It was only natural that, out of Calvin's initial statements, we should later see spring up full-fledged, Reformed resistance theories such as the *Vindiciae contra Tyrannos* in 1581 (Defence of Liberty against Tyrants) and *Rex Lex* in 1644.

That these resistance theories were of wider import than the immediate fate of the church is made clear by Professor Harold Laski when he writes that 'the moral and political liberty of the seventeenth and eighteenth centuries was the outcome of the protest against religious intolerance',[56] a struggle in which Reformed documents played a central role. So influential were documents such as the Calvinist *Vindiciae* that Laski writes, 'Practically . . . the theory of the state upon which the *Vindiciae* rests determined the character of political speculation from the end of the sixteenth century until the advent of Rousseau.'[57] The political thinkers were religious thinkers. Their religion not only gave them their political convictions, it gave them the courage to stand up for their convictions:

> It is permissible to argue that no motive save that of religious conviction would have been strong enough to inspire their effort against the inertia which made men anxious for any peace, whatever its character.

This religious fire in the belly moved these early political thinkers to translate dreams into reality.

The Calvinists, then, were able to relate God's kingdom ideas to man's civil kingdom. They related the two kingdoms easily enough but had difficulty separating them adequately (in giving spiritual oversight to the civil authorities). The Lutherans were better at separating the two kingdoms but had difficulty showing how they related. If we in the twentieth century are not totally satisfied with their final formulation of these issues we can at least be grateful that they courageously addressed them, thus moving us down the road to those freedoms we enjoy today.

In our next chapter we will examine a modern resurgence and reinterpretation of Calvinism's 'dominion means dominance': the Reconstructionists.

4

Calvin Reformed and Reconstructed

Calvin's vision of a Christian society in which God's law ruled both the church and civil society lives on today in the Reconstructionists. The Reconstructionists are Calvinist theologians who want to see God's sovereignty extended to all spheres of society. They feel that Calvin failed to apply his great core doctrine—the sovereignty of God—rigorously enough. They are more thoroughgoing Calvinists than Calvin himself! One of their writers dismisses Calvin's resistance to applying the whole of Moses' laws to Geneva as 'heretical nonsense', writing that Calvin's 'classical humanism gained ascendancy at this point' over his faithfulness to Scripture.[58] The Reconstructionists intend to make no such mistake.

'Reconstructionism' is both a mouthful and a handful. In America, Reconstructionist books and position papers pour off the presses, shaking up the church and the world. Reconstructionists are vocal, visible, and winning people over to their way of seeing things. They are out to reconstruct society and they mean business. *Christianity Today* (20 February 1986) points out that the Reconstructionists 'are regular guests on religious television shows, hobnob with a potential candidate for the presidency, testify in dozens of church/state education trials'. *Newsweek* magazine has called one Reconstructionist foundation, the Chalcedon Foundation, the think-tank of the religious right. A major religious publisher has taken to publishing their works.

And now Britain is being brought into their orbit. In 1987, at a gathering of charismatic church leaders in Oxford, a call by a well-known Reconstructionist speaker to build a society in which God's

47

laws would be taken seriously and used as the basis of legislation—in this case, the reinstitution of the death penalty for homosexuality—was met by thunderous applause.

What exactly do the Reconstructionists want?

Reconstructionists want reconstruction

First, the Reconstructionists want to see society 'reconstructed' along biblical lines. They quite rightly say that personal revival is only the first of the changes God intends. Personal change should lead to a change in the structure of society: in our law courts, in our schools and universities, in our governments.

They rebel against the narrow construction that has been put on the concept of 'building God's kingdom'. They insist that building means more than building the church. Preaching is not the only spiritual ministry. A minister can be a painter as well as a pastor, a politician as well as a preacher.

They reject the defeatism of Christians who see no hope for society until the return of Christ. They believe in the real possibility of the earthly victory of Christian principles and Christian institutions in society. Rightly, they point out that a theology of 'Satan is out and about, sin reigns, things will just get worse and worse till we blow ourselves up before the millennium' is a theology of withdrawal. It will lead to Christians withdrawing from society, at least as change-agents. Why should Christians try to apply their Christianity to society if they know in advance it won't work? Christians aren't that dumb!

They believe that not only Calvin, but the whole of the Reformation failed at this one point: it stopped short of the biblical reconstruction of society. One of the most prolific and influential of the Reconstructionist writers, Gary North (a PhD specialising in economic history), writes:

> If we're correct about the God-required nature of our agenda, it will attract a dedicated following. It will produce a social transformation that could dwarf the Reformation. This time, we're not limiting our call for reformation to the institutional church. This time we mean business.[59]

Where Anabaptists feel that the sixteenth-century Reformation went wrong in its incomplete reformation of the church, Reconstructionists feel the Reformation went wrong in its incomplete reformation of society. The Reformation failed by limiting its call to the reformation of the church. The Anabaptists wanted more focus on the church. The Reconstructionists want more focus on society. Reconstructionists want reconstruction.

Biblical law

But the Reconstructionists want more than the renewal of society by Christians. This alone would not make them so controversial. The real core of Reconstructionism lies in its insistence on 'biblical law' as the only valid law for society. And what is meant by 'biblical law' is the literal application of Old Testament civil legislation.

They argue that you have either man's law or God's law ruling society. Put like this, every Christian would opt for God's law. But just what is God's law? What is his will on land use or immigration? Reconstructionists say that 'vague principles'—'be just' or 'be compassionate'—are hopelessly general and cannot serve as firm guidelines to action. We need concrete answers from God's word. And where are these to be found but in the Old Testament? There God has spoken on land use, immigration and a host of other civil problems.

One Reconstructionist writer says:

> The law, contrary to what many Christians think, goes far, far beyond the Ten Commandments. There are over two hundred legal issues in the scriptures, and nearly two-thirds of them have to do with how God's people were to order their culture politically or socially.... Jesus said that he did not come to do away with the Old Testament Law.[60]

Another writer, in refuting that the Scriptures provide only 'vague biblical principles' for economics and government, claims, 'There is a "comprehensive biblical blueprint" for economics in Scripture.'[61] He goes on to cite various Old Testament laws as the blueprint for today.

Could all this emphasis on Old Testament literalism lead to legalism? Well, Reconstructionists say that legalism is the least of the church's worries. They insist we have the opposite problem: 'A central characteristic of the churches and of modern preaching and Biblical teaching is antinomianism, an anti-law position.'[62]

Antinomianism is a heresy which teaches that because the Christian is under grace he is now free from the law. And if no longer under the law then it is impossible to break the law. He can do what he wants—lie, steal, fornicate—as the law no longer applies to him. But the Reconstructionists have redefined antinomianism to mean the setting aside of any biblical laws, whether Old Testament or New, whether civil or moral. To them, heretical antinomianists are not just those who disregard the New Testament moral laws but anyone who ignores the Old Testament injunctions as well. Gary North writes, 'Antinomianism—the denial of the validity of the concrete application of Old Testament law in this era—has infected modern Christianity....'[63]

Reconstructionists say that the great Reformers, Luther and Calvin, failed at exactly this point of 'biblical law'. They substituted 'natural law' for the specific, concrete revelation given us in the Old Testament. Natural law consisted of those laws thought to be self-evident; laws that did not need to be specifically revealed before people recognised their validity. They were written into our natures. They were 'natural'.

Rushdoony writes:

> Luther thus paved the way for the full-fledged return of...the natural law, as did Calvin by his sometimes weak views on Biblical law.... The Bible does not recognize any law as valid apart from the law of God, and this law is given by revelation to the patriarchs and Moses, and expounded by prophets, Jesus Christ, and the apostles.... Some will deny this...having adopted a Greek and rationalistic concept of natural law.... By this thesis, to which the Reformation leaders virtually all gave assent, they denied the Reformation. Unregenerate, fallen man...is somehow able to know a law inherent in nature and make it a ground 'for the shaping of morals'?[64]

One might gulp and ask incredulously, 'Do the Reconstructionists want *all* the Old Testament civil laws reinstituted, right down to the punishments?' Read for yourself what Rushdoony has to write...

On adultery

Deuteronomy 22:22 states:

> If a man is found sleeping with another man's wife, both the man who slept with her and the woman must die.

Rushdoony writes:

Thus, the death penalty is clearly God's law for incest and/or adultery.... A godly law-order will restore the death penalty, but the church must live realistically with its absence....[65]

On witchcraft

Exodus 22:18 states: 'Do not allow a sorceress to live.' Rushdoony writes, '...the death penalty is required by Scripture for a number of offenses,' and then lists Exodus 22:18 as one of them.[66] Rushdoony would undoubtedly concur with John Calvin when he said:

The Bible teaches us that there are witches and that they must be slain...this law of God is a universal law.[67]

On incorrigibly disobedient children

Deuteronomy 21:18–21 says:

If a man has a stubborn and rebellious son who does not obey his father and mother and will not listen to them when they discipline him, his father and mother shall take hold of him and bring him to the elders at the gate of his town. They shall say to the elders, 'This son of ours is stubborn and rebellious. He will not obey us. He is a profligate and a drunkard.' Then all the men of his town shall stone him to death. You must purge the evil from among you.

Rushdoony's cryptic comment on this is, 'The law is clear enough: if only the interpreters were as clear.' He feels modern commentators evade the obvious, if unattractive, meaning of these Old Testament passages; to wit, 'Kill them!' He goes on to say:

Pity, in fact, is specifically forbidden as evil in certain cases. Obviously, in the law concerning the delinquent son, pity for the son is forbidden.

Not content with the narrow, strict interpretation of this passage in Deuteronomy 21, Rushdoony extends it to embrace even habitual criminals. They too ought to be killed. He writes:

Clearly, then, the intent of this law is that all incorrigible and habitual criminals be executed. If a criminal son is to be executed, how much more so a neighbour or fellow Hebrew who has become an incorrigible criminal.[68]

On idolatry

Deuteronomy 13:6–9 says:

> If your very own brother, or your son or daughter, or the wife you love, or your closest friend secretly entices you, saying, 'Let us go and worship other gods'.... You must certainly put him to death.

Rushdoony believes this should be applied today, saying:

> Basic to the health of a society is the integrity of its foundation. To allow tampering with its foundation is to allow its total subversion. Biblical law can no more permit the propagation of idolatry than Marxism can permit counter-revolution.... for Biblical law the foundation is the one true God, the central offense is therefore treason to that God by idolatry.[69]

Rushdoony assures the reader that this is not as limiting to the freedom of unbelievers as may first appear:

> It should be noted that Deuteronomy 13:5–18 does not call for the death penalty for unbelief or for heresy. It condemns false prophets who seek to lead the people, with signs and wonders, into idolatry.[70]

So an unbeliever is free to disbelieve if he wants; it's just that he cannot discuss his views with anyone!

Lest he be thought unrealistic in his expectations, Rushdoony adds this reasonable caveat:

> This condemnation does not apply to a missionary situation, where the land is anti-God to begin with: this is a situation for conversion. It does require a nation grounded in God's law-system to preserve that order by punishing the basic treason against it.[71]

So unbelievers cannot be killed until Christians get into power. It is uncircumspect to do so before then.

Rushdoony is insistent on the death penalty, even maintaining, on the strength of Numbers 35:31, that to oppose the death penalty is 'defying and despising the law of God...expressing...contempt of the cross of Christ, which sets forth the necessity of the death penalty in the sight of God'.[72]

Faithful citizenship

Two more aspects of Reconstructionism are worth mentioning. First is the call not just for faithful citizens but for a citizenship of the faithful. To put it baldly:

> Only those within the covenant are citizens.... Citizenship rested on faith. Apostasy was treason. This aspect of the law is...embarrassing to modern man.[73]

Rushdoony is saying that a fully biblical government will reserve the vote for Christians alone. He acknowledges that this position will be unpopular in our democratic countries, but implies that being guided by such unpopularity is unworthy of a Christian. (The question is not whether Rushdoony's position is popular but whether, in fact, it is biblical.)

Rushdoony contrasts to our modern 'heresy of democracy' the exemplary procedure of the Puritan founders of New England. These American patriarchs did not even give regular church attenders voting rights in society; these were reserved for the faithful 'elect'. (After all, church attendance was no guarantee of salvation.) Rushdoony says that if we are to be faithful to biblical law then this too will have to be written into our law books.

National covenants

The last element of the Reconstructionist approach to the Old Testament is their emphasis on 'national covenants'. Gary North writes:

> The locus of covenant blessings is the nation. This means that nations as covenantal institutions will eventually overcome the enemies of Christ.... The implicit covenantal division between sheep and goats— national entities—must be made increasingly visible over time, 'on earth as it is in heaven....'
>
> Many people have interpreted such verses as Matthew 25:31–35 (on the sheep and the goats) as referring exclusively to individual salvation, but the language of the text indicates God's judgment of collectives, not just individual souls. The text indicates...national restoration....
>
> As men strive together in national covenant to work out their salvation in fear and trembling, they extend Christ's kingdom on earth.... God's visible, external blessings cover the covenanted society. Deu-

teronomy 28 teaches that these blessings are clearly national and exter-
nal: military, weather and finances.[74]

So now we have 'Christian nations' beating non-Christian
armies due to the military blessings of God. Surely this resurrects
the very spectre of the Crusades that Luther so desperately wanted
to get away from. But let us respond more fully to the challenge of
the Reconstructionists in the next chapter.

5

The Deconstruction of Reconstruction

I wholeheartedly agree with the Reconstructionists' emphasis that God is the Lord of all of life. But I wholeheartedly disagree with their finding in the Old Testament a complete blueprint for modern societies. I disagree with them in three foundational areas: first, the relationship of the New Testament to the Old; second, the place of reason; third, the place of force.

The Old Testament

Fundamental to the whole Reconstructionist programme is their view of the Old Testament. It is what underlies their specific prescriptions on capital punishment, stopping heresy, and so on. If they are right in their view of the Old Testament then they are right in pushing these Old Testament laws. If they are wrong in their view of the Old Testament then their entire programme falls down.

The Reconstructionists, of course, believe that the Old Testament is as applicable today as it was in Moses' day. In that sense, they see no radical distinction between the Old and the New Testaments. Rushdoony writes:

> As the new chosen people of God, the Christians are commanded to do that which Adam in Eden, and Israel in Canaan, failed to do. One and the same covenant, under differing administrations, still prevails.[75]

One covenant exists, not two. That is why we are still under the original terms of the covenant given to Moses.

Rushdoony explains further: 'The law of the covenant remains; the covenant rites and signs have been changed.'[76] So all that changed with the new was the introduction of new signs and rites? Jesus came to replace circumcision with baptism and the Passover with Communion? Surely, according to this view, the 'New Covenant' is not nearly new enough! What is new—rites and signs—is far too superficial. Jesus meant more than this when he spoke of 'the new covenant in my blood' (Lk 22:20). I think he had in mind the newness of a revolution, not the newness of a reform.

Jesus came bringing good news. The gospel was not only good, it was 'news' as well. Now 'news' (I do not want to seem profound, but I'll give you both barrels anyway) is something that is new. This gospel, this good news, came as a startling new revelation to the Jews of Jesus' day. It was radically different from their Old Testament.

Evidently it had the same impact on the apostle Paul. In Ephesians 3 and 2 Timothy he was getting excited over a lot more than new rites and signs. He speaks of the 'mystery...not made known to...other generations as it has now been revealed...this mystery, which for ages past was kept hidden in God' (Eph 3:4–9). A fundamental revelation of cosmic significance was missing from the Old Testament. As Paul wrote to Timothy:

> This grace...has now been revealed through the appearing of our Saviour, Christ Jesus, who has destroyed death and has brought life and immortality to light through the gospel (2 Tim 1:9–10).

Jesus did not come to introduce new rites and signs, he came to destroy death and bring life and immortality to light. Now that is something worth getting excited about.

The entire letter to the Hebrews is in complete contradiction to the thrust of the Reconstructionist interpretation of the place of the Old Testament. Let me illustrate.

Where Rushdoony says, 'The law of the covenant remains,' Hebrews 7:12 says, 'For when there is a change of the priesthood, there must also be a change of the law.' Jesus, our Great High Priest has come, and consequently there has been a change in the law. The law does not remain.

Where Rushdoony claims that Paul's polemics against the law were in reality directed against a common 'misunderstanding' of the law, Hebrews 7:18 says, 'The former regulation is set aside because it was weak and useless (for the law made nothing perfect).' It was not the Jews' understanding which was 'weak and useless' but the law itself.

Where Rushdoony denies that a radically new covenant has been made in the New Testament, Hebrews 7:22 and 8:7 and 13 state:

> Jesus has become the guarantee of a better covenant.... For if there had been nothing wrong with that first covenant, no place would have been sought for another.... By calling this covenant 'new', he has made the first one obsolete; and what is obsolete and ageing will soon disappear.

I do not think the Bible could be much clearer concerning the radically new newness of the New Testament or the obsoleteness of the Old.

Where Rushdoony sees one covenant, the apostle Paul sees two covenants with sharp and startling differences between them. He writes to the Corinthians concerning the 'new covenant—not of the letter but of the Spirit; for the letter kills, but the Spirit gives life' (2 Cor 3:6). It was not the pharisaical twisting of the Old Covenant but the Old Covenant itself which brought death. The old was of the letter and issued in death, the new was of the Spirit and brought life.

Rushdoony maintains that 'Paul never attacked the law as the way of sanctification, but only as the way of justification'.[77] He claims that the way the Council of Jerusalem dealt in Acts 15 with the 'Judaisers' illustrates this. He writes, 'The instructions of Acts 15:20 and 29 clearly presuppose the law and emphasize how far the law was retained.'[78] These verses record the church leaders forbidding the Jewish rite of circumcision while upholding the Jewish ban on food polluted by idols, blood and the meat of strangled animals.

The question is: Is this an illustration of the law being rejected as the way of justification but retained as the way of sanctification, as Rushdoony claims? Well, if Rushdoony is correct in his interpretation of Acts 15 then the Bible contradicts itself! Of Jesus it is written:

> Don't you see that nothing that enters a man from the outside can make him 'unclean'?... (In saying this, Jesus declared all foods 'clean') (Mk 7:18–19).

Did God change his mind and decide that, after all, blood and strangled meat were not so kosher? Obviously not.

In Acts 15 the apostles are not making great theological statements about God's view on blood and meat; they are rather giving pragmatic directions to ensure peace between Jewish and Gentile believers. The Jewish believers would be offended by their Gentile brethren eating blood and strangled meat. 'So don't do it,' reply the apostles. 'They have given way to you on circumcision; now you take a half-step towards them and refrain from eating foods offensive to your Jewish brethren.' The apostle Paul advocated the same approach when he wrote to the Corinthians, 'To the Jews I became like a Jew.... To those under the law I became like one under the law (though I myself am not under the law)' (1 Cor 9:20). Paul did not have to keep the Old Testament laws but he did so in order to be on good terms with the Jews he was determined to reach.

Acts 15 is not the chapter on which to base a legalistic insistence on Old Testament observance. It goes against the whole spirit of the passage. Not only can one not base a return to Old Testament dietary laws on this chapter, one cannot even absolutely forbid circumcision on the basis of it. Paul, whose absolute opposition to circumcision was the cause for this church council in the first place, is seen in the very next chapter doing...what? You guessed it: 'Paul wanted to take him [Timothy] along on the journey, so he circumcised him because of the Jews' (Acts 16:3). Paul opposed circumcision only when it was preached by Christians as necessary to salvation. When this was not in question he could take it or leave it according to whether or not it was helpful. He was no legalist insisting on the jot and tittle. Even less was he legalistically insisting on regulations about how to eat or not eat meat. The apostle who exulted in one place that Christ had accomplished the 'abolishing in his flesh' of 'the law with its commandments and regulations' (Eph 2:15) would hardly be busily at work reconstructing those very same commandments and regulations in another place.

This distinction between the law as a way of sanctification and as a way of justification is a theologian's fiction. We do not have one way of sanctification and another way of justification. Both are accomplished by the 'obedience of faith'. Christ, Paul says, is both our 'holiness and redemption' (1 Cor 1:30). We are not justified by trusting in Christ and made holy by avoiding blood-based gravy.

Paul never makes an effort to retain the Mosaic Law as a way of sanctification. He says the Mosaic Law as a whole has passed away. He writes:

> What I mean is this: The law, introduced 430 years later [than Abraham], does not set aside the covenant [to Abraham] previously established.... What, then, was the purpose of the law? It was added because of transgressions until the Seed to whom the promise referred had come.... So the law was put in charge to lead us to Christ that we might be justified by faith. Now that faith has come, we are no longer under the supervision of the law (Gal 3:17, 19, 24, 25).

There is not a word about keeping, as a mode of sanctification, certain aspects of the law. The law is treated as a totality; as both a way of justification and sanctification. The Mosaic Law for justification and sanctification 'was added' until the promised Messiah had come. He's come, therefore we are no longer under its tutelage. Christ is now our sanctification.

The Reconstructionists understand the Old Testament law to be literally true for today. The biblical understanding, however, of the Old Testament is as a shadow of the reality. 'The law is only a shadow of the good things that are coming—not the realities themselves' (Heb 10:1). 'It was necessary, then, for the copies of the heavenly things to be purified with these sacrifices, but the heavenly things themselves with better sacrifices than these' (Heb 9:23). The Old Testament sacrifices were a shadow of Jesus, the real sacrifice revealed in the New Testament. The Old Testament earthly Temple was a shadow of heavenly arrangements brought to light in the New Testament. God's dealings with his Old Testament people, Israel, were a shadow of his dealings with his New Testament people, the church. Now that the reality is here we no longer need to insist on those institutions which were created by God as a symbol for the realities.

The Reconstructionists, in insisting on Old Testament civic legislation, confuse the shadow for the reality. The Reconstructionists also confuse the real meaning and point of Israel. They take Israel to be a model of God's dealings with all nations. But is this really what God is after? Listen to the following Old and New Covenant contrasts.

In the Old Testament God says of Israel, 'Out of all nations you will be my treasured possession... you will be for me a kingdom of priests and a holy nation' (Ex 19:5–6). In the Old Testament he looks to a nation. In the New Testament God looks to the church, saying, 'But you are a chosen people, a royal priesthood, a holy nation, a people belonging to God' (1 Pet 2:9). God's vehicle of revelation, his 'holy nation', is no longer a nation-state but a transnational body—the church. In the Old Testament Israel was the people of God. In the New Testament the church is. Israel is not, therefore, a model and foreshadowing of all nations but a model of the church.

In the Old Testament God linked himself in covenant with one ethnic people so uniquely that he was identified as 'the Lord, the God of Israel' (1 Sam 20:12). In the New Testament he sheds this covenantal relationship with a nation, so that Paul asks, 'Is God the God of Jews only? Is he not the God of Gentiles too? Yes, of Gentiles too...' (Rom 3:29). God's covenant people is the church, not 'Christian nations'. The church is God's holy nation.

To view Israel's Mosaic legislation as a model for all nations is as spiritually short-sighted as viewing Solomon's Temple as the model for all the mini-temples God wants built in 'Christian nations' living under biblical law. God has something much bigger in view. He saw the eternal church which could not be confined to national boundaries. Old Testament Israel is really a model for this church. God's dealings with Israel are a model of his dealings, not with the nations, but with the church.

Israel's legislated tithe to support the Temple service is not a warrant for modern states to impose a 10 per cent tax in order to support the church. Rather, it is a model of how the New Testament Israel, the church, should conduct itself: the leaders should teach church members to give. Similarly, Israel's criminalising of the neglect of the Sabbath is no warrant for modern states to enforce Sunday church-going. It is not a model for the state. Again, Israel's severe penalisation of idolatry was never intended as a licence to modern governments to impose upon their citizens a private relationship with God. It is a model for the church of the discipline it should impose on its own members. The apostle Paul, in 1 Corinthians 5:9–13, makes clear that Christian discipline is to be applied to fellow believers and not to the unbelieving world around us.

The minute care and attention evident in the myriad of laws God enacted for the Jews is a model of the care and attention God wants to give to the governing of his church. The content of his laws has changed but not his minute care and attention. That is the lesson for us from the Old Testament laws. They show God's ways:

his justice, mercy, power, anger, longsuffering, and so on. In none of this has he changed. But he has changed in his approach to diet (pork eating is okay), 'holy clothing' (although Deuteronomy 22:11 forbade combining wool and linen in the same garment, you can wear rayon and PVC if you want now!) and all the other minutiae of the Old Testament. Now that the reality has arrived God does not bother with all that. And neither should we.

Now that the reality has come we should no longer insist on the shadow. But that is what happens when we insist on Old Testament law. The reality is confused with the shadow. We are not meant to aim for a 'national covenant' after the fashion of the Old Testament Jews. The nation-state is no longer God's vehicle as it was in the Old Testament. That's all part of 'shadowland'.

The Reconstructionists seem anxious to rebuild the very Old Testament scaffolding that Paul worked so assiduously to tear down. Their eagerness to preserve this scaffolding contrasts alarmingly with the great apostle's own viewpoint when he wrote:

> Stand firm, then, and do not let yourselves be burdened again by a yoke of slavery... every man who lets himself be circumcised... is required to obey the whole law (Gal 5:1–3).

Paul felt that merely pointing out the implication of Christians submitting to circumcision—that it implied the acceptance of the whole law—was argument enough against it; the point being that Paul saw obedience to the whole law as something self-evidently odious. Obviously it is not so to the Reconstructionist.

The place of reason

The second foundational concept of Reconstructionism is the view of human reason as fallen and therefore useless. One of their writers puts it thus:

> The question is...the biblical doctrine of man's depravity.... This can be seen most clearly in two areas: epistemology and ethics.... Many professed Christians do not accept the biblical view that revelation and revelation alone is the source of knowledge and truth. They believe that there are at least two roads to truth—science and revelation, or reason and revelation.[79]

If 'revelation and revelation alone' can bring truth, if reason

cannot help us with forming political programmes and civic legislation, then it is no wonder that the Reconstructionists look to the
Old Testament for guidance. What else is there?

The Reconstructionists take Calvin's emphasis on the total
depravity and fallenness of humanity and apply it in a way that
Calvin himself never did. They teach that when humanity fell our
reason fell too. Fallen humanity, unable to reason properly, was
now unable to perceive truth of any sort. Reconstructionists say
that if we allow that fallen humanity can know anything apart from
God then we are conceding either that we are not, in fact, totally
fallen or that God is not totally sovereign.[80]

With this view it is only logical to insist, as do the Reconstructionists, that we base our laws on Old Testament legislation rather
than on some 'natural law' consisting of supposedly 'self-evident'
truths said to be evident even to the non-Christian, fallen mind.
Reconstructionists turn completely from reason to revelation, even
calling the concept of 'natural law' a 'truce with Anti-Christ'.[81]

Calvin could not have agreed with this formulation. He, too,
believed that God's revelation was key. However, he believed that
'natural law' was nothing but God's revelation to all people,
redeemed and unredeemed. All humanity shared this revelation in
common. He wrote:

> It is a fact that the law of God which we call the moral law is nothing
> else than a testimony of natural law and of that conscience which God
> has engraved upon the minds of men.[82]

Unredeemed people could reason accurately because they had
engraved upon their hearts godly truths which were the starting
points of their reasoning.

This is the conviction which led Calvin to forcefully reject the
Reconstructionism of his day. Mincing no words, Calvin taught:

> There are some who deny that a commonwealth is duly framed which
> neglects the political system of Moses, and is ruled by the common laws
> of nations. Let other men consider how perilous and seditious this
> notion is; it will be enough for me to have proved it false and foolish.[83]

Luther also held to the sufficiency of reason within its proper
sphere. We have noted earlier his emphasis on 'two regiments' and
two kingdoms. He said God's spiritual kingdom was ruled by the

gospel and revelation while God's worldly kingdom was ruled by the law and reason. Thus reason had a perfectly valid role.

It seems to this author that the views of Calvin and Luther are more consistent with the Scriptures than are those of the Reconstructionists. The scriptural view is that reason is fallen yet useful. Sin has twisted the human mind but it has not obliterated it altogether. Humanity may be fallen but is still in the image of God.

God himself reasons with sinful, fallen humanity; something he would hardly do if it was an exercise in futility. He says to faithless Israel, even before the New Covenant outpouring of the Holy Spirit has been made available to them, 'Come now, let us reason together' (Is 1:18).

The apostle Paul reasoned with unregenerate, fallen sinners, apparently convinced that this was no pointless activity and that sinners were able to reason about spiritual truths. This is how he evangelised the Thessalonian Jews and Gentiles: 'He reasoned with them from the Scriptures, explaining and proving that the Christ had to suffer and rise from the dead' (Acts 17:2–3). Indeed, we know that his reasoning was far from useless for, as a result, 'a large number' are said to have believed.

Godly wisdom does not scorn reason. In fact, one of the characteristics distinguishing it from 'earthly, unspiritual' wisdom is that it is 'reasonable' (see James 3:15, 17, NASB).

And as for the doctrine of natural law being a 'truce with Antichrist', it would be more accurate to view it as a reformulation of Romans 2:14–15 which states:

> Indeed, when Gentiles, who do not have the law, do by nature things required by the law, they are a law for themselves, even though they do not have the law, since they show that the requirements of the law are written on their hearts, their consciences also bearing witness.

The scripture could scarcely speak more clearly. Unbelievers are not hopelessly in the dark about God's moral law. They do have a dim grasp of God's ways and God's law even if they rebel against it. 'It is written on their hearts.

God does not negate the contribution unregenerate minds can make to the building up of our earthly society. More startling still, he even allowed unregenerate minds to contribute, at times, to the construction of his divine society, the people of God. We see, in Exodus 18, Moses, the man of God, receiving important help and advice from pagan Jethro. Jethro is not only unregenerate, he is a pagan priest to boot—'Jethro, the priest of Midian' (Ex 18:1).

See, in 1 Kings 7:13–14, how Solomon, before he ever drifted into apostasy, drafts into his service Huram of Tyre. Huram was only partly Jewish, his mother being from the tribe of Naphtali and his father from Tyre. But that did not prevent Solomon from utilising his talents in the Temple. Huram made all the bronze artifacts for the Temple, 'so many, the weight of the bronze was not determined' (1 Kings 7:47). God used his contribution. How much more today can he allow the contributions of unregenerate minds to build earthly kingdoms and human governments.[84]

The Reconstructionists overstate the inadequacy of reason; it is not as unable to find truth as they claim. Equally, they overstate the exhaustiveness of Scripture. In the words of theologian Cornelius Van Til, 'The Bible is authoritative on everything to which it speaks. And it speaks of everything.' The Bible is God's word but it does not speak comprehensively about everything under the sun. Paul may have said that a little wine is good for the stomach (1 Tim 5:23), but that does not mean this is the last word on the subject. It does not mean that Rennies or Settlers are unscriptural. The Bible never purports to give us a complete medical programme, neither does it purport to give us a complete political programme.

Where Scripture is silent, people are free to work out as best they can what they think is the right way forward. This is a God-given freedom. Reconstructionists who insist that we must not venture further than Old Testament legislation have a similar approach to the Bible as one sincere Christian who told me, 'I think clapping hands is good and biblical but swaying is out; after all, where in the Bible does it say anything about that?' The whole approach here is wrong. The Bible gives us the general framework in these areas and then leaves it to us to work out the details.

It is this 'freedom principle' that a Reconstructionist such as David Chilton misses when he writes:

> The prophets therefore took their stand firmly in terms of biblical law.... they never advocated statist policies to remedy the situation. You will never read of an Old Testament prophet calling for rent controls, minimum wage laws, or guaranteed jobs.[85]

Chilton's reasoning is unconvincing. Old Testament prophets never called for faith in Christ, evangelisation of the heathen, no taxation without representation or a host of other principles we would now consider important. Does that mean we, today, should not call for them? Obviously not. We can and should be doing things not specifically mentioned by the Old Testament prophets. God has given us freedom within a certain framework. Because the Reconstructionists' framework does not allow for this freedom it is far too narrow. One preacher said it well: 'The gospel cannot be too narrow or God would not recommend it for footwear.'

Reconstructionists find concrete blueprints for action in the Old Testament where other Christians find only 'general principles'. Reconstructionists suspect these Christians of using this 'general principles' approach as a ruse to escape the plain and obvious meaning of the Old Testament. But the apostle Paul was resorting to no ruse in digging general principles out of the Old Testament.

In 1 Corinthians 9:9–10 Paul writes:

> For it is written in the Law of Moses, 'Do not muzzle the ox'.... Is it about oxen that God is concerned? Surely he says this for us, doesn't he? Yes.

Paul here looks deeper than the first meaning and sees that what God intends for New Testament Christians to understand from this passage is that Christian workers are worthy of financial support. He gets a general principle from oxen—no small feat!

And in Romans 9:7–8 Paul writes:

> 'It is through Isaac that your offspring will be reckoned.' In other words, it is not the natural children who are God's children, but it is the children of the promise who are regarded as Abraham's offspring.

Again, Paul digs a general principle out of a specific, concrete, historical situation. The concrete situation—Abraham fathering a race according to the promise of God—is of some historical interest, but the general principle—becoming children of promise through Christ—is vitally, 'life-changingly' important. The general principle is more important than the concrete specifics.

We Christians need to be reading our Old Testaments with active minds, asking the Holy Spirit for guidance. We need to learn and relearn God's principles, his ways as shown in his dealings with the children of Israel. 'Principle hunting' is biblical. Principle hunting is critical to the pursuit of godly politicking. How can we be Christlike in our politicking if we do not understand God's priorities or God's ways? Chapters 7 through 9 will explore some of these key biblical principles.

To discover and apply God's principles we must study his word and carefully observe his world. You cannot do that without an active mind. Although the human mind is fallen it is not useless. Revelation is vital but it is not exhaustive, nor is it the only avenue to truth. While it is the only avenue to spiritual truth, to the understanding of redemption in Christ, it is not the only avenue to natural truths. That is why we should not deny its place in the art of politics.

The place of force

One gets the uneasy feeling in reading Reconstructionist literature that they want to return to the bad old days when a heretic was a heretic and was treated as such by being burned at the stake! I exaggerate for effect, but there is no escaping the fact that Reconstructionists see the state to have a role in enforcing religious faithfulness.

In fairness to the Reconstructionists, I should say that in several places they specifically disavow any wish for a state-imposed religion. Gary North writes:

> Let's get this straight: Christian reconstruction depends on majority rule. Of course, the leaders of the Christian reconstructionist movement expect a majority eventually to accept Christ as savior. If this doesn't happen, then Christians must be content with only partial reconstruction and only partial blessings from God. It isn't possible to ramrod God's blessings from the top, unless you're God.[86]

Reconstructionist Gary DeMar echoes this sentiment when he writes:

> God's kingdom is a kingdom of the heart, not a top-down centralized power that crushes the lawful desires of men, thereby creating rebels.[87]

Rousas Rushdoony takes a similar line:

> This condemnation [of false prophets to death] does not apply to a missionary situation where the land is anti-God to begin with: this is a situation for conversion. It does require a nation grounded in God's

law-system to preserve that order by punishing the basic treason against it.[88]

But this is just what I fear! Rushdoony is saying that while a nation does not have a Christian government, or a largely Christian society, it can allow heresy to flourish. But once sufficient Christians come to power then we can legislate the system we really want. Then we can punish heresy and suppress false religions. But *is* this the system we really want and is this really Christlike governing? Is this approach consistent with DeMar's opposition to 'top-down centralized power'? Once we get 51 per cent of the vote and outlaw heresy will the 49 per cent eligible for execution and banishment—for 'treason against God's law order'—really believe in our protestations against top-down imposed religion?

The Reconstructionists do not have a principled theology of religious toleration. Tolerance and pluralism are not highly valued. One fears that the Reconstructionists' affirmation of democratic tolerance is more in the nature of a tactical concession than a deeply felt, principled stand; something in the nature of Thomas Aquinas' concession that 'under certain circumstances heresy [may] be tolerated; when heretics and unbelievers are numerous, the church may tolerate them in order to avoid disturbance of the peace'.[89] According to this way of thinking, once our numbers are up all necessity for tolerance and pluralism disappears.

In other words, Reconstructionists would never grant that an individual has a 'right' to practise his religion; he only has a 'concession' from the government—a concession which can cease the moment the government decides it can suppress this religion without causing a 'disturbance of the peace'. Once the government can get away with it, it is free to restrict heretical religions.

The Reconstructionist objection to top-down, government-imposed religion is not based on firm principles but on a free-floating pragmatism. This, it seems to me, falls far short of what a Christian political philosophy ought to advocate. How can the religion of the cross be imposed by the sword?

I fear the seeds of oppression sown so clearly in Reconstructionist doctrine. Given their system, the steps to oppression are only logical:

Step 1: A narrow platform. Gary DeMar writes:

When man's laws, based upon the independent reasoning of the creature, are made equal with revelation, we can be assured that the new law system [a pagan system of law] is in place. Christians must know that there can be no so-called system of law.[90]

All law not specifically derived from Scripture is rejected as pagan.

Step 2: Deviance as treason. All deviance from this narrow platform is seen as 'treason', the subverting of God's order in the nation.

Step 3: Leaders do their duty. Leaders must do their duty, which is to rule according to God's law-order (the narrow platform) and to protect the society from treason. A government leader does not have the option to tolerate a 'little bit of treason';[91] he has a duty to suppress it. Religious dissent and heresy would thus have to be suppressed. This is oppression.

Although the Reconstructionists are not opposed to democracy,[92] there is some question as to how it would fare in their hands were they ever to hold the reins of power. For instance (the scenario is absurd but let's just follow the logic through to its ridiculous end), what would stop Reconstructionists from outlawing all non-Christian political parties, any party that would not affirm a biblical base? If they are not averse to executing heretics how much easier to imagine this far less drastic measure. The reasoning would be exactly the same: that a party wishing to put the state back on to secular principles would be leading the nation astray into apostasy and would be committing treason against God's law-order. Surely they would see it, then, as their duty to cleanse the land from any such evil.[93]

Neo-Reconstructionism

While the direction in which Reconstructionist rule would take us is somewhat bleak, some of the developments within Reconstructionist thinking are more encouraging. Most hopeful of all is a new development I shall call Neo-Reconstructionism.

Neo-Reconstructionism is a reworking of traditional Reconstructionism. Neo-Reconstructionists follow their Reconstructionist sires in believing that the Mosaic civil law is still valid for society today. But their depiction of the actual contents of the Mosaic Law differs radically from traditional Reconstructionism. For instance, one Neo-Reconstructionist explained to me that yes, Exodus 22:1 and 4[94] was applicable as a theft law today but that its instructions concerning the fivefold restitutionary payment for a stolen ox, the fourfold restitutionary payment for a stolen sheep and the twofold restitutionary payment for any stolen-but-recovered item were not to be taken literally. Indeed, he insisted, they were not even taken literally in the days of Moses. These multiples of repayment were, instead, to be understood as approximate guidelines.

Imagine, for instance, a cattle rustler working your neighbourhood in Jerusalem. At the end of the day he finds himself blessedly richer by two cows: 'Old Bess'—your next-door neighbour's emaciated, blind, lame one-step-away-from-being-beefburger cow—and 'Blue Ribbon Belle'—your own prize cow valued in the five figures for her pedigree. Supposing the thief had slaughtered both for steak, would justice be served if the thief were to repay you and your neighbour the same amount according to the literal rendering of Exodus 22:1—five new cows? Hardly; not today and not in Moses' day and age either.

My Neo-Reconstructionist friend explained to me that what was especially relevant for us today from the restitutionary repayment scheme of Exodus 22 was not the concrete details—five cows or four sheep—but the principles underlying these details. What were these principles? That the victim of the theft needed to be compensated for his actual loss, for any pain and suffering involved in the theft, for investigation costs, for future investment lost. All these were to be considered when deciding how much restitution to make.

This is eminently reasonable—but distinctly different from the traditional Reconstructionism which eschews the search for 'general principles'. Here is a form of Reconstructionism which believes that the Old Testament was always meant to be read as embodying general principles. The usual 'principle approach' to the Old Testament says that with the advent of the New Testament, the Old Testament laws no longer literally apply, that they need now to be reinterpreted in the light of New Testament general principles. The Neo-Reconstructionists say that this 'principle approach' is no New Testament innovation; rather it was the Old Testament approach itself. The Old Testament was never meant to be woodenly applied and interpreted even in the days of the patriarchs! Far from disagreeing with the proponents of the 'principle approach', and far from accusing them of introducing a radical, new innovation in biblical interpretation, the Neo-Reconstructionists have actually beaten the 'principlists' to the punch by 3,000 years, saying that this approach is as old as the Bible itself.

Neo-Reconstructionism opens up the possibility of a rapprochement between the Reconstructionist school and the more traditional approaches to Christian politicking. There are enough common convictions for meaningful working coalitions to be formed. This is a sign of cheer.

After all, Reconstructionists are Christian brethren with whom we should be able to work, even if in some cases that unity takes on the tone of the eighteenth-century American General, Charles Lee, who left instructions that he was not to be buried near any Anabaptists or Presbyterians as 'I had so much bad company while living that I do not choose to continue it while dead'! General Lee disapproved, but at least he had sense enough to lump together differing bands of Christian believers.

Reconstructionists are to be applauded for the fact that they take God seriously and they take his word seriously. Their vigorous assertion that a 'whining negativism is not enough' is commendable. None should disagree with their declaration that God is the Lord of all life. Nor can we quibble with the good works that are being accomplished under the impetus of Reconstructionist theology.

It is their underlying Old Testament framework that I deny. Until the Reconstructionists renounce their allegiance to an Old Testament approach to government, their teachings will always cast the shadow of tyranny; a tyranny of the righteous, perhaps, but still a tyranny. It's a shadow that the New Testament does not cast. As such, it is no model for Christians to follow.

6

Libertarians versus Moralitarians

G.K. Chesterton once darkly warned his readers that all-out war between telescopists and microscopists was imminent.[95] Doubtless such a prospect fails to daunt; of more concern in our day and age is the war between libertarians and moralitarians. The battle is on between libertarians who venerate individual freedom and moralitarians who venerate morality. Libertarians understand politics to be the art of maximising and protecting freedom. Moralitarians understand politics to be the art of promoting and protecting morality. When these two very different visions of the political enterprise meet there is bound to be conflict.

In the last chapter we criticised a style of Christianity too eager to impose its narrow vision of Old Testament legislation on society. In this chapter we criticise a libertarianism grimly determined to impose its own brand of amoral politics on society; a libertarianism which grows hysterically vocal the moment morality presumes to tiptoe into the public arena. Apparently, individuals must be free to act immorally but politicians must not be free to legislate morally. Libertarians want an 'open' society, but foolish is the person who then presumes to assume that this openness extends to morality. A crusading liberalism turns out to be no more tolerant than a crusading Christianity.

Consider some of the following real-life situations. How do you think they should be handled?

The Sunday Telegraph of 24 January 1988 reported that the Isle of Man, last outpost of Victorian values...where homosexual acts can incur heavy prison sentences; faces a serious liberal assault from a 43-year-old doctor's wife...who...proposes to legalize homosexuality between consenting adults.... Reform has long been urged by the British government which is uneasy that a Crown dependency preserves sexual laws similar to those in Rumania, Libya and Chile.

Evidently the residents of the Isle of Man think differently. What do you think? Should freedom be allowed or morality imposed?

A draft bill published by the Labour Campaign for Lesbian and Gay Rights included, among other items, a proposal for legalising sexual relations with animals and a proposal for legalising conduct of a sexual nature in a public place, whether between members of the same sex or members of the opposite sex.

In the United States of America similar moves were afoot as the pro-homosexual lobby sought to turn sodomy into a 'civil right' protected under the Constitution's Bill of Rights. Moreover, all six candidates for the 1988 Democratic nomination for President came out in favour of a 'national gay rights bill'.[96] Thankfully, George Bush said he would veto such a bill.

Gore Vidal is a novelist and playwright who crafts pernicious ideas in beautiful prose. He toured the United States during the 1972 presidential election giving his own 'State of the Union' address. Here is his gospel:

Roughly 80 per cent of police work in the United States has to do with the regulation of our private morals. By that I mean, controlling what we drink, eat, smoke, put into our veins—not to mention trying to regulate with whom and how we have sex, with whom and how we gamble. As a result, our police are among the most corrupt in the Western world.... Therefore, let us remove from the statute books all laws that have to do with private morals—what are called victimless crimes. If a man or woman wants to be a prostitute that is his or her affair. It is no business of the state what we do with our bodies sexually.[97]

Vidal goes on to reassuringly point out, 'Obviously...the virtue of our animal friends will continue to be protected by the S.P.C.A.' But then, Vidal had not yet heard of the Labour Campaign for Lesbian and Gay Rights. What do you think? Should we adopt Vidal's across-the-board liberalism?

The evangelical right pressed in the early 1980s for laws prohibiting unmarried couples from booking into motel rooms. Consider that as recently as 1948 the Boston police recorded 248 arrests for adultery.[98] Is this an unwarranted intrusion by the state into an area which should be left to private ethics or is this the state carrying out its proper task of protecting morality?

The issue of Sunday trading brought a split within the very Conservative Party which was proposing it. Journalist Noel Malcolm, commenting on the furore occasioned by this particular issue at the 1987 Conservative Party Conference, wrote:

> The real division within the Conservative Party is undramatic, but nevertheless profound.... The real division...is between those who think that it is not the business of government to interfere in people's lives by imposing moral, cultural and religious values on them, and those who think that's just what government is for. 'Libertarians' is a good label for one side of the argument; 'moral majority' is a cumbersome phrase for the people on the other side, so I shall coin the word 'moralitarians'.... Both sides...could all unite in attacking the excesses of municipal socialism: libertarians denounced it for imposing its doctrinaire values on people's lives, and moralitarians denounced it for imposing the wrong doctrines.[99]

Moralitarians vie with libertarians and at the centre of their debate is the question: When does sin become a crime? Earnest libertarians would say, 'Never.' Unduly fanatical moralists would say, 'Just about always.' Common sense would say, 'Sometimes.' Godly extremists feel compelled to impose God's will while ignoring the individual's right to choose. Libertarian extremists defend the individual's right to choose at all costs while ignoring society's right to defend itself against decadence and God's right to rule his universe.

The classical libertarian position was put forward by John Stuart Mill over a century ago in his essay *On Liberty*:

> The only purpose for which power can rightfully be exercised over any member of a civilised community against his will is to prevent harm to others. His own good whether physical or moral is not sufficient warrant.[100]

Freedom was the bottom line. Its only limitation was if it brought harm—specifically physical harm—to someone else.

Mill's thinking, shocking to his Victorian peers, predominates today. It can be seen, for instance, in the Wolfenden Report of 1957 which suggested a change in English legislation. On the basis that 'unless a deliberate attempt is to be made by society...to equate the sphere of crime with that of sin, there must remain a realm of private morality and immorality which is...not the law's business', the Wolfenden Report recommended that 'homosexual behaviour between consenting adults in private should no longer be a criminal offence'.[101] Though not immediately accepted, the report found its way into English law. Parliament eventually followed its lead and decriminalised homosexuality.

The Wolfenden Report brought about a lively exchange of views between Lord Devlin, a judge of the Queen's Bench, and H.L.A. Hart, Professor of Jurisprudence at the University of Oxford. Lord Devlin disagreed with the Wolfenden Report while Professor Hart defended it.

Lord Devlin pointed out that if the report's standard of no public morality—morality as a strictly 'private affair'—was taken seriously, not only homosexuality, but euthanasia, suicide, duelling, abortion, and incest between brother and sister would have to be legalised too. All are acts which can be done in private and without offence to others and need not involve the corruption or exploitation of others (I would disagree with Devlin's saying abortion does not exploit the foetus). However, society would not tolerate the legalisation of such acts. Indeed, even the members of the committee making the Wolfenden Report would find this repellent. But why? Devlin finds his answer in the fact that, like it or not, lawmakers do operate according to a certain public morality which cannot be transgressed. And this is only natural, says Devlin.

Lord Devlin defends the right of a society to legislate certain core values, saying:

> What makes a society of any sort is community of ideas, not only political ideas but also ideas about the way its members should behave...without shared ideas on politics, morals and ethics no society can exist.... For society is not something that is kept together physically; it is held by the invisible bonds of common thought. If the bonds were too far relaxed the members would drift apart.... The bondage is part of the price of society; and mankind, which needs society, must pay its price...then society may use the law to preserve morality in the same way as it uses it to safeguard anything else that is essential to its existence.[102]

Society has the right to protect itself against treason—to limit the citizen's freedom in order to preserve the freedom of the society as a whole—for treason threatens a society's existence.[103] Equally, society has the right to protect itself against moral dissolution.

Mill was totally arbitrary in limiting his 'harm principle' solely to the physical realm. Why should not moral harm also be included? It is just as real and just as destructive. Indeed, where moral harm has been left to breed, physical harm is sure to follow. That is why those who are truly concerned about protecting citizens from harm will legislate against immoral deeds.

The Christian believes with Devlin that governments should punish wrongdoing because a common morality holds society together. But Christians have another less utilitarian reason for believing that governments ought to punish transgressions against the common morality. (After all, common immoralities, and lies held in common, also hold society together. A Christian would not, however, hold that these should be upheld.) We believe evil deeds ought to be punished because we understand this to be part of government's God-given role. Romans 13:4 says, 'He [the one in authority] is God's servant...an agent of wrath to bring punishment on the wrongdoer.' God has so decreed it.

How are we to decide the sort of wrongdoing that government ought to punish from the sort it ought to leave alone? Let me suggest eight principles and considerations to guide us in answering this question.

Humanity was created free

Our very first point is that humanity was created free. This is old ground from Chapter 3 that we do not want to cover all over again. Nevertheless, the fact that humanity was created free is such a key consideration in the biblical view of government that it needs to be stated. When William Wilberforce was fighting for the halt of the slave trade, he was accused of advocating compulsory conversion to Christianity. His reply was:

> Compulsion and Christianity! Why, the very terms are at variance with each other—the ideas are incompatible. In the language of Inspiration itself, Christianity has been called the 'law of liberty'.[104]

God is the all-powerful Sovereign who allows each puny individual a measure of sovereignty over his own life. A person can freely choose his direction and his destiny. God's governing of humanity is not characterised by totalitarian control. If God, who is pure in motive and unlimited in wisdom, does not exercise total control over humanity, why should his creatures, who are sinful and unwise, attempt it?

The results are always unpleasant when a human being attempts to play God. The results are even worse when people attempt to play God in a manner that God himself would not recognise, ie, by allowing no freedom to sin. Religiously motivated totalitarianism is not really what God is after.

The libertarians are right to put a high premium on liberty. God does.

This freedom is limited

Freedom, however, is not the first and last principle of God's governing style. The libertarians are wrong in absolutising this one principle. Our second principle is that freedom is limited. Yes, God respects human freedom but he also respects his own right to rule the universe. One of the most obvious of God's limits on humanity's freedom is the establishment of a Judgement Day. At that time each individual will have to face the consequences of his freely taken choices. All debts will be called in. Every person has been given the right to choose his way, but he has not been given the right to choose the attendant consequences. These are up to God to parcel out. Individuals have freedom but it is within very definite limits.

God also limits people's freedom by establishing governments. 'Everyone must submit himself to the governing authorities.... The authorities that exist have been established by God' (Rom 13:1). 'No man is an island,' the poet John Donne said and he was quite right. God has created men and women to be in society and that society, to survive, must have some order which they fit into and submit to.

The Englishman's home is his castle, yet planning regulations dictate what that castle should look like and where, if at all, it can be extended. You are free to live in the sort of home you would like—within limits. You are free to drive where you want and at the speed you want—within limits. If everyone invented his own traffic rules the result would be chaos (witness Paris and Rome!). Living in society means that we give up total individual freedom.

Societies and their governments continually seek to determine the proper boundary line between individual freedoms and governmental duties to restrain individuals. The result is countless border wars.

In 1987, California banned smoking on all its internal airline flights and on all buses and trains. It was decided that the individual smoker had no right to endanger the community's health. This did not sit so well with one pipe-smoking State Senator who called the bill's proponents 'health fascists'.

London's *Evening Standard* reported the story of a German judge banning two plastic garden gnomes from a seventy-two-year-old man's front garden because of a complaint by a woman in a neighbouring block of flats. She claimed that the two cheeky figures—with their pointed red hats and grey beards—offended her aesthetic sense. After a four-year legal battle an Appeals Court judge sided with her saying, 'It is legally wrong for this woman to have to tolerate objects which upset her,' giving the gnomes' owner a month to find them a new home.[105] There may be many who would disagree with this court's decision (what about the rights of the gnomes?) but few who would disagree with the deeper presupposition underlying the court's very existence: namely, that it exists to restrain the freedom of those who are wronging their neighbour.

The threefold jurisdiction

Our third principle is that as individual freedoms are limited, even so are governmental freedom and authority limited. Government without limits is tyrannical government. Just what are these limits?

James Madison's famous *Memorial and Remonstrance* (1785)—an essay that did much to ensure religious liberty was preserved in the commonwealth of Virginia—addressed itself to the proper role and limits of government. Madison wrote:

'Religion or the duty which we owe to our Creator and the Manner of discharging it, can be directed only by reason and conviction, not by force or violence.' The Religion then of every man must be left to the conviction and conscience of every man; and it is the right of every man to exercise it as these may dictate. This right...is unalienable; because the opinions of men, depending only on the evidence contemplated by their own minds, cannot follow the dictates of other men.[106]

Madison was saying that government had no jurisdiction over

people's hearts and minds but only over their deeds. People's actions are properly subject to the government's lawmaking power. 'Actions' includes deeds that physically harm and deeds that morally harm. What individuals think, believe and worship, however, is not under the government's jurisdiction. Here each person has freedom to follow his whims and insights.

In other words, we could look at humanity in three departments: his deeds; his mind—what he thinks; his heart—what he is devoted to. The government has jurisdiction over people's deeds (Romans 13:4: 'the wrong*doer*') but not over their mind and heart. Here they are to be free from government imposition.

Creator/Redeemer distinction

Professor Amos of Virginia's Regent University has pointed out to me the pertinent doctrine of the Creator/Redeemer distinction. Calvin wrote:

> The Lord first appears, as well in the creation of the world as in the general doctrine of Scripture, simply as a Creator, and afterwards as a Redeemer in Christ—a twofold knowledge of him hence arises.[107]

The relevance of this doctrine for us here is twofold. First, although not everyone is related to God as Redeemer—and hence cannot be expected to live according to redemptive mandates—all people are related to God as Creator. Every person, therefore, can be expected to live up to the general laws which God gives as Creator. Eighteenth-century English jurist William Blackstone—author of a work held by some to be 'the most important legal treatise ever written in the English language'[108]—reminded his readers of the universal obligations to obey the Creator:

> When the Supreme Being formed the universe, and created matter out of nothing, he impressed certain principles upon that matter.... governed by laws.... Man, considered as a creature, must necessarily be subject to the laws of his creator, for he is entirely a dependent being.... This will of his maker is called the law of nature.[109]

It makes no difference whether the individual is Muslim, pagan or Christian; he is subject to the same laws of nature. Both Muslims and Christians must live by the laws of gravity. Both Muslims and

Christians must live by the equally binding law of nature—albeit a moral law—which states, 'Thou shalt not kill.'

The second ramification of the Creator/Redeemer distinction comes to light when we consider the operative principles of these two realms. The order of redemption works along radically different lines from the order of creation. The order of redemption operates according to grace, special revelation, and the personal, intimate dealings of individuals with God. By contrast, the order of creation operates according to law and general revelation.[110] For government to intrude with its sword into the arena of redemption would be a denial of the very nature of the redemptive order. However, it is totally consistent with the order of creation.

There is an absolute morality underlying society's laws

Our fifth principle rubs up against the spirit of the age: the age of relativism. The apostle Paul wrote in Romans 13:3-4:

> For rulers hold no terror for those who do right, but for those who do wrong.... if you do wrong, be afraid, for he [the one in authority] does not bear the sword for nothing. He is God's servant, an agent of wrath to bring punishment on the wrongdoer.

Paul talks in terms of wrong/right here, not in terms of order/disorder. The role ascribed to government has highly moral overtones. The government is to stop what is 'wrong'. The government is described as an 'agent of wrath'. Surely the only appropriate target of God's wrath is moral evil. God's wrath is not aroused over a little bit of disorder.

Libertarians say, 'You cannot legislate morality.' Romans 13 says, in effect, 'You *must* legislate morality.' In fact, what is legality but legislated morality? We need only think of our laws against murder, theft, child-battering, libel, and so on, to see this.

Very few libertarians would be as rigidly consistent as libertarian economist Dr Murray Rothbard who suggested that, in a truly free society, libel, slander and even blackmail would not be illegalised:

> Blackmail would not be illegal in the free society. For blackmail is the receipt of money in exchange for the service of not publicizing certain information about the other person. No violence or threat of violence to person or property is involved.[111]

Libertarians, in fact, want to legislate morality as much as any seventeenth-century Puritan. It's just that they want to legislate *their* morality rather than a seventeenth-century morality. The frustration is that they hide this fact from the public. The comedy is that they hide this fact from themselves.

Twentieth-century morality is rooted in moral relativism—a conviction that mortal man cannot know, with certainty, what God's (if he is even there!) absolute moral laws are.[112] Tolerance is king. Black and white pronouncements on morality are taken as sure indicators of a distastefully provincial mind. Moral relativism is an intellectual hothouse in which political libertarianism breeds and prospers. After all, how dare we legislate on the basis of moral uncertainties?

This is the line of reasoning undergirding John Stuart Mill's libertarian doctrine. When I wrote earlier that Mill's limiting his 'harm principle' to physical harm was purely arbitrary, I was not strictly speaking the truth. It was a logical and reasonable conclusion given his starting point of moral relativism. He wrote:

> The same reasons which show that opinion should be free, prove also that he should be allowed, without molestation, to carry his opinions into practice at his own cost. That mankind are not infallible; that their truths, for the most part, are only half-truths; that...diversity not an evil, but a good, until mankind are much more capable than at present of recognising all sides of the truth.[113]

Mill asserted that human moral certainties were only half-truths (and doesn't everybody know a half-truth is more dangerous than an obvious lie?), that they were essentially unknowable. The Bible, of course, asserts that humanity has been made privy to God's absolutes. We have his laws written on our hearts (Rom 1:19; 2:15), and we have the special revelation of the Scriptures. We are not hopelessly lost in moral relativism. Human beings do not create their own morality; they discover God's morality. Morality is not a human invention that man is free to change as he 'progresses'; morality is a divine fact to which man must submit.

The biblical view is that human governments are to reflect God's government. God governs according to absolute moral standards, so human governments are to govern according to absolute moral standards.

People can distort and run from God's absolute morality but they can never completely eradicate its presence in their hearts.

That is why, try as they might, libertarians actually turn out to be firm moralists. Let us see the libertarian morality at work.

H.L. Mencken, journalist extraordinaire in the early twentieth century, violently objected to Christians using the government to impose their morality on others. In a piece entitled 'The Believer', he dismissed faith as 'the illogical belief in the improbable' and the man of faith as 'not a mere ass; he is actually ill'.[114] Did this mean that Mencken was not a man of faith himself? Of course not! His faith—held no less tenaciously than the faith of the fervent Christian—was crystalised in the following credo: 'I believe in only one thing and that thing is human liberty.... I am against any man and any organization which seeks to limit or deny that freedom.'

This is not the voice of the sceptic speaking; this is the voice of the true believer (note his 'I believe') who has seen the light and is willing to risk life and honour for his cause. This is not the voice of the reasonable man suspending belief until more evidence is in; this is the voice of the prophet declaring revealed truth. Liberty is his particular morality and liberty is his faith. And, clearly, this is the morality he wants to impose on the public square.

Mencken's blend of scepticism concerning blind faith and blind faith in his own scepticism reminds me of an aphorism I once saw hanging from someone's wall. It ran, 'Those of you who think you know everything are annoying to those of us who do.'

Professor Hart may have defended the Wolfenden Report's stated principle that 'private morality...is not the law's business', but he was actually unable to keep his own morality private. His basis for supporting the Wolfenden Report was that it chose as its guidelines for lawmaking the avoidance of human misery and the maximising of human freedom. In the words of Professor Hart, 'I have also assumed...the critical principle, central to all morality, that human misery and the restriction of freedom are evils.'[115] This, then, is Professor Hart's morality, a morality which he places at the very centre of his theory of legislation. All legislation is to be judged by how it violates or is in accord with his two central moral principles: the avoidance of human misery and the maximising of human freedom.

In a similar vein we have Gore Vidal, who shocked his middle-class audiences by suggesting the legalising of drugs and sexual perversion. One might think that here is a case of pure libertarianism opposed, on doctrinal grounds, to the legislating of morality.

No again. At the bottom of Vidal's suggestions lies his own peculiar morality.

He writes, 'Recognize that bisexuality was once our culture's norm and that Christianity's perversion of this human fact is the aberration and not the other way around.'[116] Homosexuality is normal and healthy! Christianity is what is perverted! In his mind, he is not advocating the legalisation of perversion but the legalisation of what is normal. Morality is very much at the bottom of his suggestions. Vidal contests America's puritanical sexual laws not because they reflect moral standards but because they do not reflect *his* moral standards. Vidal turns out to be yet another closet moralist seeking to craft legislation in the image of his own particular set of values.

In other words, the libertarian/moralitarian debate cannot be framed in terms of reason versus faith or in terms of neutral, value-free secular rationality battling judgemental, stuck-in-the-mud, irrational morality. What we are really seeing is moralities in conflict. One, indeed, may be stuffy and the other progressive but make no mistake, they are both moralities.

While progressive intellectuals argue about the wrongs and rights of legislating morality, society gets on and simply does it. With a common sense deeper than 'expert opinion', society knows that it cannot avoid legislating morality and does not bother trying. Our anti-racism laws are clear examples of this. There is an undiluted moral fervour behind such legislation that no one even bothers to hide. Indeed, we even glory in it.

But outside of certain narrowly defined spheres (racism and business greed to name two) we tend to keep our moralism under wraps. This moralism with a bad conscience (for daring to hold a morality in the first place and, second, for daring to show its face publicly) is evident in the Wolfenden Report's proposals on prostitution. The report concluded that the current view of the law should be upheld: prostitution was legal; poncing (pimping) and running a brothel were not. Even the liberal Wolfenden Report wanted to retain the illegal status of ponces and brothels, but the really revealing item is the reasons they gave for their stand. They opposed brothel-running as 'exploitation'. Now there's a good progressive word escaping all ugly moralistic overtones. It sounds 'caring' (another progressive word) rather than judgemental. But this exploitation is a pure fiction. Most prostitutes enter the profession in the same manner that others enter a trade; no more or less willingly. They may not love their trade but 'Ya gotta earn a living.'

The Wolfenden Report claims that the brothel-keeper and the ponce exploit 'the whole complex of the relationship between prostitute and the customer; they are, in effect, exploiting the human weaknesses which cause the customer to seek the prostitute and the prostitute to meet the demand'.[117]

Surely this is legal word sorcery. Exploitation has to do with coercing people against their will. It has to do with forcibly depriving people of a just return for their labours. Is this happening to prostitutes' customers? Hardly. You have only to observe the cars on the prowl down at London's King's Cross, drivers eagerly scanning the pavement for an evening companion to know there is no compulsion involved. The supply is only meeting the demand. These customers would not be there if they felt exploited and if they felt they were not getting a fair return on their fee.

No, exploitation is a weasel word behind which the report hides its morality. If one separates all moral overtones from prostitution then one would have to say that brothel-keepers are no more exploiting their customers' appetite and weakness for commercial sex than supermarket chains are exploiting their customers' appetite and weakness for food. Both supermarkets and brothels provide a service by meeting people's physical needs. It is only our very special ideas about sex—moral ideas—which make us treat the two differently. The Wolfenden Report thinks commercialised sex distasteful because it finds it morally offensive. All this is hidden under the word 'exploitation'.

The report cannot bring itself to say that brothel-keeping should be illegalised because it is morally wrong. Yet even one of the meanings of the word 'exploitation' carries this moral connotation. *Webster's Dictionary* defines it as 'to make unethical use of for one's own advantage or profit'.

While we shout the language of freedom, we practise a code of moral restraint. What we really believe in is freedom within limits. This is biblical, natural and right. Pure libertarianism is contradicted by libertarian theorists themselves, by our society at large and by Romans 13. We should not be ashamed of our convictions on moral restraints any more than we are of our convictions on freedom. Civil society is possible only when both are in operation. Tolerance needs to be hedged by principle; freedom by duty.

There will be irreconcilable conflicts in values—expect war

Our sixth principle starts off with a recognition of the truth of Amos 3:3: 'Do two walk together unless they have agreed to do so?' This verse has also been translated: 'Can two walk together unless they are agreed?' The point is that common effort demands common agreement. Human endeavours demand unity as well as diversity. Diversity without unity leads to chaos. Unity without diversity guarantees a mediocrity both bland and rigid.

Democracy, a political experiment seeking to embrace diversity, is not possible without a basic unity. Proponents of the 'open society' are right to champion the individual's liberty but wrong to downplay the need for conformity on core issues and the need for a certain amount of 'closedness'. All values and standards of behaviour cannot be up for grabs.

Democratic societies value openness and tolerance; they also value givens and truth. Professor Willmoore Kendall points out:

> In order to practice tolerance on behalf of the pursuit of truth, you have first to value and believe in not merely the pursuit of truth but truth itself.... The all-questions-are-open-questions-society cannot do that.[118]

There are many issues that can be settled by compromise; issues where absolute agreement is not imperative for the survival of the political enterprise. But there are core issues where compromise is not possible; issues that cannot be fudged; issues on which society has to come down on one side or the other. This is not undemocratic; this is just the nature of reality, political reality included. As somebody has put it:

> Pluralism does not mean that all positions must be afforded equal weight and equal value. Pluralism simply means that all positions deserve to be fairly heard. Democracy then requires that a choice be made.

For Christians to insist uncompromisingly on certain values in the public square is not an essential violation of democracy. Secularists insist on their values; why cannot Christians fight for their values? William Wilberforce's crusade against slavery was just such a battle. On one side stood Wilberforce with his biblically grounded values and on the other side stood the forces of unfet-

tered profit. One tactic was to deny Wilberforce the right to introduce Christian piety into politics. Lord Melbourne said at the time,
'Things have come to a pretty pass when religion is allowed to
invade public life.' The Earl of Abingdon concurred, saying,
'Humanity is a private feeling, not a public principle to act upon.'[119]
But Wilberforce pushed on anyway and England was a better place
because of it.

Christians need to know those values which they cannot see
compromised in the public square; then they need to do everything
within their power—using the media, the ballot box, the courts—
to see those core values prevail. That's politics.

Gospel transforms culture; legislation preserves it

This seventh principle—that the gospel is what transforms culture
whereas legislation only preserves it—reminds us to beware the
political illusion. Politicians for ever promise more than they can
deliver; it seems to be the very nature of the political beast. Today,
when Christians are reclaiming their dominion mandate in the
realm of politics, we need to remember not to expect more than we
ought.

If Jesus had thought that grabbing governmental power was
central to building the kingdom then, when his followers rushed to
make him king by force (Jn 6:15), he would have eagerly jumped at
the chance. As it was, he was indifferent. More, he hid himself. He
did not confuse political power with kingdom power. We need the
same kind of clarity.

We can never legislate our way into an ideal world. We will
never pass laws which will transform our sinful world into some sort
of angelic haven of purity and peace.

Purity and peace come to a culture to the degree that there is
purity and peace in the hearts of transformed individuals. That is
the work of the gospel. The order is: first transformation, then
legislation. Legislation can only preserve the gains won by gospel
transformation. Legislation can only reflect the values and goals of
society. It cannot put holy goals into people's hearts.

Perhaps I slightly overstate my case to make a point. I say
'overstate' because if it were literally true that legislation could
only preserve gains won by the gospel then pagan societies ought to
be without laws restraining evil. Not only do we know that this is
simply not the case, we also know—from Acts 17:26 and Romans

13:1–7—that it *ought not* to be the case. Even the unredeemed are expected to govern according to God's moral law.

No, even in the absence of the gospel, legislation serves a useful, God-ordained purpose. Legislation will not save a culture but it can help a culture. Specifically, legislation can accomplish two salutary effects: first, it can restrain evil and, second, it can teach. These are not to be sniffed at. Surely we are all thankful for the laws which protect us from violent and unscrupulous men. A society where evil is restrained is far preferable to a society where it runs at will.

Legislation is also a powerful teaching tool. So certain was the Swedish government of the teaching potential of legislation that in 1979 it passed an 'anti-spanking' law which, interestingly, had no special legal penalty. A law without a sanction! The Swedish Information Service explains that the law never meant to punish 'transgressors' but that 'the rule is chiefly only of educational significance'.[120] The government wants to teach parents not to physically discipline their children.

Legislation moulds the minds of the citizens growing up under that legislation. It teaches them what is permissible and what is not, what is shameful and what is not. Surely racism is far less acceptable in America's south due to decades of civil rights legislation. Legislation does teach.

In saying that legislation cannot accomplish everything we must be careful not to say it can accomplish nothing.

Principled pragmatism

Pragmatism is not a dirty word. God is a pragmatist. He tempered his idealistic and demanding expectations of his people Israel with pragmatic concessions to their sinful hearts. He was legislating for sinners, not saints. No one knows that better than God. His is a principled pragmatism which combines a strict moral outlook with realistic what-will-work mentality. This is our eighth guiding principle.

See how Jesus responded to the Pharisees' challenge on divorce. The Pharisees had reacted to Jesus' teaching forbidding divorce by challenging him from an Old Testament teaching: 'Why then did Moses command that a man give his wife a certificate of divorce and send her away?' Jesus' reply was that 'Moses permitted you to divorce your wives because your hearts were hard. But it was not this way from the beginning' (Mt 19:7–8).

In other words, God lowered his standard to make it more accessible. He accommodated human sin. He legalised what he did not approve of. Divorce was against God's will but he still allowed it. He did not throw the floodgate completely open—there were laws governing divorce—to humanity's rebellious inclinations, but humanity's rebellious desires were not, in this particular instance, completely outlawed either.

God's principled pragmatism was also at work in his response to the Israelites' desire for a monarchy. God's intention was to direct them through the prophetic office—as with Moses and Samuel. But when they said they wanted a king instead his response to Samuel was, 'It is not you they have rejected as their king, but me' (1 Sam 8:7). The Israelites' plan was both a rejection of God's plan and of God himself. But did this mean that God had the earth open and swallow them whole? No, first he reasoned with them, showing them the cost of a monarchy—higher taxes and the loss of their independence. When they still persisted he said, 'Listen to them and give them a king' (1 Sam 8:22).

Governing in a sinful world entails not only listening to God but listening to people. It means not only respecting God's moral standard but also responding to people's hard hearts.

Surely it was a principled pragmatism which prevented the apostle Paul from fighting for the abolition of the slave trade in his own day. He obviously thought slavery was undesirable as he urged slaves, where possible, to win their freedom (1 Cor 7:21). He firmly condemned slave traders, equating them with perverts, murderers and liars (1 Tim 1:9–10; see the *niv*). He also knew, from Leviticus 25:41–43, the passage in which God forbade the Israelites to enslave fellow Israelites, that slavery was not God's ideal. Despite all this he did not, like the eighteenth- and nineteenth-century Christian reformers in America and Britain, forthrightly condemn and fight slavery. Why? I can only think it was because he was pragmatic. He knew he could not possibly win a battle against this entrenched social custom until there had been a moral and spiritual revolution. Only then would people's standards and viewpoints change.

Eighteenth- and nineteenth-century Britain and America had had such a spiritual revolution. The gospel had been preached there for centuries. A Christian standard could be appealed to. But there was no such generally accepted Christian standard in Paul's day. Paul had first to transform the culture of the Roman empire through the dynamite of the gospel before he could go on to challenge slavery. He knew his priorities and he stuck to them.

Unprincipled pragmatism

A Christian pragmatism is to be a principled pragmatism rather than the unprincipled pragmatism of this world. Worldly pragmatism is willing to do anything which 'works' (whatever that means; you cannot decide if something is working until you first have some ideal [the opposite of pragmatism] standard by which to judge it). This inevitably results in the 'end justifies the means' syndrome.

Ours is to be a principled pragmatism, a pragmatism strictly limited by moral constraints and guided towards ethical goals. The principled pragmatist has ethical endpoints in mind. He knows where he is going; he is just prudent about how to get there.

By contrast, unprincipled pragmatism, having no ideals to guide it, does not even know where it is going. It may talk of 'progress' but the question remains: Progress towards what? In the pointed words of G.K. Chesterton:

> Progress should mean that we are always changing the world to suit the vision. Progress does mean (just now) that we are always changing the vision.... We are not altering the real to suit the ideal. We are altering the ideal; it is easier.[121]

The pragmatism I espouse is not the anti-Christian pragmatism of a Charles Sanders Peirce or of a Chief Justice Oliver Wendell Holmes, Jr. It was Holmes who said that 'truth is the majority vote of that nation which could lick all others'.[122] Doubting that puny human beings could ever have access to real, absolute truth, pragmatism was all that was left to Holmes. Not content with having consigned truth to the scrap-heap of discarded illusions, Holmes went on to discard any notion of real law as well:

> The life of the law has not been logic; it has been experience. The felt necessities of the time...even the prejudices which judges share with their fellow-men, have had a good deal more to do than the syllogism in determining the rules by which men should be governed.[123]

Law, in Holmes' view, reflects not the absolute morality written on every man's heart but simply our sociological needs.

Pragmatism threatens liberty

What has been insufficiently considered is that this progressive pragmatism threatens the very liberty libertarians so cherish. Political liberties have not been won by the shifting counsels of moral relativists. Political liberties have been fought for and won by those convinced of the truth, righteousness and justice—rather than the mere 'usefulness'—of their cause. Only consider some of the central moments in Anglo-American history: Magna Carta—a document limiting the power of the government and securing individual rights—was forced on King John by nobles outraged at an injustice, namely that their property rights had been violated through the king's arbitrary seizure of their property.

Furthermore, England's Bill of Rights (1689)—the culmination of both the Puritan revolution (1640–1660) and the bloodless Glorious Revolution (1689)—was established through the efforts of those convinced that not only was their cause 'useful', but that it was just in an ultimate sense. The language of the document—it speaks of 'evil...cruel...arbitrary power...subvert liberties...violation of rights'—breathes the air, not of pragmatism, but of moral absolutism.[124]

And what shall we say about America's War of Independence? The colonists' *Declaration of the Causes and Necessity of Taking Up Arms* (1775) fairly smokes with a sense not just of injured pragmatism but of outraged injustice. The document rages against the British Parliament's 'cruel purpose', 'oppressive legal domination', 'inordinate passion for power', 'their intemperate rage for unlimited domination', and their 'deserting...truth, law, and right'.[125]

The American War of Independence would probably never have occurred had pragmatism been the reigning philosophy. At the time of the revolution, America was steeped in the legal thinking of William Blackstone. Historian Daniel Boorstin has written, 'In the history of American institutions no other book—except the Bible—has played so great a role as Blackstone's *Commentaries on the Law of England*.'[126] Edmund Burke

pointed out, on the eve of the Revolution, that nearly as many copies of the *Commentaries* had been sold in America as in England. That legal training, he said, gave the Americans the habit of thinking in terms of principles rather than mere grievances.[127]

'Principles rather than grievances!' Here is the essential difference between the pragmatist—who only thinks in terms of interests and felt needs—and the absolutist—who thinks in terms of right and wrong. The Americans had been brought up on the milk of the natural law (as opposed to law as a purely human creation). Americans had learned, under Blackstone, to view human law as an extension of divine law. Blackstone had written:

> This law of nature being co-eval with mankind and dictated by God himself, is of course superior in obligation to any others...no human laws are of any validity, if contrary to this.... Upon these two foundations, the law of nature and the law of revelation, depend all human laws.[128]

With this sort of legal foundation it is not surprising that, in justifying their revolution, the American colonists appealed to the 'laws of nature and nature's God'.[129] And perhaps it is not surprising that legal pragmatists such as Jeremy Bentham viewed Blackstone's teaching as a 'dangerous maxim'.[130] Bentham saw, in these appeals to natural and divine law, incitements to sedition. And he was right inasmuch as the teaching of natural law holds governments accountable to a higher standard, a standard by which they can be found wanting!

Bentham opposed to Blackstone's natural/divine law, teaching his own

> principle of utility...that principle which approves or disapproves of every action whatsoever, according to the tendency which it appears to have to augment or diminish the happiness of the party whose interest is in question.[131]

It is only natural that Bentham, who elevated utility over principle and viewed natural law and natural rights as mere fictions,[132] should dismiss America's *Declaration of Independence* as a 'hodge-podge of confusion and absurdity'.[133] The *Declaration*'s appeals to 'unalienable rights' and the 'laws of nature' were just so much nonsense to him.

But without laws of nature and unalienable rights there is nothing to limit the authority of a ruler save the appeal to force. Sovereignty is considered to be unlimited—indeed, this is just what Bentham believed.[134] But if sovereignty is unlimited our individual liberties simply disappear; or rather, they are simply granted at the gracious goodwill of the state instead of adhering to our persons as unalienable rights. Here is where pragmatism leads. In seeking ultimate independence (from law and truth) we actually lose our independence. It is only the biblical concept of a law-ordered universe—a law-order to which even kings must submit—that preserves the very liberties libertarians so value.

A Christian approach to politics would mix principles with practicalities, idealism with pragmatism. Idealism and pragmatism need each other. Pragmatism saves idealism from unrealistic, utopian fantasies; idealism saves pragmatism from sinking into an unprincipled, mean selfishness. Pragmatism's plaguing vice is its moral cowardice; the unwillingness to pay a price for a moral gain. Idealism's plaguing vice is a loss of perspective and humanity; a desire to go down in flames rather than plod along with second-best; a propensity to treat people like devils if they do not behave like angels.

We need wisdom to balance idealism and pragmatism. We need wisdom to know how to mix the eight biblical principles of government that we have been discussing in this chapter. And wisdom is just what we will be looking at in our next chapter.

7

Boiling Water's One Thing— Making Soup's Another

When baby number one entered the Miller family, my wife and I diligently prepared for parenthood by reading books on child discipline. Discipline became the operative word—the missing key to effective parenthood. It was Spock versus spanking with spanking winning hands down... and bottoms up.

We soon learned there was more to child-rearing than discipline. Love and mercy were helpful too. The problem with this new insight was that instantly parenting became a more difficult proposition. Instead of there being a sure-fire response to every situation—spank him or thank him—a number of valid responses became possible. Alas, one needed wisdom more than rules. There were no rules exactly explaining when mercy should triumph over justice or when the rod should be preferred to a 'let's sit down and talk about it' time. One had to ask for God's wisdom.

Politics is exactly the same. If only there were some cast-iron rules to tell us what to do in each situation it would all be so much simpler. If only it could be like boiling water: just put the kettle on the stove and turn on the heat. But it turns out that politicking is more like making soup; both involve a host of ingredients demanding artful blending. It takes wisdom to know how to blend together our eight principles of biblical government.

Newsweek columnist George Will has written that the four most important words in politics are 'up to a point'.

Are we for liberty, equality, military strength, high employment, low inflation, environmental protection? Sure—up to a point. The point is where the cost to other values is disproportionate to the incremental gain.[135]

We are in favour of all Chapter 6's principles of government—'up to a point'. It is wisdom which will show us just where that point is. It is wisdom which will show us when to violate freedom and insist on moral absolutes or, conversely, when to relax moral absolutes and allow for freedom.

It was wisdom which enabled King Solomon to rule so effectively. At the very beginning of his reign he turned to God and requested 'a discerning heart to govern...and to distinguish between right and wrong' (1 Kings 3:9). He had God's written word but that was not enough. He needed wisdom to know how to apply it, to know what part applied and when.

That God answered his request abundantly is immediately evident from his handling of two prostitutes. Both had had a son. The son of one of them had died and the remaining son was being claimed by each as her own. The Bible was clear that justice had to be done. The Bible, however, was silent as to how to administer justice in this case. It said nothing on how to discover which of the two women was telling the truth. There was no concrete test prescribed as there was, for instance, for a wife suspected of being unfaithful (Num 5:5–31). But there was a divine provision of wisdom. That was all Solomon needed.

Solomon was a man gifted with wisdom, not only in the 'religious' sphere but also in the 'secular' sphere. He grasped the workings of the political sphere and spoke with equal insight on the world of nature (see 1 Kings 4:33). He ruled well because in addition to his knowledge of the Bible 'God gave Solomon wisdom and very great insight, and a breadth of understanding as measureless as the sand on the seashore' (1 Kings 4:29). This wisdom was marked by both depth and breadth. He was familiar with a wide-ranging field of intellectual disciplines. But, no mere dilettante, he could see beyond the surface into the very heart of issues in each of these fields. He had insight.

Insight is defined by *Webster's Dictionary* as 'the ability to see and understand clearly the inner nature of things'. The Greek philosopher Aristotle could not rate this ability too highly. Michael Novak comments on Aristotle's view, writing:

Aristotle saw early that in practical judgments concerning what to do and how to act, general rules are not enough. One must have a particular insight into which rule to apply and how to apply it, in each particular, contingent, unprecedented, and irrepeatable situation. Mere logic and conceptual clarity will not work. Ethical judgment (in action) is always about singulars. 'Insight' or 'perception'—'hitting the mark'—is necessary. 'The crux,' Aristotle writes in the Nicomachean Ethics (III, vii, 3), 'lies with perception.'[136]

Aristotle is only saying what every Christian ought to know, that general rules are not enough. For instance, Jesus gave the general rule that his way was to 'turn the other cheek'. Yet this same Jesus cast the money-changers out of his Father's house with braided cords swinging and money-tables flying! His general rule did not seem to apply in this particular situation. Jesus was guided by the Spirit of wisdom who showed him how to apply God's laws in each particular situation. This is the same insight that we need.

Solomon had great quantities of this wisdom and insight. So much so that the Aristotles of his day came to sit at his feet and marvel: 'Men of all nations came to listen to Solomon's wisdom, sent by all the kings of the world, who had heard of his wisdom' (1 Kings 4:34).

It was wisdom which made Ahithophel such an effective counsellor to King David (2 Sam 15:12). So full of wisdom was Ahithophel that the Bible says, 'Now in those days the advice Ahithophel gave was like that of one who enquires of God' (2 Sam 16:23). Ahithophel was not a prophet who heard from God. Nevertheless, his advice was so impregnated with the gift of wisdom that it was 'like that of one who enquires of God'. It was a wisdom which enabled him to discern between the plausible and the true, between the right way and the apparently right way. Discerning this difference was often the difference between defeat and victory.

Absalom found this out too late. When Ahithophel deserted David to become Absalom's counsellor, he advised Absalom to strike out at David immediately; to strike while David was weak and his men scattered. Hushai's counter-advice was that Absalom should wait, assemble a large army and then strike with overwhelming force. Hushai's advice was plausible but bad. It made sense but it did not match the reality of the situation. Wisdom sees below the surface and discerns what the real need is. In fact, it sees the invisible (David's actual condition, though far out of sight); no mean feat.

Absalom followed Hushai's advice. The result? Defeat, as

Ahithophel had predicted. Ahithophel was so sure that this would be the outcome that he had already committed suicide even before the battle. He knew he was a dead man anyway for having betrayed David.

The difference between the plausible and the true is subtle but monumental; not unlike Mark Twain's comment that 'the difference between the right word and the nearly right word is the difference between lightning and the lightning bug'. The difference becomes meaningful when told you are about to be struck by one or the other!

Wisdom discerns the difference. And wisdom is a gift of God's Holy Spirit. God makes it available to the church: 'To one there is given through the Spirit the message of wisdom' (1 Cor 12:8). God has wisdom in abundance and he is willing to give it to his people.

So how do we come by this wisdom? James 1:5 says, 'If any of you lacks wisdom, he should ask God, who gives generously to all without finding fault, and it will be given to him.' Just ask for wisdom and God is ready to grant it. Sounds simple! It also sounds biblical.

The wisdom highlighted by James is not just for 'religious' issues but is wisdom for conducting all of life. That includes politics. It is the same wisdom Solomon asked for and received in guiding the civic/political life of his nation. It was a wisdom which was not only deep but broad, ie, it covered many subjects other than religion:

> God gave Solomon wisdom and very great insight, and a breadth of understanding as measureless as the sand on the seashore.... He described plant life.... He also taught about animals and birds, reptiles and fish (1 Kings 4:29–33).

But this wisdom is not simply to be found in our prayer closets. Not only will God grant wisdom in response to our prayers for it, he will also grant it as we listen to one another. Searching for wisdom is not a solitary affair: 'Plans fail for lack of counsel, but with many advisers they succeed' (Prov 15:22). God wants us not only to listen to him but to listen to others. That entails humility, a willingness to learn from others, a readiness to drop even some of our most cherished ideas should they be shown to be wrong.

We may pray for wisdom and still not find it straight off. We may not get it right the first time. Prayer does not guarantee infallibility. God will often teach us wisdom the hard way—

through our mistakes and errors. God teaches us through experience.

With regard to this there is an eye-opening series of remarks made by the prophet Isaiah:

> Listen and hear my voice;
>   pay attention and hear what I say.
> When a farmer ploughs for planting,
>   does he sow continually?
> Does he keep on breaking up and harrowing the soil?
> When he has levelled the surface,
>   does he not sow caraway and scatter cummin?
> Does he not plant wheat in its place,
>   barley in its plot, and spelt in its field?
> His God instructs him and teaches him the right way.
> Caraway is not threshed with a sledge,
>   nor is a cartwheel rolled over cummin;
>   caraway is beaten out with a rod,
>   and cummin with a stick.
> Grain must be ground to make bread;
>   so one does not go on threshing it for ever.
> Though he drives the wheels of his threshing-cart over it,
>   his horses do not grind it.
> All this also comes from the Lord Almighty,
>   wonderful in counsel and magnificent in wisdom
>
> (Is 28:23–29).

Several points are made in this passage. First, we see once again that God is concerned about the temporal, earthly affairs of his people. Heaven in the by-and-by is not his only focus. Food, farming, agricultural techniques and tools are equally his province.

The next point this passage makes is that God's specific response to people's temporal, earthly needs is to give them wisdom. God will not do everything for us; rather he will give us 'instruction', 'counsel', and 'wisdom' to enable us to get on with it ourselves.

Third, we note that the nature of this wisdom is that it respects creational givens. Wisdom does not attempt to ignore God's givens; it rather tries to adapt to the nature of reality around us. It is no good wishing cummin were different, nor will it do to resent the fact that caraway cannot be threshed with a sledge; much better just to change your methods to suit the situation. This point rebukes both relativists—who do not believe in a God-given order of nature—and the sort of supernaturalists who think they can dismiss the natural world and natural revelation. Wisdom conducts herself otherwise.

Fourth, it is instructive to ask just *how* God grants this wisdom. We immediately notice that the wisdom God grants here is not specifically biblical knowledge. We search Leviticus and the Song of Songs in vain for detailed prescriptions on the art of cummin grinding or state-of-the-art methods of designing threshing carts.[137] God's wisdom here comes primarily through the *observation and experience of nature*. We are to learn by doing, by observing what works and what does not work.

This, in fact, is just what has happened. Farmers learned, when crops failed, about heeding the rhythm of the seasons. They learned, when crops rotted, about the need to bring things out of the rain. They paid attention to what was happening in the natural world. As they did that they were heeding the counsel of God. Professor Albert Wolters comments upon this passage, 'This is not a teaching through the revelation of Moses and the Prophets, but a teaching through the revelation of creation.'[138]

Relating this to the political sphere we can say that not only do we need to know the biblical principles of government, not only do we need to know God's voice so we can heed his specific instructions, but we also need experience of the political realm—the practical observing of what works and what does not—if we are to walk in God's wisdom. Experience will temper utopian expectations. Experience will try our ideas in the furnace of reality. Experience will teach us how to translate good ideas into practice. Then and then only will we be useful and wise.

We need a wisdom which will see into the heart of each situation confronting us, a wisdom which can discern the true problem and devise the true solution. General biblical principles, while providing the essential starting point and the final goal, are not enough. They need to be complemented by the guidance of the Holy Spirit and the Holy Spirit's gift of wisdom. For instance, the Bible gives us the general principle that 'there is a time to be silent and a time to speak' (Eccles 3:7), but that does not tell us what time it is *now*. Wisdom will tell us that. In directing the affairs of a nation it is helpful to know that 'there is a time to kill and a time to heal' (Eccles 3:3), but our very next burning question in a time of crisis is: Yes, but what time is it *now*? Wisdom will tell us that.

God has promised to meet our need for wisdom as we enter the public arena. 'If any of you lacks wisdom, he should ask

God... and it will be given to him.' We do not need to go in alone or unprepared.

Wisdom is not all that we need, nor is it all God has promised. In the next chapter we will look at more of what God has promised for us in the governmental realm.

8

The Promise of Participation

In previous chapters we have looked at faulty conceptions of the Christian's role in politics. We have seen that we need to steer away from inflated, utopian dreams on the one hand and despairing resignation on the other. But what do we need to steer towards? What is our proper goal? What do we have a right to expect from participation in politics? Let me list three things.

God's name glorified

God's name is glorified, not when his people retreat from society, but when his power, wisdom and grace are allowed to shine into each of the mind-moulders through our participation in them. Psalm 19:1 says, 'The heavens declare the glory of God; the skies proclaim the work of his hands.' Created things can be a witness to God. Cannot things created by man and woman, the image-bearers of God, also declare the glory of God? In the mind-moulder areas we might not always be able to preach, any more than the skies and the heavens can, but we can still show forth his excellencies.

How are unbelievers to see God at work if we confine him to the churches; churches to which they never go? Christians need to take the presence of God within them out to the marketplace, the media, the government.

This is what Demos Shakarian did in the business realm. Shakarian, at one point the owner of the largest dairy farm in California, founded the Full Gospel Businessmen's Fellowship in order to penetrate the business world with the gospel. In his autobiography, *The Happiest People on Earth*, he recounts an incident which perfectly illustrates how God is glorified and the way prepared for the gospel when we take our faith into the mind-moulders.

To us [dairy farmers] it's [cattle breeding] the most fascinating topic in the world: the search for that elusive perfect animal who will invariably pass his good qualities on to the next generation....

I remember walking through those spotless calf barns for the very first time, looking for the little bull who would introduce this line into our herds. The first animal I stopped to admire was priced at $25,000—many times more than I could pay. There were animals among these two- and three-month-olds selling for $50,000, others the same age going for $1,000.

And suddenly I saw him. In a pen along the south wall of the barn, a sturdy little fellow who stood out from the others as though a light had shone on him. It was the same phenomenon that never ceased to amaze me at meetings of the Fellowship, where in a roomful of four hundred people I would suddenly 'see' the man I was to call on next. Now this two-hundred pound youngster stood out the same way.... His name was 'Pabst Leader'....

'I'll take Pabst Leader,' I said when the farm manager caught up with me.

Mr Sylvester looked at me curiously. Breeders never made up their minds so quickly—only after extensive consultations with their advisers. 'Are you quite sure? I wanted to show you some animals in the next barn, and Mr Pabst thought you'd be interested in....'

'Quite sure, Mr Sylvester.'

...Generally a bull's first ten daughters give an accurate picture of what he will do. Every one of Leader's first ten inherited her father's superior qualities: appearance, disease resistance, the high quality milk production of his strain. Even some of our spindliest little cows produced offspring with none of their own shortcomings, all of his assets. Over the fifteen years that we bred him, he sired five thousand daughters, every one stamped with their father's unmistakable quality. Pabst Leader was that animal-in-a-million with the ability to pass on his own likeness every single time....

It was not an isolated experience. Every bull we bought from the Pabst farm proved to be a top investment. Witness? I couldn't help it.

I remember the day Mr Sylvester leaned across the table in the farm dining room, very serious and solemn. 'Come on now, Shakarian. You're not making these choices on the spot the way you pretend. You have an adviser, don't you? Someone who travels ahead of you and makes recommendations?'

'Well, Mr Sylvester, as a matter of fact, yes, I do.'

He glanced triumphantly around the table. 'I knew it! Who is he? Come on! We won't raise the price on you because we know the one he's looking at.'

'You mean you really don't know who my Adviser is?'

'No, really! We get buyers and brokers through here by the dozen, all the time. Your man's obviously a pro.'

'Knows more about animals than all of us in this room together.'

'An old-timer, eh?'

'He's been in the business longer than anyone. . . .'

Of course, I kept it up as long as I could. By the time I gave them the name of my advance man I couldn't have had a more breathless audience. 'The Lord Jesus made these animals,' I told them. 'You and I can only look at pedigrees. He sees what's inside an animal—and a man too.'

It was the perfect opening into the hearts and minds of those men. The chance to show God alive in the world a man knows—that's what the Fellowship is all about.[139]

Do you suppose God was glorified through this incident? Well, I suppose he was.

Consider an example of God being glorified from another mind-moulder area: the media. Several Christmases ago I saw a television film called *Shadowlands* which told the story of C.S. Lewis finding a wife late in life, only to have her snatched away from him by cancer three years later. There was no overt preaching in the film but Lewis' Christian faith was evident throughout. He was realistically shown grappling with doubt and despair and then winning through to peace and hope. Nobody could have turned off his set that night thinking that Christianity was a Pollyanna faith unwilling to grapple with the hard questions of life; a faith that was irrelevant to the realities of the modern world. This programme literally glorified God. It made Christianity attractive, and this is crucial if people are ever to begin seriously to consider the claims of Christ.

Os Guinness talks about the difference between 'verifiability' and 'plausibility' in evangelism. Verifying has to do with proof, with strict intellectual reasoning. It's the world of Christian apologetics, of examining historical, archaeological and philosophical evidences. Plausibility is a softer word referring to whether something is generally believable rather than strictly provable. It asks not whether a thing has been rigorously argued but simply whether it seems true or sounds good. Does the proposition sound stupid, ridiculous, outlandish—in fact, 'implausible'? It asks not whether a thing is true but whether it seems true.

Verifiability is different from plausibility but is related to it in this manner. If people judge our convictions to be highly implausible they will not give us the time of day as we try to explain them. People will only think seriously about ideas that seem serious. If the Bible world of demons and angels, heaven and hell seems a world fit for infantile minds and superstitious medievals, one can hardly expect a self-styled sophisticated modern to give our heartfelt personal testimony a respectful hearing.

Every one of us has been brought up within a certain 'climate of opinion', with ideas not so much proved to be true as assumed to be true. Our environment bolstered these ideas. The institutions within which we grew up—the schools, the media, the business and governmental world—all seemed to take these truths for granted. These ideals, values and beliefs were not so much consciously taught as they were unconsciously packaged in every activity. Radically different beliefs were ignored. They seemed irrelevant and unrealistic; in a word, implausible.

Guinness points out that 'plausibility comes from a world of shared support'. He points out that

> Parisian skepticism was more likely to seem true on the Left Bank than on the Right. On the Left Bank it was a whole, shared world, not just an intellectual idea. In the same way, Roman Catholicism is more likely to seem true in Eire than in Egypt, just as Mormonism is in Salt Lake City than in Singapore.[140]

Eventually a climate is created whereby 'a thing's seeming to be true is often mistaken for its being true'.

Now here's the point: Christians need to work at plausibility as well as at verifiability. We need to prepare the way for the gospel. We need to pre-evangelise as well as evangelise. We need not only to preach the gospel and argue the gospel (verifiability), we also need to work at setting up an environment in which the gospel can be more easily received. We need to work on plausibility. Plausibility precedes verifiability.

It is at this point that the seven mind-moulders are absolutely crucial. Outside of individual holiness and a dynamic corporate church life, the mind-moulders are the key to setting up a favourable climate of opinion for the gospel. It is they which convey and reinforce the values, goals and assumptions of each generation. We need to penetrate the schools, the media, business, the government, and so on, with Christian salt. It is here that plausibility is won or lost. When God's name is honoured here then the gospel preached in the pulpits is more likely to receive a serious hearing.

C.S. Lewis, in *God in the Dock*, puts the case for Christian participation in the mind-moulders crisply:

> I believe that any Christian who is qualified to write a good popular book on any science may do much more by that than by any directly apologetic work. We can make people (often) attend to the Christian point of view for half an hour or so; but the moment they have gone away from our lecture or laid down our article, they are plunged back into a world where the opposite position is taken for granted. As long as that situation exists, widespread success is simply impossible. We must attack the enemy's line of communication. What we want is not more little books about Christianity, but more little books by Christians on other subjects—with their Christianity latent. You can see this most easily if you look at it the other way round. Our faith is not likely to be shaken by any book on Hinduism. But if, whenever we read an elementary book on geology, botany, politics or astronomy, we found that its implications were Hindu, that would shake us. It is not the books written in direct defence of materialism that make the modern man a materialist; it is the materialistic assumptions in all the other books. In the same way, it is not books on Christianity that will really trouble him. But he would be troubled if, whenever he wanted a cheap popular introduction to some science, the best work on the market was always by a Christian. The first step to the reconversion of a country is books produced by Christians.

That C.S. Lewis' theory was more than just good theory/bad reality is evident from my own conversion. I was in India pursuing Eastern religions when I met a Christian who piqued my curiosity. The next day I found myself browsing through a Christian bookshop still wary of this narrow, hide-bound faith with its ranters and charlatans. I was reluctant to buy any book until I came across one whose author I recognised—you guessed it, C.S. Lewis. Years before I had read his science fiction trilogy, so when I spotted his name in the bookstore I thought, 'I know him. He's no nutty fanatic' (simply a sane one!). So I bought *Mere Christianity*. Only a week later I too entered the Christian fold.

Daniel is a prime example of God's name being glorified in the mind-moulder of government. Daniel had every reason to resist participating in the politics of the Babylonians: they were pagan people, they were idolatrous, they were the ruthless conquerors of his beloved, devastated nation, and they were the nation God had called him to! There must have been many discouragements working in such an environment, as can be imagined from King Nebuchadnezzar's response to Daniel in Daniel 4:18, where the king calls upon Daniel's help 'because the spirit of the holy gods is in you'. Despite two earlier manifestations of Jehovah's unique power, the king is still able to confuse things and understand Daniel's miraculous ministry in terms of a pluralistic pantheon of pagan 'gods'.

Regardless of this, Daniel soldiers on, plugging away at his job. The result of his faithful participation in his calling of government is seen in Daniel 4:34–37. Nebuchadnezzar says:

> Then I praised the Most High.... His dominion is an eternal dominion.... Now I, Nebuchadnezzar, praise and exalt and glorify the King of heaven, because everything he does is right and all his ways are just.

Nebuchadnezzar recognises the one true God. He sees there is only one God who is really God and who rules over all. He bows before him. God is glorified in the life of this pagan. All because of Daniel's obedience.

So struck is Nebuchadnezzar with the greatness of God as manifested through the life of Daniel that at one point we read:

> Then King Nebuchadnezzar fell prostrate before Daniel and paid him honour and ordered that an offering and incense be presented to him. The king said to Daniel, 'Surely your God is the God of gods and the Lord of kings and a revealer of mysteries, for you were able to reveal this mystery' (Dan 2:46–47).

That's what I call bringing glory to God's name. And all because Daniel followed his call to participation in this mind-moulder of government. We, like Daniel, are the 'salt of the earth' (Mt 5:13). Salt is useless unless it is mixed with the substance it is meant to be preserving and flavouring. But get the salt out of the saltshaker, then God can be glorified.

This does not, of course, mean that we will never make enemies. The fact that political participation on the part of Christians may result in strong opposition should never of itself lead us to conclude that this participation is wrong and that it is failing to glorify God.

The very nature of politics ensures enemies; its policies help one side and hurt another. With bracing realism, John Wesley wrote:

> I know mankind too well. They who love you for political service, love you less than their dinner; and they that hate you, hate you worse than the devil.

Daniel himself, the great God-glorifier, had enemies—specifically because of his political involvement. Daniel 6—the story of the lions' den—details his escape from some of his jealous rivals. The more God blessed him and used him the more upset these political rivals became. He had enemies not because he was doing the wrong thing in the wrong sphere, but because he was doing the right thing in the right sphere.

Christian activity in any sphere creates enemies. Look at Jesus. He did not fail to glorify God. He was also killed on a cross.

God does not promise his people a trouble-free road as we up and follow him. We do, however, have this assurance:

> But thanks be to God, who always leads us in triumphal procession in Christ and through us spreads everywhere the fragrance of the knowledge of him (2 Cor 2:14).

'Everywhere' includes the corridors of political power. Those called to tread there have this mandate: to exude the fragrance of heaven where normally presides the stale air of realpolitik. Realpolitik is a good advisor but a bad ruler. These corridors need a fresh blow of the Spirit of God. God wants Daniels today. Daniel was never meant to be a dinosaur on exhibit—very awesome and very extinct. He was meant to be a model to emulate. Then God is glorified.

Evangelism

The second expectation and result of Christian participation in politics is evangelism. Evangelism has been described as 'one beggar giving bread to another beggar'. But how can we give bread to someone who is out of reach and far off?

Of the non-Christians who come to a Billy Graham crusade, 80 to 90 per cent are brought by a friend. They won't come on their own but they will with someone they know. How does one befriend non-Christians if one withdraws from all the areas they are involved in? Friendships are built out of common interests and common activities, out of working and playing together. If we retreat to the church and the family and abandon the other five mind-moulders we will have cut ourselves off from a world that, whether it knows it or not, needs our salt.

Politicians need salt too. They need to be evangelised. One way that will be done is as they are in contact with other Christian politicians; Christians who have similar concerns and interests.

Evangelism is not just a matter of vast crusades or Sunday night guest services. Evangelism can sometimes happen more effectively through the other 'non-churchy' areas of life. It can erupt into our secular jobs.

Norman Vincent Peale is a pastor famous for his book *The Power of Positive Thinking*. Peale not only pastors a church, he also speaks at secular sales rallies and business conventions. He is not invited to evangelise but does this mean he never has the chance to share the goodness of the King? Answer for yourself as you read the following account:

One day four other speakers shared the platform with me in a huge sports arena type of auditorium near the Minneapolis airport. Nearly 18,000 persons filled the arena to overcapacity for what the promoters called a Positive Mental Attitude Rally.

Going along routinely in my speech doing the best I could, all of a sudden something happened to me. It was as if time stood still; a deep hush settled the big crowd. The people seemed silhouetted in sharp, clear light. Everyone appeared immobile and frozen into place, and all eyes seemed to bore straight into me. They seemed to have a pleading air, as if each one was saying, 'Please, please say something to me, something that will help me. Give me real answers, not words— answers that really answer.'

The spell lasted but a minute, perhaps barely even that. Maybe it was only a fraction of a second. But I was shaken by those faces...mutely demanding something.... On that October day I caught myself saying to this vast crowd...'I can only tell you how I found what I deeply wanted. I decided to be a true follower of the way of life set forth in the Bible by Jesus Christ. I determined to do everything His way. It wasn't all that easy, but the more sincerely I tried, the better I did with my life. And I felt Him close and very real, helping me over the rough spots. In finding Jesus Christ personally in this way, I found what I really wanted from life.' Then I went on with my speech on the subject, 'Positive Thinkers Get Positive Results.'

Finishing the speech, I left the platform and headed for a car waiting to take me to the airport. But I was overtaken by a young woman. 'Oh, please, wait. I must speak to you,' she cried. I saw that she was weeping. Struggling to control herself, she managed to say, 'As I sat in that audience just inside the door from the stage...I was completely despondent. My life has been a failure. My marriage has broken up. I went into business, into sales work, and here again I have failed.'

By this time she was more composed and I noticed a kind of radiance reflected on her face, at least that is how it appeared to me—sort of like sunshine coming through the rain. 'I haven't known what I wanted,' she said. 'My heart and mind were empty. I wanted something meaningful that would change my error-and-failure life pattern and give me some happiness. Then when you gave that brief but obviously sincere witness about your own finding of yourself through commitment to our Lord Jesus Christ, something flashed through my mind like a bright light. "This is it," I said to myself; "this is it." Right then and there, with all my heart, I gave my life into the hands of the Lord. I just wanted you to know that you reached one mixed-up, unhappy person. But I'm different now, very different. I have found me at last by finding Him.'[141]

Norman Vincent Peale's example was in the area of business. But why could not the same thing happen in the arena of politics? Is anything too hard for God? The God who could glorify his name through Daniel in a hostile, pagan land can also open up opportunities to spread the message of the cross in the unlikely arena of politics. We don't have to force it. God can make it happen. He wants his good news to go everywhere.

Service

The third result Christians can expect from participation in politics is effective service. As Christians, we have been called to a life of service. We have been called to good deeds as much as we have been called to evangelism. Paul wrote to the Ephesians that 'we are God's workmanship, created in Christ Jesus to do good works, which God prepared in advance for us to do' (Eph 2:10). Good works are obviously important to God as he created us specifically with these in mind. So keen was he on them that rather than leaving them to happenstance, he has prepared them in advance for us to do.

God not only created us to speak and evangelise, but to do and to serve. Paul went on to write:

It was he who gave some to be apostles, some to be prophets, some to be evangelists, and some to be pastors and teachers, to prepare God's people for works of service... (Eph 4:11–12).

The spiritual ministries are not only preaching and teaching. Far from it. Paul is here saying that ministries such as that of the prophet and teacher are not ends in themselves but only means of equipping God's people so that they can serve. That's the real end.

Can politics be an effective form of service? You bet. God not only cares for our inner peace and heavenly righteousness, he cares too for the rule of peace, order and justice here among people on earth. Now the preservation of peace, order and justice is the political task (see Romans 13:1–7 and 1 Timothy 2:2). That's what politics is supposed to be about. And God cares about these issues.

This is plainly evident, for instance, in his response to his captive people in Egypt. He is moved and concerned not only by their spiritual needs but by their human needs:

The Lord said, 'I have indeed seen the misery of my people in Egypt. I have heard them crying out because of their slave drivers, and I am concerned about their suffering' (Ex 3:7–8).

See, too, what moves God to anger and judgement. The reason for God's severe judgement upon the earth in Noah's day is revealing: 'I am going to put an end to all people, for the earth is filled with violence because of them' (Gen 6:13). It was not simply man's spiritual shortcomings, his idolatry and turning his back on God, which brought judgement, but man's inhumanity to man.

The same emphasis comes through in the disasters and judgements foretold by the prophet Micah. Part of the reason God is moved to judge the people of Israel is because of their sins against God in his heaven with their 'high places' and 'idols' (see Micah 1:5, 7). Equally galling to God, however, were their sins against people on his earth. He denounces them because:

They covet fields and seize them, and houses and take them.
They defraud a man of his home, a fellow-man of his inheritance.
Therefore the Lord says: 'I am planning disaster....
Lately my people have risen up like an enemy.
You strip off the rich robe from those who pass by without a care,
      like men returning from battle.
You drive the women of my people from their pleasant homes.

You take away my blessing from their children for ever'
(Micah 2:2, 8–9.)

Micah is describing a corrupt people loaded with an equally corrupt government. The sins he describes were all issues that good government would have dealt with. A corrupt government, however, learned to wink at them provided the right palms could be sufficiently greased.

God's concern for godly government can be seen in his leading both Joseph and Daniel into government service. Joseph, of course, was the head of the Department of Social Services in Egypt, his specific brief being to prepare for and administer government famine relief. Daniel started out as a lowly civil servant in Babylon (Daniel 1:19), then moved up to be a provincial governor (2:48), and finally became the chief administrator over one third of the empire.

We remember these men for their dramatic supernatural acts, but it must be remembered that the majority of the time they were chained to their desks, fulfilling mundane administrative roles. Their priority time involvement was given to meetings and memos rather than to prayer meetings. They were administrators, not official court prophets. As such, they were there to ensure the smooth working of the machine of government. They were working for peace and order in everyday life.

Governmental service has as much to do with the little things—poor local services, noise, pollution, and so on—as it does with the great crusading issues that capture our imagination—the fight against slavery and inhumane working conditions in the nineteenth century and the fight against abortion in our own. God is interested in both levels of service. He wants his people to be involved at both levels.

The result will be that people will be blessed and God uplifted: 'In the same way, let your light shine before men, that they may see your good deeds and praise your Father in heaven' (Mt 5:16). Note that it is service and good deeds that elicit praise. People are impressed with deeds more than with words.

So it was with Lord Shaftesbury's political service in the nineteenth century. Shaftesbury sacrificed political advancement in order to devote himself to the cause of the poor in England. His devotion to good deeds was not lost on those he served. It resulted in praise to God and respect for his faith. John Pollock tells the story that so devoted were the poor to him that on one occasion, when a gold watch of much sentimental value had been picked from his pocket in London, he

> appealed to his friends in the underworld. A few nights later a large, squirming canvas bag was deposited on his doorstep. Shaftesbury and his butler opened it. A small urchin was inside along with the watch and a note from other vagabonds pinned to the boy's rags demanding that the thief should get what he deserved. Shaftesbury placed him in a school.[142]

Winning people's hearts with our good deeds is one step towards winning their hearts to God.

Christians need to be involved in government because through that involvement God's name can be glorified, because it can serve as a useful platform to evangelism, and because it is one avenue of godly service.

It is instructive to consider the different types of governmental service God opened up for his servants in the past. They can teach us the manners of service God wants to open to us today.

Esther—the godly influence

Esther had an important role; she was raised by God to a position of governmental influence in order to save her nation: 'And who knows but that you have come to royal position for such a time as this?' (Esther 4:14). Due to her wise use of this position a vast slaughter was averted and a great evil avoided.

We note, however, that her service was more in the form of influence than it was in the actual exercise of governmental authority. She, in fact, had no governmental authority. She was simply the king's consort. Although she had no political authority, she had plenty of personal influence. She was the king's wife! She had access to the king's ear and heart.

Some who will never hold government office will be granted personal influence with those who do. Much good can be done here if, like Queen Esther, this influence is used for service and not for personal gain.

Joseph—the godly administrator

Joseph was another who, through his role in government, played a vital part in the outworkings of God's design. God had a nation to save from famine and another fledgling nation to move. All this he accomplished through Joseph.

Unlike Esther, Joseph's gifts funnelled directly through his governmental office. It was as an administrator that he was such a blessing. Of course, he was an administrator with a difference! He had received a revelation of God's goals and of God's chosen means. Joseph knew what God was going to do—bring on famine—and what he needed to do about it—store up grain during the seven good years. Where Esther was gifted to operate outside and alongside the wheels of government, Joseph's gift was to operate these very wheels of government. In doing so he served Egypt, Israel and God.

Daniel—the godly prophet-cum-administrator

Daniel was like Joseph in that he, too, was called into government service. That is where he exercised his ministry. He was an administrator in the Babylonian empire and a very fine one at that (Dan 6:3). Daniel was different from Joseph, however, in that his most vital ministry was not actually his governmental service.

As helpful as his administrative gifts undoubtedly were, his most noteworthy contribution was through his prophetic gifts; prophetic gifts that operated alongside rather than directly in his official function. Joseph, as we have seen, exercised his prophetic gift through his office; his prophetic gift told him what and how he should administrate (the famine relief project).

Daniel was firstly a prophet and only secondarily an administrator. Government service was the platform from which he could exercise a prophetic gift which was aimed at the personal lives of the most powerful rulers of the day. With this prophetic gift he challenged and shook these kings to their core.

Moses—the godly legislator

Lastly, we look at Moses, yet another who served in government. Moses was unlike Joseph and Daniel in that where they administrated affairs at the direction of kings, Moses actually directed affairs. Joseph and Daniel were administrators; Moses was a legislator. Joseph and Daniel did not touch the laws—the political heartbeat of a nation—of their respective kingdoms; Moses shaped Israel's laws through and through. He brought the heart and mind of God to bear on the guiding principles of an entire nation, with the enviable result that the surrounding peoples 'who...hear[d] about all these decrees...say, "Surely this great nation is a wise and understanding people" ' (Deut 4:6).

There is still a place for the ministry of Moses today, for bringing godly legislation to pass in our respective nations. God has not changed. He is still raising up godly influencers, godly administrators, godly prophets-cum-administrators and godly legislators.

'And who knows but that you have come to royal position for such a time as this?'

9

Principles of Participation

God gives us promises for participation; he also gives us principles for participation. Perhaps we could expand on the quaint formula—'Where God appoints, he anoints'—by adding 'and points'. He appoints us to a task, anoints us with his Spirit of power, and then points out the way we need to go. Job placement (appointing) and job ability (anointing) achieve little without job training (pointing).

God, in his word, has pointed out four key principles which the Christian involved in politics needs to abide by if he wishes to be effective for the kingdom. These four principles can be seen at work in the lives of Joseph and Daniel.

Joseph and Daniel are not just handy examples of biblical political involvement; they are unique examples. Their special relevance for us today arises out of one simple fact: they served in situations identical to ours today. Unlike the Nathans, the Samuels, the Hoseas—who served in an Israel which was based on the word of God—Joseph and Daniel served regimes based on the word of man. So today we serve secular governments based on the word of man. Why even America, with its ardent Bible Belt and millions of evangelicals, outlaws prayer in its state schools. It's okay—as long as you do it under your breath! Joseph and Daniel served in pre-Christian times; we serve in post-Christian times. Let us see, then, how they went about doing their work in government.

Government is a calling

Government is a calling; it's a vocation not meant for everyone. It was Joseph's; it wasn't John the Baptist's. It was David's; it wasn't Jesus'.

While the burden of this book is to encourage and funnel Christian participation in politics, it must not be read to elevate government service above all other callings. It is not our greatest priority. We cannot all rush off to run for office. We must focus our energies on what God has called us to do.

In both Joseph's and Daniel's lives it is obvious that it was God who elevated them to their respective positions in Egypt and Babylon. God, who spoke so often to Joseph in dreams, gave him a dream while just a young man of his family bowing down before him (see Genesis 37:5–10), a prediction of what God intended for him in Pharaoh's courts. He served with Pharaoh, not because it was his idea, but because it was God's idea.

And so with Daniel. He could see God's hand of blessing on everything he did in government. Not only did he see general blessing, he witnessed the dramatically supernatural equipping of God for effectual service; an equipping which opened the door to kings. Clearly God wanted him in politics. He had the call of God upon his life.

Moses had to learn the importance of calling the hard way. He was a man who early in his life was caught in the enthusiasm for a political project and promptly rushed off to accomplish it without seriously consulting with God. Moses had a good idea—to deliver Israel from oppression—and decided he knew how and when to execute it. He didn't seek God, nor ascertain his call. Such a good idea must surely be God's! 'Moses thought that his own people would realise that God was using him to rescue them, but they did not' (Acts 7:25). His presumption landed him in the wilderness for forty years. How differently everything goes forty years later when his involvement is based on the call of God.

Integrity

That integrity is essential goes without saying. Yet, what is unsaid can go unheard and, being unheard, find itself disregarded. So let us say something about integrity.

Involvement in any one of the mind-moulders lays us open to

two very different temptations. The first one is guilt; guilt that one is spending time and energies on temporal affairs rather than eternal ones; guilt because one is concentrating on earth rather than heaven. I know of a pastor who felt called to leave his pulpit and go into business. Then, even though he knew the call of God and saw the blessings of God (through his successful patents he was able to give millions to the work of the kingdom), battled for years with guilt over leaving the pastorate. This was a temptation not a virtue. It was a manifestation of an oversensitive, 'weak conscience' the apostle Paul refers to (1 Cor 8:10, 12), which feels bad about things it ought freely to accept. This ex-pastor had to follow God's call, not his feelings. Guilt can be a temptation.

Compromise is the other temptation typically accompanying the call to the mind-moulders. Jesus wanted us to be 'in' the world but not 'of' the world. He said:

> My prayer is not that you take them out of the world but that you protect them from the evil one. They are not of the world, even as I am not of it. . . . As you sent me into the world, I have sent them into the world (Jn 17:15–18).

Now, it is easier to resist being 'of' the world when you are not 'in' the world. It's easy to be different at a distance. There's no pressure then. It's easy to wear hermit's rags in a cave; not so easy when you are working nine to five down in the City. The special danger here is that God's call and mission get drowned out by the incessant and clamorous demands of our profession. Compromise comes in.

Many years ago I met a young Englishman in Amsterdam who was very gifted in music. He could play several instruments, sing, write and arrange music. He told me he had, while quite young, experienced a call to glorify God's name through music. At first he played strictly Christian music. Soon, however, he felt he should branch out and play in secular groups. Years down the line, by the time I met him, he was managing a Dutch, non-Christian group that went by the name 'Lucifers'! (A play on words, as in Dutch 'lucifers' means 'matches'.) He had travelled far from his original calling. He had lost his way seeking for success. Making his mark musically had become more important than glorifying God. Compromise had set in.

Compromise is equally a temptation in the mind-moulder of

government. A politician out of office is a politician without a point. From this premise it is all too easy to move to making the winning of office our number one priority. But when ambition for office and career success outstrips our ambition for God then compromise lurks just around the corner. Indeed, it has already begun.

Daniel was a man 'in' the world of politics yet not 'of' the world of politics. He was sold out for God. His ambition was for God. He put God first and let God take care of his servant's success. And succeed he did. He held high office under King Nebuchadnezzar of Babylon, Darius the Mede and Cyrus the Persian. He was first promoted under Nebuchadnezzar to be the governor of the choice province of Babylon (Dan 2:48). Under Nebuchadnezzar's son, Belshazzar, he was appointed the third highest ruler in the whole Babylonian kingdom (Dan 5:29), a position he continued to hold under Darius the Mede (Dan 6:1–2).

We first meet Daniel in his youth when he has just been entered into the Babylonian civil service. We see that right from the outset he set himself never to compromise God's call, even in the little things:

> But Daniel resolved not to defile himself with the royal food and wine, and he asked the chief official for permission not to defile himself in this way (Dan 1:8).

How much easier not to cause waves, to blend in and be like everybody else. Daniel knew that in calling adverse attention to himself like this he was risking his plum job in the king's service with all its status, power and privilege; but he was undeterred. He set his heart on being faithful to God.

Later, we see Daniel called into the presence of King Nebuchadnezzar to interpret a dream. Again he refuses to compromise and water down God's message. He gives it to the king with both barrels:

> Renounce your sins by doing what is right, and your wickedness by being kind to the oppressed. It may be that then your prosperity will continue (Dan 4:27).

It's not that he is forgetting that he is addressing the most powerful ruler on the world scene; it's simply that he remembers he is ultimately serving the most powerful ruler on the universal scene.

If God said, 'Flatter,' he'd flatter; if God said, 'Flatten,' he'd flatten. The latter seems more often the prophet's lot.

Daniel again renounces compromise when, in the reign of Darius, the king's counsellors trick the king into passing an edict forbidding prayer for thirty days. What does Daniel do? 'Three times a day he got down on his knees and prayed, giving thanks to his God, just as he had done before' (Dan 6:10). Daniel had long ago settled whether survival and success were more important than faithfulness, and he was not about to alter his decision now.

No wonder God could entrust him with significant responsibility. No compromise had spoiled him for God's use. The problem with compromise is that if we have used it to wangle our way into office, by the time we arrive we have nothing to say; we will have lost our message on the way. From one angle there's nothing sillier than a messenger who arrives breathlessly, wearied by a long, dangerous journey, only to reach into his dispatch-case to find—no message. From another angle, there is nothing more tragic.

I mentioned earlier Lord Shaftesbury as a more contemporary example of a Christian who fought to maintain, without compromise, his call to help the powerless in England. To do this meant a willingness to sacrifice ambition for high office. John Pollock recounts the struggle he had in refusing the call by his stepfather-in-law, Lord Palmerston—the then Prime Minister—to a cabinet post.

> A month later Palmerston suffered several resignations and again turned to Shaftesbury. The newspapers wanted him, the Queen hinted that she would take it as a personal insult if he refused, his mother-in-law, busy Cabinet-making with her husband, wrote a hurried note telling him to come in, and Minny [his wife] was imploring: 'I do beseech you,' she wrote from the country, 'not to refuse. Reflect how much more weight everything has coming from a Cabinet Minister.'
>
> 'I was at my wit's end,' recalled Shaftesbury many years later. 'On one side was ranged wife, relations, friends, ambition, influence; on the other, my own objections, which seemed sometimes to weigh as nothing in comparison with the arguments brought against them. I could not satisfy myself that to accept office was a divine call; I was satisfied that God had called me to labour among the poor.'[143]

Shaftesbury never did become a cabinet minister, in the process severely disappointing the likes of the Duke of Wellington who expected him to be a future Prime Minister. But Shaftesbury was not disappointed because his ambitions centred on God's call rather than on career advancement. That is why he was able to resist compromise.

Joseph is another biblical character who achieved political success. He rose to the highest political office in Egypt outside of the Pharaoh himself. So Pharaoh said to Joseph, "I hereby put you in charge of the whole land of Egypt."... He had him ride in a chariot as his second-in-command.... "I am Pharaoh, but without your word no one will lift hand or foot in all Egypt" (Gen 41:41–44).

He, like Daniel, had an integrity which kept him from compromise and led him into sacrifice. He went to prison rather than betray his master's trust through adultery. He put God's ways before making his own way. While in prison he refused to lapse into bitterness but selflessly extended a helping hand to both the warden and his fellow prisoners. Despite two years of imprisonment, years in which he must have had many an opportunity to doubt that integrity was really a key to career effectiveness, he held on to his faith in God. And then, overnight, his circumstances changed. Pharaoh released him from prison, sought his help and finally elevated him to high office over all of Egypt.

Because Joseph had not compromised he was ready when Pharaoh called on him. He could stand as God's representative boldly declaring, 'I cannot do it...but God will give Pharaoh the answer he desires' (Gen 41:16). Holding to his convictions was costly, but compromise would have been costlier still. It would have cost him his political career. He never would have become Pharaoh's right-hand man.

Chuck Colson tells the story of one Judge Bontrager. It serves as a powerful contemporary example of the sort of refusal to compromise needed today by Christians wishing to serve in public office.

Fred Palmer [was] a young Vietnam veteran who accepted Christ in 1977 while in jail awaiting sentencing for a string of house burglaries. His offense carried a mandatory ten- to twenty-year sentence in Indiana, though that law, already acknowledged as harsh, was changed just eighteen days after his arrest.

Judge Bontrager, who had himself been converted to Christ a year earlier, reviewed Palmer's case carefully. He realized that the mandatory ten-year sentence would destroy rather than rehabilitate Palmer, so he declared it unconstitutional. Bontrager ordered him to serve one

year in the state penitentiary and then, upon release, to reimburse those
he had robbed and provide community service.

Palmer did just that. He was a model prisoner; after release he was
reunited with his wife and family, and began paying back his victims.
The case seemed closed, a model of justice, restitution and restoration.

But the Supreme Court swung into action; claiming that Judge
Bontrager had erred, they ordered him to send Palmer back to prison—
for at least nine more years!

For Bontrager, the order was clearly a case of choosing between the
law of man and the law of God. He had been reading the Old Testament
prophets; the words of Amos seared his conscience. He knew the
Supreme Court's order didn't meet God's standard of justice and righteousness, but would instead punish a man twice for the same crime,
merely to satisfy a technicality of the law.

So Bontrager stepped aside, turning the case over to another judge.
A nightmarish sequence of events followed. The Court slammed Palmer
into Westville Correctional Center, declared Bontrager in contempt,
fined him $500, and sentenced him to thirty days in prison. Though that
sentence was suspended, proceedings were begun to remove him from
the bench. Rather than allow his own case to endanger Palmer's appeals
for release, Judge Bontrager resigned.

His resignation was not without cost. Bill Bontrager gave up a
comfortable salary, the judgeship he had always wanted, a position of
respect. His radical talk about obeying God, not man, raised eyebrows
in his community as well...clients for his small firm have been very
scarce.

So it was that I invited private citizen, ex-judge Bill Bontrager and
his wife to accompany me to services at Westville on Easter morning.
Bontrager said nothing as we waited for guards to unlock the entrance
to the auditorium, but as the steel doors swung open he bolted ahead of
me and made his way into the crowd of waiting inmates. Seconds later
he found Harry Fred Palmer—and the tall, lanky ex-judge embraced
the young ex-burglar in prison denims, as tears rolled down their
cheeks.[144]

Let the supernatural in

Our modern world squirms uncomfortably when there is talk about
mixing the supernatural with politics; and that includes the modern
Christian too.

The Times reported the recent revolution in Fiji under the
bemused headline: 'Rabuka invokes God's blessing on his
republic'; the headline registering politely restrained wonder at the
novel and curious thought of bringing God into politics. If an

antiseptic 'blessing' can cause such astonishment, what will a full-blooded miracle provoke?

If Christians aspire to maximum effectiveness for God, we cannot shut up the supernatural to our private, devotional lives. We must let it out into our professional lives.

Joseph's and Daniel's whole influence was due to the supernatural. Integrity and lack of compromise formed the foundation for their ministries, but what launched them was the manifestation of the supernatural.

It was Joseph's ability to interpret dreams which brought him to Pharaoh's attention. So, too, with Daniel in Babylon. This supernatural ability won respect for their pronouncements and brought them high governmental office in pagan regimes:

> Then Pharaoh said to Joseph, 'Since God has made all this known to you, there is no one so discerning and wise as you. You shall be in charge of my palace, and all my people are to submit to your orders' (Gen 41:39–40).

In Daniel's case we read:

> The king said to Daniel, 'Surely your God is the God of gods and...a revealer of mysteries, for you were able to reveal this mystery.' Then the king placed Daniel in a high position and lavished many gifts on him. He made him ruler over the entire province of Babylon and placed him in charge of all its wise men (Dan 2:47–48).

Both of these men were prophets—a prophet not being someone who foretells events so much as being someone who 'forthtells' God's truth. A prophet sees events from God's perspective. He has God's heart and God's mind—and whatever may come, he is going to tell you what it is. He sees behind the scenes because he is in touch with the divine Producer of our earthly drama.

The prophetic gift seems the supernatural gift most fitted to governmental services. We have already noted that Daniel and Joseph were prophets who heard from heaven. Other noted leaders, such as Moses and Samuel, were prophets. David is called a prophet in Acts 2:30. Even when Israel switched to being ruled by kings, they were never without prophetic guidance to challenge them and direct them in God's paths. The prophet was an essential part of the king's cabinet, part counsellor and part gadfly, but always there. John the Baptist was simply continuing the traditional Old Testament linkage of prophet to king when he sought Herod out to face him with truth.

Although all the supernatural gifts of the Spirit are important, they appear almost incidental to the working of government. The prophetic gift on the other hand, by virtue of its role in bringing God's mind to bear on national direction, was central to good government. Elisha's fantastic healing ministry, for example, clearly had dramatic consequences for the individuals touched by it, but was almost completely irrelevant to the general course of the nation. What he foretold and forthtold was of more consequence to the king and the government than any hundred lepers healed or dead men raised.

Does this have any application today? Is there a place for the prophet today? Should modern governments be non-prophet organisations? I can imagine someone complaining that it was much easier in days gone by for a prophet with a revelation to get a hearing than it is today. Both Pharaoh and Nebuchadnezzar had supernatural worldviews which acknowledged the existence of a non-material, spiritual world with which one could communicate. That's why they both had their court magicians and diviners to guide them. Today, by contrast, we live in secular times where reason, science and evidence are king; heavenly guidance is dismissed as silly superstition.

All this is very true. However, there were multiple difficulties in days gone by as well. It may have been easier to speak up, but it was also harder to be heard. With so many other diviners and magicians already giving their advice to the king, these young Jewish prophets would have been just lone voices among the many. Their voices simply joined the din. Today the competition is less. In this sense, it is easier to be heard.

And we must not imagine that the early pagan rulers Joseph and Daniel dealt with were naïvely credulous, ready to believe at the drop of a 'thus saith the Lord'. See the hard-headed scepticism of Nebuchadnezzar when, to root out any charlatans among his court diviners, he tells them not only to interpret the dream but even to describe the dream. He says, 'So then, tell me the dream, and I will know that you can interpret it for me' (Dan 2:9). He wants proof of their supernatural ability. The cry for evidence is not so modern after all.

Daniel was able to break through this sort of scepticism and there is no reason why Christians today cannot do the same;

provided, that is, we follow the biblical principles of presenting prophecy to pagan cultures.

Presenting prophecy to pagans

Acts 27 shows how the apostle Paul presented to his pagan travelling companions a prophetic warning about their forthcoming shipwreck. Paul, at this point, is being taken under guard to Rome where he is to stand trial for his faith. Their ship has been forced by contrary winds to proceed slowly and everyone is anxious to hurry on and reach Rome before the onset of bad winter weather.

Paul warns them, 'Men, I can see that our voyage is going to be disastrous and bring great loss to ship and cargo, and to our own lives also' (Acts 27:10). God has supernaturally revealed to Paul the outcome of the next leg of the voyage. On one side we have Paul the prophet with a divine revelation. On the other side we have arrayed the time pressures (v 9), natural circumstances pointing to the opposite conclusion (v 12) and the weight of expert opinion (vv 11–12). We are not amazed to find that they followed the 'experts' rather than the prophet. People 2,000 years ago were no different from people today.

When a favourable wind begins to blow, making it possible for them to leave their present poor harbour, they weigh anchor and sail off—right into hurricane-force winds which batter them for the next fourteen days and nights till their ship sinks. The prophet had been right; the experts wrong. God had spoken to Paul. Interestingly, God had spoken to Paul about a non-spiritual event, a storm, that did not seem immediately connected with evangelism. He was not preaching the gospel to his shipmates, just telling them how to sail their ship! In a similar vein, God had spoken to Joseph about a non-spiritual event, a famine, and to Daniel about the rise and fall of secular kingdoms. 'Are you saved?' is not God's only question. His wisdom and care cover all of life.

Now let us notice several key approaches Paul takes in bringing this divine revelation to bear. First, he expounds his revelation in a way that is easy to accept. He says, 'I can see that our voyage is going to be disastrous.' He is low-key in his approach and uses naturalistic language. He does not stand from the bow pulpit with sparking eyes (aren't sparking eyes standard equipment for even the beginner prophet?) and bellow, 'Thus saith the Lord who at this very time tomorrow will smite the seas with the rod of his wrath....' No, he uses language and a tone that they can easily accept. He is almost conversational.

Not only does his approach make it easy for them to accept, though, it makes it easy for them to disagree. 'He sees one thing,' the pilot might say, 'but I see another.' This is exactly what the shipmates did say. They were soon to find out that there is a big difference between what man sees, handicapped by finitude, and what the infinite God sees. Paul, the seer (often used in the Old Testament interchangeably with 'prophet'), sees with God.

Paul displays tact in handling these soldiers and sailors. One definition of tact in the *Oxford English Dictionary* is, 'A ready and delicate sense of what is fitting and proper in dealing with others, so as to avoid giving offence or to win goodwill.'

The prophet Daniel shows this aptitude for tact in his own dealings with unbelievers. When Daniel resolves not to defile himself with non-kosher foods he does not simply dig in his heels and sullenly defy the official over him. He does two things. First, he very politely asks him for permission not to eat the proposed foods (Dan 1:8). Next, he offers him an alternative as a solution (vv 12–14). The official feels respected and he sees a reasonable way out of his dilemma. That's tact.

US Congressman Mark Siljander relates the story of how his lack of tact lost him an election. Late in the congressional race he was sending out a tape to his Christian supporters asking for prayer. At one point in the tape he talked about the need to 'break the back of Satan' through prayer. When he spoke the words he felt a check in his spirit as if this was not a wise thing to put down on tape, even if it was true. But in the rush of last-minute events he let it go. Within a few days his opposition had got hold of the tape and leaked it to the press. The press, smelling a sensational story, blew it up to be some spooky remark in which Siljander posed as the force of light crusading against the malevolent forces of darkness, ie, his opponent. It lost him the election. Tact and wisdom are important.

The second tactical manoeuvre Paul uses in presenting prophecy to pagans is a refusal to force the situation. He lets God open the way. Notice the total absence, when his prophetic warnings go unheeded, of thunderous denunciations of their hard hearts. As his starting point he takes for granted their hard hearts. They wouldn't be pagans otherwise. He does not turn huffily away from them muttering doom and gloom. He relaxes and lets God ripen the situation.

If God has given Paul a word then he can also trust God to open the way for that word. God is a God who will 'go before you and will level the mountains; [he] will break down gates of bronze and cut through bars of iron' (Is 45:2) in order to see that his word comes to pass—though sometimes more subtly than by bashing bronze and rolling over iron barriers. The point is that the God who reveals the path you are to take is the God who 'will make your paths straight' (Prov 3:6). He will iron out the kinks that prevent you from realising his will. That is what Paul was trusting in.

Neither Daniel nor Joseph had to force his revelation upon an unwilling sovereign. Quite the contrary: in both cases these rulers came to them asking for help. God had engineered circumstances so that they felt their need for divine guidance. And this is exactly what he does in Paul's situation in Acts 27. By verse 20 the crisis has been brought to a head. The ship's company are now at the end of their own personal, human resources: 'When neither sun nor stars appeared for many days and the storm continued raging, we finally gave up all hope of being saved.' Now they are ready to heed Paul.

At this point Paul, who has been patiently biding his time, swings into action again. He says, 'Men, you should have taken my advice not to sail from Crete' (v 21). He cannot resist a little 'I told you so'. More seriously, he is reminding them of his prophetic credentials. He then foretells that they will all be saved even though they will lose the ship by running aground on an island. He encourages them not to give up, saying that they will soon be safe.

It is worth pointing out here the non-fatalistic nature of the prophetic gift. Originally God had said through Paul that if they took this sea voyage then all hands would be lost. Now he is saying that all will live if they heed him. We do not know if this change in outcome is in response to Paul's intercessory prayer, even as Moses interceded with God for disobedient Israel and saw them spared. The Scriptures do not say. The pertinent point is that prophecies are not completely iron-clad, fixed and unchangeable. God is fixed, but his plans for people change with the circumstances. Prophecy should never lead to despairing fatalism. It should lead to understanding and hope. Now we know how to proceed and how to pray. How God responds is up to him. After all, he is God.

Third, we need to notice that prophecy is not all mysticism; it does not negate the necessity of intelligent action. The world cannot understand a completely other-worldly mysticism, but intelligent action it does understand. Paul does not gather the whole crew and instruct them to sing and pray without ceasing that they might be rescued. Pray certainly, but also drop four more anchors over the side—that is Paul's approach (v 29). Paul cannily perceives the attempted escape of the frightened sailors and prevents them, saying, 'Unless these men stay with the ship, you cannot be saved' (vv 31–32). Paul does not reject the natural for the supernatural. He sees that they need the sailors' natural skills if they are to escape death. This does not contradict his faith in the saving ability of God. Finally he encourages them to eat some food, saying, 'You need it to survive' (v 34).

Paul combined faith with a pragmatic realism. He was no mystic floating two feet above reality. And this leads us into our fourth and last principle of biblical politicking:

Don't keep nature out

Although the prophetic gifting was central to the political effectiveness of both Joseph and Daniel, the more naturalistic giftings—administration and an understanding of civil affairs—were also vital. Daniel's initial entrance into government service was not his grasp of spiritual issues but his grasp of secular issues. He was given a place in the Babylonian civil service training programme because his pagan masters could see that he showed an 'aptitude for every kind of learning, [was] well informed, quick to understand' (Dan 1:4). He was sharp. And then, after three years of training, he was approved for a government position because in 'every matter of wisdom and understanding about which the king questioned them, he found them ten times better than all the magicians and enchanters in his whole kingdom' (Dan 1:20). What did Daniel, along with Shadrach, Meshach and Abednego understand so well? It must have been the 'language and literature of the Babylonians' (Dan 1:4) in which they had been schooled for the preceding three years. Nebuchadnezzar was not in the least interested in Daniel's grasp of the Bible; he was very interested, however, in Daniel's grasp of civil affairs. He wanted to know if Daniel had understanding of the way in which the Babylonians needed to run their empire. He had heaps of it.

Joseph, too, did not allow the supernatural and miraculous to crowd out the natural. His success in government owed as much to his superb administrative skills as to his ability to interpret dreams. He administrated the business affairs of Potiphar with such adroitness that Potiphar 'left in Joseph's care everything he had' (Gen 39:6). While in prison his administrative gifts were so obvious that they were used by his own jailers to run the prison! (see Genesis 39:21–23). And then as Pharaoh's chief aide, if he had won his position by his supernatural ability to foresee the famine, he only retained it because of his ability to organise and administrate the mammoth task of seven years of food gathering and seven years of food distribution.

Spirituality is not enough for government service. Good intentions are not enough. Being a sincere Christian, a great preacher or a humble prayer warrior is not enough. We also need the gifting and skill for government.

David succeeded as king not only because of his good heart but because he was skilled at the art of governing. 'And David shepherded them with integrity of heart; with skilful hands he led them' (Ps 78:72).

When Moses looked for people to fill governing positions in Israel he sought for 'capable men from all the people—men who fear God, trustworthy men who hate dishonest gain' (Ex 18:21, 24, 25). He looked for both character and ability. Availability was not enough! Those selected had to be available and able. Here's an overly cute yet wholly accurate rubric: availability plus ability results in utility.

To believe in the importance of skills and ability is not to doubt that God can and does use anybody, especially the 'weak and foolish' (1 Cor 1:27). Rather, it is to recognise how God usually works. One indication that God has chosen a person for a task is that he or she can do it! That person must have not only good intentions, but good abilities. God gives us the abilities we need to do the job he has called us to. These abilities are called 'gifts of the Holy Spirit' (1 Cor 12:1–7). These gifts—prophecy, administration, service, and so on—are simply tools to get a job done. We are to do what we are gifted for, not what we are not gifted for: 'Each one should use whatever gift he has received to serve others, faithfully administering God's grace in its various forms' (1 Pet 4:10).

To believe in the importance of skill and ability is not to retreat from a reliance on God's Spirit. It is simply to believe that where the Holy Spirit leads, he also equips with the requisite skill. The very first time anyone is mentioned being 'filled with the Spirit' the result is that he is endowed with 'skill, ability and knowledge' (Ex 31:3). Interestingly, the skill imparted by the Spirit was in the areas of crafts and metal-work—another reminder that God is interested in the secular and 'non-spiritual' world. It is also a reminder that the more mundane gifts such as administration are actually no less supernatural than the prophetic gifts; they only appear so. All gifts come from a supernatural God, and nothing that comes from God can be unspiritual.

Two sorts of gifts and skills are necessary for government service. First, one needs the ability to implement solutions. Administration again! Government is actually the art of administrating good ideas. A good idea that remains just that helps no one. Ideas need to be implemented. Joseph was Pharaoh's second-in-command not only because he foresaw problems but because he saw solutions. More, he knew how to implement those solutions and bring them into reality.

Second, one needs a gift of wisdom and understanding; an ability to grasp issues. Before you can implement good ideas you need to have some. This is where wisdom comes in.

Government service requires the qualities ascribed to the tribe of Issachar during the reign of David: 'men...who understood the times and knew what Israel should do' (1 Chron 12:32). They understood not just eternity but 'the times'—their unique spot in human history. Consequently, they understood Israel's role and how the nation ought to proceed to fulfil that role.

Without this gift of wisdom and understanding it is worse than useless to attempt to serve in government. To govern is to lead; and to lead is to take people from point A to point B. If a leader lacks the understanding of where point B is and how to get there, he cannot possibly lead. So the very nature of leadership demands a gift of wisdom.

Moreover, the sensitive nature of the governing relationship demands wisdom. How do Christians govern non-Christians when they hold fundamentally different worldviews, speak a different language and are motivated by different goals? Part of the answer is that while there is much that divides us from non-Christians, there is also much we hold in common—our common humanity to start with. The rest of the answer is found in God's gift of wisdom.

God's wisdom will clear up misunderstanding, overcome friction and gain goodwill. As it was for Joseph, so it can be for God's people today: 'God...gave Joseph wisdom and enabled him to gain the goodwill of Pharaoh king of Egypt' (Acts 7:10).

MP Michael Alison tapped God's wisdom in relating his convictions to the political sphere. Chuck Colson recounts the following incident:

> In 1979 Michael was named minister of state for Northern Ireland, a responsibility that included administration of Ulster's notorious prisons. Then, in the late fall of 1980, young Catholic terrorists in Belfast's Maze prison began to starve themselves to death in protest of British rule in Northern Ireland. By Christmas the first prisoner had gone nearly two months without food and was near death. Worldwide attention focused on Belfast. Would the British government allow this young inmate to die, or would they force-feed him once he slipped into a final coma?
>
> The prison doctor came to Michael Alison for the decision. It was, of course, a Hobson's choice. To force-feed the protestor would cause riots among the Irish Republican Army faithful; to let him die would be callous.
>
> Michael had been praying for weeks for wisdom in the horrible situation. 'Go to the prisoner's fellow hunger strikers,' he told the doctor. 'Ask them to make the decision.' The other protestors could not have their brother's death on their consciences, but in the process of putting him on life-support equipment, they saw the inconsistency of their own position. The hunger strike ended, the crisis averted.[145]

Christians can make a vital contribution to the political arena, even in this age of the pluralistic and secular state. But the type of Christians we need involved are Christians who are called, Christians who refuse to compromise, Christians who are open to God's supernatural power, and Christians with the needed skills and gifts for politics. Then God will be glorified even as he was in the days of Joseph and Daniel.

IO

Partial Participation

Evangelism and church growth are political events. While the central thrust of this book is the urging and delineating of biblical involvement in government, it needs to be seen that even the politically uninvolved Christian is, in fact, inadvertently involved— if not up to his eyeballs then up to his neck (which is why non-politicals such as the Anabaptists were apt to lose theirs!). Vital Christians, even those who are only minimally involved in the political process, unknowingly possess and exercise tremendous political impact. How so?

Consider these words of Abraham Lincoln:

> Public sentiment is everything. With public sentiment nothing can fail; without it, nothing can succeed. Consequently he who molds public sentiment goes deeper than he who enacts statutes or pronounces decisions. He makes statutes and decisions possible or impossible to be executed.[146]

The Christian faith is not a political programme on which to form a government; it is, however, a faith which moulds and shapes the sentiments. It furnishes values, virtues, a sense of the priorities and goals of life—the things that are the bedrock of government. Government only organises and administrates society's movement; it does not originate movement. Religion does that. Religion provides the context within which government can function. It is the oil which makes possible the smooth running of the machinery of government.

John Adams, second President of the United States, said:

> We have no government armed with power capable of contending with
> human passions unbridled by morality and religion. Our constitution
> was made only for a moral and religious people. It is wholly inadequate
> to the government of any other.[147]

The skeletons of government structures are lifeless and useless
without the life-force of moral and spiritual forces. Lawlessness will
reign when the spirit of lawlessness is loose among the populace, no
matter how many edicts Parliament decrees. Government needs
the value-shaping role of religion. Without that it cannot do its job.
Here is the political impact of the church.

James Madison, a key framer of the American constitution,
argued against the vanity of supposing that a state can govern in the
absence of virtue among its citizenry, saying:

> Is there no virtue among us? If there be not, we are in a wretched
> situation. No theoretical checks, no form of government, can render us
> secure. To suppose any form of government will secure liberty or
> happiness without any virtue in the people is a chimerical idea.[148]

The church nurtures this virtue so necessary to the prospering of
a nation. The church needs the government and the government
needs the church.

It was the much maligned Victorians who were the architects of
the liberal society in England (liberal in the sense of being anti-
authoritarian, of freeing the populace from excessive state control
and restriction). The Victorian Age gave birth to England's Liberal
Party and ushered in such reforms as universal male suffrage and
freedom of conscience.[149] The Victorians were only able to build a
society with liberty at its heart because they also placed morality at
its heart. It was their insistence on morality and self-control which
made it all possible. Gertrude Himmelfarb, distinguished Professor
of History at the City University of New York, writes:

> ...far from promoting social control, the [Victorian] ethos had the
> effect of promoting self-control. This was at the heart of Victorian
> morality: self-control...self-discipline. A liberal society, the Victorians
> believed, depended upon a moral citizenry. The stronger the voluntary
> exercise of morality on the part of each individual—the more inter-
> nalised that morality—the weaker need be the external, coercive
> instruments of the state. For the Victorians, morality served as a sub-
> stitute for the law, just as law was a substitute for force.[150]

Historians Halevy and Lecky credit the saving of Britain from a bloody revolution, similar to that which overtook France in 1789, to the Methodist Revival under Wesley and Whitefield. Lecky, the rationalist, claims that the evangelicals

> infused into the Church a new fire and passion and devotion, kindled a spirit of fervent philanthropy, raised the standard of clerical duty and completely altered the whole tone and tendency of the preaching of its ministers.[151]

The French historian, Halevy, adds:

> We shall witness Methodism bring under its influence first the dissenting sects, then the Establishment, finally secular opinion. We shall explain by this movement the miracle of modern England, anarchist but orderly, practical and businesslike, but religious and even pietist.[152]

The Methodists had no political designs but by their preaching they stamped a gospel imprint on to the beliefs and morals of England; beliefs and morals which channelled England's political forces into peaceful change and reform.

No wonder that Irving Kristol, editor of the influential US magazine *The Public Interest*, in viewing the alarming breakdown of the family among the nation's blacks, suggested:

> What is wanted is a black John Wesley to do for the 'underclass' in the ghettos what Wesley did for the gin-ridden, loose-living working class in 18th-century Britain. Reformation has to be on the agenda, not just relief.[153]

Reformation needs to go hand-in-hand with relief, or there will be no real relief. Moral crises profoundly affect government but government cannot affect them. Another force is necessary: God's Spirit working through his church.

Moral crisis is not confined just to the ghettoised blacks. Daniel Bell, Professor of Sociology at Harvard University, sees the whole of Western culture under the strains of what he calls 'the cultural contradictions of capitalism'; strains which have arisen within the last 125 years. He observes a discordance between the ideals driving the political realm, the economic realm and the cultural realm, a discordance which threatens to rip our society apart. Efficiency and bureaucracy govern the economic realm (as opposed to tradition in earlier times), equality rules in the political realm (as opposed to the earlier principle of hierarchy), and self-gratification and hedonism dominate the cultural realm (as opposed to an earlier transcendent ethic which limited individuals).

Bell observes that tension arises out of the disjunction between the norms of the economic realm and the political realm: one insists on hierarchy, the other on equality. An even more fundamental contradiction arises out of

> the disjunction between the... norms demanded in the economic realm, and the norms of self-realization that are now central in the culture. The two realms which had historically been joined to produce a single character structure—that of the Puritan and of his calling—have now become unjoined. The principles of the economic realm and those of the culture now lead people in contrary directions.[154]

The Puritan ethic of delayed gratification, the ethic which made possible the tremendous economic growth of the West (by encouraging saving, investment for the future, trustworthy contracts, and so on), has been exchanged for an ethic of self-gratification. How long can the West's economy flourish in such an environment?

Bell believes that Western culture is now at a watershed; that it cannot contain these contradictions much longer. Something will have to give. And what solutions does he offer for this crisis in the West? His analysis of the solution is even more interesting than his analysis of the problem. Let me quote:

> The real problem of modernity is the problem of belief. To use an unfashionable term, it is a spiritual crisis, since the new anchorages have proved illusory and the old ones have become submerged.... What holds one to reality, if one's secular system of meanings proves to be an illusion? I will risk an unfashionable answer—the return in Western society of some conception of religion.... What religion can restore is the continuity of generations.... Yet such a continuity *cannot be manufactured* [my emphasis].[155]

What this eminent Harvard sociologist is saying is that he can give us the problem but he cannot give us the solution. He can analyse the problem; he can even analyse the solution; what he cannot do is implement the answer. But *the church can!* That is precisely its role and its mission. This is what evangelism, discipleship and church growth are all about. The church was left behind by a risen Christ to meet the spiritual crisis raging on earth. Jesus died to resolve this crisis. He left a living church to continue his work.

One result of the church doing its job, as Bell points out, is that the life-springs of a healthy society will be revitalised; an ethic is diffused through society which makes trust possible, promotes harmony and limits the destructive influences of sin. In revitalising the church we revitalise the whole society. That is why I said at the outset that even the politically inactive Christian unwittingly makes a tremendous political contribution just by living out his faith. Partial participation transformed the Roman empire (the early Christians did not bother with politics); it can do the same today.

Bell, in calling for 'the return ... of some conception of religion', comes dangerously close to President Eisenhower's celebrated remark that American government makes no sense 'unless it is founded in a deeply felt religious faith—and I don't care what it is'.[156] But this will never do! First, you cannot want a 'deeply felt' faith and still not 'care' what it is. That's like the preacher who rose up on his soapbox to announce, 'I was going to preach against apathy, but I can't be bothered.' Second, just what faith one relies on matters quite a lot. We need to care deeply about which faith and which morality we choose to adhere to. Faiths and moralities come in all stripes and colours.

Two ideologies responsible for the greatest butcheries of the twentieth century—Naziism and communism—held very firm moralities. Historian Paul Johnson comments:

> Hitler also appealed to the moralistic nature of many Germans, that is, those who had a keen desire for 'moral' behaviour without possessing a code of moral absolutes rooted in Christian faith. Himmler, the conscientious mass-murderer, the scrupulous torturer, was the archetype of the men who served Hitler best. He defined the virtues of the SS, the embodiment of Nazi 'morality', as loyalty, honesty, obedience, hardness, decency, poverty and bravery. The notion of obeying 'iron laws' or 'a higher law', rather than the traditional, absolute morality taught in the churches, was a Hegelian one. Marx and Lenin translated it into a class concept; Hitler into a race one.... Service to the race, as opposed to the Marxist proletariat, was the basis of Nazi puritanism, marked by what Rudolf Hess, commandant at Auschwitz, termed the 'cold' and 'stony' attitude of the ideal Nazi, one who 'had ceased to have human feelings' in the pursuit of duty.[157]

There are puritans and then there are Puritans. It makes a difference which you get. The Nazis had a morality—duty, self-sacrifice, loyalty, obedience, and so on—but it was a misdirected one. The same is true for the communist puritan. The memoirs of a Guatemalan guerrilla, Mario Payeras, ring with a sense of a moral imperative. His little band not only fight the enemy without, they fight the enemy within; they hold each other to account by conducting self-criticism meetings where 'such sins are confessed and discussed as licking the empty sack of sugar instead of boiling it—when one is nearly dying of starvation—for the collective coffee, as revolutionary morality demands'.[158] The sin of individualism must be ruthlessly stamped out. Where the sin cannot be stamped out then, reluctantly, the sinner must be.

The guerrillas serve history, not God. When one of their little band begins to suspect that this god may fail—when his faithfulness to 'revolutionary morality' flags—they are obliged to bring him in line with history. They execute him. The sinner strayed and history must be served. Listen to the high moral tone of this extract from Payeras' memoir:

> We exhausted our ability to save him.... We tried to appeal to his better judgment and win him over again for the group.... In his desire to live, he promised loyalty and many other virtues.... We shot him one April morning when many birds were singing. This was one of the world's lovely sounds that he would no longer hear.... We returned to our posts. A profound silence reigned. The unit had reached maturity. Perhaps from that moment each of us was a better person.[159]

This is the sort of unflinching devotion to duty that wiped out millions in Russia, China and Kampuchea. Morality cut off from its Christian underpinnings can be worse than no morality at all. Society needs more than vague 'values'; it needs Christian values.

It is doubtful that Western morality can long survive without its Christian base. Morality is rooted in theology. Dry up the theology and sooner or later the morality will follow.

The moral descent of certain literary/political families in Victorian England is illustrative of what happens in the wider culture. In the first generation we find the staunch evangelicals of the Clapham Sect (Wilberforce was a guiding light in this group). The next generation jettison their fathers' theology while holding on to their morality. These are the Victorian moralists who see no reason why they cannot maintain a secular code of ethics—the code of the

'gentleman'—without an underlying biblical faith. The next generation see every reason. The third or fourth generation come along
and wonder, in the absence of a transcendent Lawgiver, what
makes their parents' Victorian morality anything more than a convention. If it is just a convention, well then, when it becomes
inconvenient it can be changed for a new convention. And that is
just what they did. They jettisoned conventional morality along
with conventional theology. They started, not the 'Clapham Sect',
but the Bloomsbury Group.

The Bloomsbury Group were an influential literary/cultural cli-
que of the early twentieth century (named after the area of London
where its members met and lived) who rejected the late Victorian
ethic of duty to God, king and country. They worshipped at the
altar of beauty and art; elevated the individual over society; vener-
ated sensation and experience; and lived promiscuously homosexual lives.

Their ringmaster, Lytton Strachey—whose father had been a
general in India for thirty years—went before a tribunal in 1916 for
his stand against conscription into the armed forces. 'Tell me, Mr
Strachey,' he was asked by the tribunal chairman, 'what would you
do if you saw a German soldier attempting to rape your sister?' 'I
should try to come between them,' he replied.[160] He could mock
conventional morality in his high, squeaky voice because he, with
the rest of the Bloomsbury Group, thought of himself as having
progressed beyond it. Conventional morality might be well and
good for 'timid natures who dare not allow their souls free play',
but not for Bloomsbury artistes.

Maynard Keynes, a 'Bloomsberry' (their term), a writer on
economics and a seminal thinker behind much twentieth-century
economic practice, said about Bloomsbury:

> We repudiated entirely customary morals, conventional and traditional
> wisdom. We were, that is to say, in the strict sense of the term immoral-
> ists.... I remain, and will always remain, an immoralist.[161]

Many of these immoralists of the Bloomsbury Group descended
from the moralists of the Clapham Sect. For instance, Henry
Thornton was a banker, philanthropist, Member of Parliament and
a founder member of the Clapham Sect. In fact, the sect met in his
home in Clapham (hence the name). As faith in biblical theology
deserted his family over the generations, so did biblical morality.

His great-grandson was E.M. Forster, eminent novelist, Bloomsbury 'fellow-traveller' and, of course, homosexual.

Then there were the Macaulays. Zachary Macaulay, a fervent evangelical of the early nineteenth century, was the father of Thomas B. Macaulay, one of England's greatest historians. Thomas lacked his father's biblical faith but held on to the moral and civic virtues that stemmed from it. Two generations later, he might have been shocked to find his grandson, the minor poet R.C. Trevelyan, an advocate of Bloomsbury immorality.

The same decline can be seen in the family of James Stephen. James Stephen was a convinced evangelical who took Wilberforce's widowed sister to be his second wife. His grandson, Leslie Stephen, distanced himself from evangelicalism, saying, 'I now believe in nothing, but I do not believe the less in morality etc, etc. I mean to live and die like a gentleman if possible.'[162] There's step two in the progression. Step three comes in the next generation: all three of Leslie Stephen's children were Bloomsbury members. One of them, Virginia Woolf, wrote of her move to Bloomsbury, 'Everything was going to be new; everything was going to be different. Everything was on trial.'[163] Morality was put in the dock and found wanting.

There we have it: Clapham to Bloomsbury in four generations. The self-denying, others-regarding morality of the evangelicals, when stripped of its biblical underpinnings, had nothing to support it and inevitably degenerated into the narcissistic decadence of Bloomsbury. Decadence may be momentarily thrilling but it does not fuel the reforms and advances every society needs to make if it is to survive and thrive. That is the lesson of the Clapham to Bloomsbury Express.

A society needs spiritual input if it is to escape the cloying grip of decadence. The church can provide spiritual input. In providing, it makes society possible. And that is why the church is a political heavyweight even before it goes to the polls. Even partial participation is a blessing.

II

The Myth of the Third Way: Rejected and Resurrected

Myths delight children, motivate adults and madden scientists. They can cloud reality, sending us off in pursuit of hopelessly illusory goals, or they can clarify reality, thereby launching us into the building of a better world. All this is true of that most tenacious of Christian myths: the myth of the Third Way.

The myth of the Third Way states that there is a uniquely Christian programme in politics which is radically different from secular programmes. 'Why borrow from the world? Can't God supply his own?' Third Wayists look for a revealed politics set apart from worldly, non-revelational politics.

American historian Herbert Schlossberg once echoed the hopes and dreams of Third Wayists everywhere when he wrote:

> The participants... insist that we have to choose between left and right on every issue, that there is no third way. But...there must be a third way.[164]

British sociologist Andrew Walker takes up the theme, saying:

> A Christian 'third way' in politics, I believe, is to transcend the dualism of the Enlightenment children, the collectivist and the individualist man.... our third way should be directed by the Trinitarian nature of God.[165]

He wants uniquely Christian approaches which do not stem from the secular political philosophies of right and left. He wants uniquely Christian categories of thought.

Harry Blamires, student and friend of C.S. Lewis, also wants to see the development of uniquely Christian categories. He writes:

> There is no longer a Christian mind. There is still, of course, a Christian ethic, a Christian practice, and a Christian morality. But as a thinking being, the modern Christian has succumbed to secularization.... we Christians in the modern world accept, for the purpose of mental activity, a frame of reference constructed by the secular mind and a set of criteria reflecting secular evaluations.[166]

Blamires feels that, for the purpose of evaluating contemporary political and social life, we ought to find and use specifically Christian categories expressed in a recognisably Christian vocabulary.[167] Otherwise, we are selling the gospel short.

The attraction of Third Wayism is that it takes God seriously and promises that our faith is relevant to everyday life. What Christian could fail to be sympathetic to Third Wayist challenges which run like this:

> A week-end Gospel is a weakened Gospel. Is your God just the God of your week-ends or do you let him speak his programme into your workaday world?

> He is Lord of all or not at all.

> How big is your God? Is he big enough to cover the political arena? If we are not 'of this world' then why do we use the world's politics?

I have noticed two frustrating patterns constantly recurring in Third Wayist literature. The first pattern is that Third Wayists, when they finally move from eloquently affirming the need for a Third Way to actually describing the Third Way, end up describing something remarkably similar to some already existing secular model. For instance, when Blamires actually offers up some samples of what the Christian mind might look like, we find him saying just what secular politicians are saying. In his complaint that 'the tragic keynote of our age is atomism', he is only maintaining what any good Marxist sold on alienation and the need for group solidarity would maintain.[168] In lashing out at our educational institutes for their 'revolt against authority in favour of popularity, against quality in favour of quantity', he is condemning what any good traditionalist Tory would condemn.[169] And in excoriating modern man for 'increasingly living his day-to-day life in servitude to mechanical contrivance', he only echoes the identical complaint of Romantics from earlier centuries and Greens from our own.[170] What happened to the uniquely different Christian mind? I am not saying that any of Blamires' critiques are wrong; I am simply saying that they are not uniquely Christian.

Gary North meets the same fate. He writes, 'Is there such a thing as distinctively Christian economics? Yes.' He is a firm believer in the Third Way. However, in the very next sentence he goes on to say, 'Are there explicitly Christian economic teachings that no secular economist has written about? So far, probably not.'[171] He affirms his belief in a distinctively Christian programme while quickly adding that it is not quite as distinctive as one would hope. In fact, so far, it looks exactly like other secular programmes! The Third Way slips away. North is theoretically a Third Wayist who, when it comes to actually constructing an economic system, turns out, in practical terms, to be a non-Third Wayist conservative (ie, he believes in the market economy, individual freedom, limited government, protection from redistributionist polities, and so on).

Even more frustrating is the second trend constantly met with in Third Wayist writings: Third Wayists who believe in a uniquely Christian way but cannot even begin to tell what it is. Dr Paul Marshall is Senior Member in Political Theory at the Institute for Christian Studies in Toronto. He has written a book on the biblical perspective on government in which he starts out strongly, saying, 'Much Christian comment about politics was "either pious generalities with which it would be difficult for anyone to disagree, or over-specific prescriptions which owe more to the author's political ideology than his Christian faith".'[172] Now this looks promising. Here is somebody who is going to steer us between vague banalities on the one hand and worldly politics on the other in order to give us God's politics. Great is our disappointment when, after eagerly reading through seventy-five pages in search of his Third Way, one arrives at page 76 to read:

> We must develop means of understanding society which themselves flow from our Christian faith. At this point in the book I should perhaps go on to describe such means of Christian social analysis. But I shall not do so, for the simple and embarrassing reason that such means do not exist.[173]

Well, this is a let-down. 'Such means do not exist!'

I have a simple suggestion which would explain these recurring patterns in Third Way literature: *The Third Way in the form sought does not exist.* It is a myth.

The 'different' myth

I do not say that Blamires et al are wrong-headed in seeking Christian categories of thought. I say they are wrong-headed in seeking *unique* Christian categories of thought. That is, the error lies in believing Christian political categories will be essentially different; that their essential characteristic should be that they are 'other than' secular offerings.

But why should this be their primary characteristic? Surely their key feature should be that they are biblical; whether or not they are also 'different' is incidental and secondary. For instance, a Christian position on murder is that it is both morally wrong and legally punishable. Why should it disturb us that pagan cultures untouched by the gospel also say the same? Do we need to look frantically for a uniquely Christian position different from the pagan position? Some Third Way? Of course not.

Creator/Redeemer distinction

We are brought back once more to the Creator/Redeemer distinction as a frame of reference for our thinking on this issue. God rules all his creatures, Christian and non-Christian alike, as their Creator. To effectuate his rule he has given general revelation to all humanity: 'They show that the requirements of the law are written on their hearts' (Rom 2:15).

This does not mean that humanity lives up to the truth God has revealed, or that it does not 'suppress the truth by . . . wickedness' (Rom 1:18). It simply means that God has made available to everyone through general revelation a knowledge of basic moral rights and wrongs. Christians share this with non-Christians. It is not surprising, therefore, that in these areas we would find much to agree upon with non-Christians (and even where we disagreed, we would be talking the same language and understanding one another's categories).

What differentiates Christians is their acceptance of God's special revelation, a revelation that covers his redemption plan in Christ. This is where, by definition, anyone who was not a Christian would disagree with the Christian position (that is, if he agreed with the fact that redemption was only in Christ then he would be a Christian).

Structure/direction

Professor Albert Wolters picks up, in his helpful little book *Creation Regained*, John Calvin's twofold distinction between the 'order of creation' and the 'order of sin and creation'. He builds on this basis with some of his own thoughts on 'structure' and 'direction':

> Structure refers to the order of creation, to the constant creational constitution of any thing.... Structure is anchored in the law of creation, the creational decree of God.... Direction, by contrast, designates the order of sin and redemption.... Anything in creation can be directed either toward or away from God.[174]

Christians analysing any issue would want to look at both these considerations. Does it agree with God's structures (the family, private property, the government, and so on), and is the policy aimed in a Godwards direction (are the motives godly)? Some policies are well-intentioned (ie, they are aimed in a godly direction) but are ill-conceived in that they violate creational realities. Other policies are selfishly directed but are consonant with God's creational structures. They fit with the way God has created the world. Thus, we may not agree with the intention of the policy but we can agree with the policy itself.

Certainly this is the way we would view the remarks, for instance, of journalist Noel Malcolm on family policy. In a *Spectator* article he contrasted traditionalist Tories who support the family for pragmatic reasons with 'the *Kinder, Kuche und Kirche* Tories, the Christian moralists for whom the family is not just a handy socioeconomic unit but an ordinance of God'.[175] One may not agree with the pragmatic intention of some Tories—to support the family merely as a traditional and efficient economic institution—while yet agreeing with the policy itself, ie, that of strengthening the family. The family is a godly structure, no matter how you arrive at it.

This structure/direction viewpoint will help us as we look at an issue raised by Harry Blamires.

Recovering roots

Harry Blamires remarks that 'as a thinking being, the modern Christian has succumbed to secularization.... we Christians in the modern world accept, for the purpose of mental activity, a frame of reference constructed by the secular mind'.[176] But there are two very different ways of looking at this claim of secularisation. The first is that the godly have succumbed to the ungodly through accepting their categories. The second is that the ungodly cannot but use God's categories—creational standards given to all through general revelation—when they think. That is, the *direction* of the policy may not be Godwards but the *structure* may be a God-ordained creational reality. If the second viewpoint is true then the secular world is actually using godly categories! If so, it is no great shame to use the secular categories.

I agree with Blamires that secularisation has swept our modern world (only a fool wouldn't, and I have no desire to join that unhappy company). However, it seems to me that the primary locus of secularisation is not the categories themselves but rather in the roots of these categories: we have lost our biblical roots; roots that gave birth to our present categories. To undo secularisation is not only, or even mainly, to rethink our categories but rather to rediscover their godly roots.

This is exactly the approach Professor Amos takes in his challenging book *Defending the Declaration*. He looks at the five ideas central to America's Declaration of Independence—the laws of nature and nature's God, self-evident truths, unalienable rights, government by the consent of the governed, divine providence—and, in the face of those who would dismiss these as pagan constructs, defends them as categories which had their birth in the Bible and Christian theology as it developed over the centuries. To be faithful to the Bible it is not necessary to jettison these concepts. To do so would be a misunderstanding of the process of secularisation. (This process of rediscovering biblical roots will help us to discover the 'Christian mind' that Blamires, quite rightly, is so keen for us all to have.)

Concepts and values

To recap, then, I reject the Third Way as it is commonly understood, ie, as the search for 'different' and unique concepts. I fully embrace it, however, as the search for Christian concepts. There are biblical concepts bearing political implications. Third Wayists, such as contributors to the British Christian magazine *Third Way*, are right to seek to identify them and, having identified them, to seek to apply them to our political life.

Of course the Bible is not a political primer, nor is it a source book of detailed political programmes. It is not a party manifesto. It deals first with our relationship to God and then with our moral responsibilities to our fellow men and women. It teaches us godly values and moral principles.

However, when we analyse these values and moral principles we find that implicit in them are very clear concepts about men and women in both their private and public roles. Now concepts about our public life are concepts eligible for a political reading. For instance, when the Bible says, 'Do not steal,' we are given not only a clear statement about our private moral responsibilities; we are also given to understand the legitimacy of the concept of private property. It is a biblical concept. The immediate political implication of this is that legitimate government will include in its role a protection of individual property; conversely, it means that any political philosophy which rejects this notion—such as Marx's statement, 'Communism may be summed up in the single sentence: Abolition of Private Property'[177]—should be rejected as false to the creational givens that God has ordained.

Some of the most obvious moral commands carrying clear political concepts are in Romans 13. We are told to 'submit...to the governing authorities, for...authorities...have been established by God' (v 1). From here we learn the base legitimacy of the very idea of governing; a concept which undercuts the alternative philosophy of anarchy. We are also told the government 'bears the sword' (v 4), a scripture legitimising the use of force by the authorities. We are also (unfortunately!) told, 'Give everyone what you owe him: If you owe taxes, pay taxes' (v 7). Thus we learn the government has the right to tax.

In Romans 13, the political connection of biblical ideas is explicitly made for us by the writer. It is not so everywhere. In many places we have to dig and do our own work. Indeed, I am one who believes that just such 'digging out' work can be seen in the interrelated development of Western political thought and Christian theology.

Biblical impact on Western law over the centuries

French sociologist Jacques Ellul claims that 'the essential, undeniable fact is that the West was the first civilization in history to focus attention on the individual and on freedom'.[178] In other words, in the West the rule of law was supreme; not just a rule of law with a view to maintaining order[179] but a rule of law aimed at protecting the rights and liberties of the individual.

What gave birth to these characteristics in the West? Did they find their origins in Greek philosophy and Roman legal thinking or did they find their origins in Christianity? I would suggest the latter. Biblical thinking held tyranny in check by denying that any individual, including the king, was above the law (see, for instance, Deuteronomy 17:18–20[180]). By contrast, Greek thinking, as passed down to us by Aristotle, said, 'That for men of preeminent virtue there is no law—they are themselves the law.'[181] Aristotle, in his realism, immediately qualified this point by adding that, as there were no such men of pre-eminent virtue in actual fact, then the rule of law must prevail. However, in setting up the ideal of the virtuous man superior to the law, Aristotle shows where the real heart of Greek thinking lay.

Roman thinking, despite their famed law codes, is no better a source for the concept of the rule of law. Richard Tuck, a lecturer in history at Cambridge University, identifies the 'classical Roman view: all moral relationships belonged to the stage of civilisation'.[182] Morality was considered to be an expression of humanity's developing social circumstances rather than a reflection of an eternally fixed and absolute moral code. Civil laws could not reflect absolutes (they do not exist!); they are purely civil creation. But what man has made, man can break—and there goes the rule of law. Even Cicero, the supposed bastion of natural law thinking in Roman jurisprudence, has been discounted by some to be, in fact, a real sceptic; one who doubted that civil laws could ever reflect any natural law.[183]

Another contribution of Christian theology to Western political development—particularly its stress on the freedom of the individual—has been the carving out of a realm of conscience inviolable by the state. It was nineteenth-century historian Lord Acton who acclaimed Luke 20:25—'Then render to Caesar the things that are Caesar's, and to God the things that are God's' (RSV)—as the great turning point in humanity's historic efforts to establish true liberty.[184] Acton meant that Christ clearly differentiated between the authority of the political sphere and that of the spiritual sphere. Unlike Graeco-Roman thought, Christ taught that the state could not swallow up the religious sphere of life; it could not dictate to the individual what his relationship to God would be. This duty and role was not one of 'the things that are Caesar's'. In Acton's words, 'Christianity divided the functions. Its distinctive action on politics was to restrict authority.'[185]

William Ebenstein, professor at the University of California, Santa Barbara, is no great friend of Christianity yet he admits:

> Christianity introduced a revolutionary principle into communal life by destroying the previous equation of personality and citizenship, and by postulating the autonomy of a spiritual sphere, independent of, and even superior to, political authority.[186]

The Greeks have no such concept of a religious realm independent of the state. Sir Moses Finley, Professor Emeritus of Ancient History in the University of Cambridge, points out that America's First Amendment concerning the non-establishment of religion 'would have been incomprehensible to an Athenian; or, if understood, abhorrent. Greek religion was thoroughly enmeshed with the...state.'[187]

The Romans were no different. We read that 'the religion of Rome was intimately connected with the civil polity.... The king was at the head of the religious body.... Every division and subdivision of the State...had its own peculiar sacred ceremonies.'[188]

In 1864, Numa Denis Fustel de Coulanges, Professor of History at Strasbourg, wrote what was destined to become a classic of French historical writing: *The Ancient City: A Study on the Religion, Law, and Institutions of Greece and Rome.* Seeking to shed light on the true nature of pagan Rome and Greece, he wrote:

> The city had been founded upon a religion, and constituted like a church. Hence its strength; hence, also, its omnipotence and the absolute empire which it exercised over its members. In a society established on such principles, individual liberty could not exist. The citizen was subordinate in everything, and without any reserve, to the city; he belonged to it body and soul.... A man had no chance to choose his belief. He must believe and submit to the religion of the city.... The ancients, therefore, knew neither liberty in private life, liberty in education, nor religious liberty.[189]

It is Christianity which introduced the idea that the political state was not sovereign in all areas. It was Christianity which carved out for the individual a sphere of inalienable rights beyond the jurisdiction of the state. This movement towards freeing the individual conscience from state control started, as Acton observed, with Christ himself.

The next development came with Pope Gelasius' fifth-century formulation of the 'two swords' doctrine.[190] Here we see the institutional church applying the implications of Christ's words to the political structures of the day. While acknowledging the political sphere's proper authority over people's temporal affairs (the first sword), Pope Gelasius claimed ecclesiastical authority (the second sword) over their spiritual and religious welfare. The effect of this was to limit the spiritual pretensions of secular authorities.

The next significant development came in 1075 when Pope Gregory VII asserted, and largely won, the independence of the clergy from secular control. So monumental were the reforms instituted by Gregory that Harvard professor Harold Berman does not hesitate to label this entire reform period (1075–1122) the 'Papal Revolution'.[191]

Centuries after Pope Gregory came a further development, when Protestant Reformers advanced the notion of *Sola Scriptura*—the teaching that the Scriptures alone were to be the believer's authoritative source of doctrine and practice. In elevating the Bible over church councils and church tradition the Protestant Reformers were also elevating the individual's conscience; the individual was responsible to God and his book, not to man and his traditions. Though Calvin and Luther did not follow up the religious liberty implications of the doctrine of *Sola Scriptura*, their later disciples did. For instance, Elisha Williams (1694–1755), one-time Congregational pastor and judge of the Connecticut Supreme Court, wrote a pamphlet in 1744—a pamphlet which had emblazoned on its cover the scripture Matthew 22:21: 'Render unto Caesar...'—in which he stated:

> That the sacred scriptures are the alone [*sic*] rule of faith and practice to a Christian, all Protestants are agreed in; and must therefore inviolably maintain, that every Christian has *a right of judging for himself* what he is to believe and practice in religion according to that rule: Which I think on a full examination you will find perfectly inconsistent with any power in the civil magistrate to make any penal laws in matters of religion [emphasis in the original].[192]

Elisha Williams believed that the logical political conclusion of the doctrine of *Sola Scriptura* was that government had no right to enforce religion. If church councils could not bind individual consciences in matters of belief, how much less could secular councils.

Here is the dynamo that led to religious liberty in the West. It is a mistake to credit religious scepticism with the growth of religious toleration. Religious liberty was not won by sceptics who thought religion too unimportant to legislate; religious liberty was won by those who thought it so important that it was a matter best left between a person and his God alone. Religious liberty was a religious accomplishment, not a secular one. In the words (noted already in Chapter 3) of the late Harold Laski, the one-time socialist Reader in Political Science in the University of London:

> The political liberty of the seventeenth and eighteenth centuries was the outcome of the protest against religious intolerance.... it is permissible to argue that no motive save that of religious conviction would have been strong enough to inspire their [the Protestant Reformers of the sixteenth and seventeenth centuries] effort against the inertia which made men anxious for any peace, whatever its character.[193]

Biblical thinking has political repercussions. We can see this legal/political influence of Christianity in the law codes of King Ine (688–726) of Wessex and King Alfred (871–899) of Wessex,[194] in Archbishop Langton's key role in the drafting of the Magna Carta (1215),[195] in the century-long Dominican/Franciscan theological debate which resulted in a resounding justification, through the papal bull *Quia Vir Reprobus* (1329), of the concept of private property (the foundation, Locke suggested, for modern constitutional government),[196] and in the Calvinist covenantal theories of government which both undercut divine-right-of-kings theories and prepared the way for our modern contractual views of government.[197]

Impact today

These Christian concepts of the rule of law, the limited state, and the freedom of individual conscience make a notable difference to the way politics is conducted. In our own century we have seen what happened when opposite concepts were adopted. World War II was largely triggered by two countries, Japan and Germany, which built their foreign policy on anti-Christian elements.

Germany's case is well known but we ought also to recognise, as does historian Paul Johnson, the connection between Japan's brutal, lawless expansionism and her failure 'to absorb the notions of individual moral responsibility which were the gift of the Judaic and Christian tradition'.[198]

The case of communist Russia is a morality tale told with bold strokes. The lesson? Christian concepts make a difference. Unfortunately, Lenin and his successors actually took Marx seriously when he boasted, 'Communism abolishes eternal truths, it abolishes all religion, and all morality';[199] when he dismissed 'notions of freedom, culture, law' as just so much 'bourgeois claptrap'; and when he spurned Western jurisprudence as 'but the will of your class'.[200]

With this sort of anti-Christian philosophy—specifically its substitution of 'class guilt' for the notion of individual guilt—it should come as no surprise that Stalin instituted a system of arrest quotas per district. A designated number of arrests needed to be made irrespective of the somewhat academic question of the actual guilt of the accused individuals.[201] Nor should it come as a shock to read *Pravda*'s justification of Russia's invasion of Czechoslovakia in 1968:

> Those who speak of the action of the allied socialist nations in Czechoslovakia in terms of 'violation of rights' forget that in class society there is not and there has never been a classless law. Laws and legal procedures obey the class struggle, the laws of social development.... Formal legal considerations should not lose the class point of view.[202]

Note how easy it is to airily dismiss law as merely 'formal legal considerations' when one has lost the concept of civil law mirroring divine law; of civil law being connected to eternal law. It is Christianity which made this connection in the West.

Convictions and consensus

If unbelievers refuse to acknowledge the existence of divine law and if believers will not acknowledge the existence of Christian political concepts—not only the existence of Christian values—then the possibility of conducting conviction politics will have been eradicated. All politics will become consensus politics. The art of the possible will have triumphed over the art of the permissible.

Now, consensus building is a necessary part of politicking, but consensus building unrestrained by proper convictions ends in com-

plete immoralism. It leads to following the path of least resistance—Pontius Pilate's operative principle when dealing with an
aroused mob yelling for Jesus' blood. This leaves the public square
a much poorer place.

Consensus parades as 'realism' and pooh-poohs the starry-eyed
idealists who think to make the world a better place. These 'realists' want to accept the world as it is, saying cast-iron convictions
have no place in the hard-nosed world of power-broking politics.
But consider that it was 'realism' triumphing over principle, consensus over conviction, which paved the way for the appeasement
of Hitler in the 1930s; a policy that turned out to be highly impolitic.[203]

And consider the dramatic changes that have taken place in
Eastern Europe as the 1980s shifted into the 1990s before deciding
that 'realists' have the corner on political relevancy. The changes in
Eastern Europe have not been brought about by vacillating con-
sensus-builders but by conviction-based dissidents unwilling to set-
tle for current reality.

Lech Walesa addressed a joint session of Congress in which he
recalled the early days of Polish resistance to communism:

> In those days, at the beginning, many warnings, admonitions, and even
> condemnations were reaching us from many parts of the world. 'What
> are those Poles up to?' we heard. 'They are mad, they are jeopardizing
> world peace and European stability. They ought to stay quiet.'[204]

Realists wanted the Poles to stay quiet, to accept the inevitable,
to sacrifice convictions for consensus (a few tanks can be extremely
persuasive). Western realists thought it wisest to cut off ties with
the Eastern bloc dissidents, to simply grant the Russians the right
to impose their hegemony over 'their' Iron Curtain countries. One
recalls that 'Chancellor Schmidt declared in 1981, [that] challenging
its [Soviet Union's] right to intervene in those countries meant
"revising Yalta" and thus "endangering the peace" '.[205] Walesa
had this sort of remark in mind when he said the Poles waived
discouraging counsels aside in their determination to follow their
convictions.

Realism and unprincipled pragmatism are unable either to
understand or shape the real world. William F. Buckley, Jr, once
wrote that 'pragmatists never know what they are doing, because

they never know why they are doing it. Without theory the facts are dumb.'[206]

I tremble to make mention of Maggie Thatcher but it cannot be denied that here is yet another case of the supreme relevancy and power of conviction politics. The British Prime Minister was what she was because of her convictions. She explained in a 1977 television interview:

> For years now in British politics you have needed to use the word 'consensus'.... It's a word you didn't use when I first came into politics. We had convictions.... Provided you had convictions, politics was more than merely a matter of multiple manoeuvrings to get through the problems of the day.[207]

We need convictions if politics is not to descend to the level of mere power-broking; a level where politics becomes the 'continuation of war by other means'.[208] Lutheran social commentator Richard John Neuhaus says that in the absence of a social normative ethic, the dominant surrenders to the deviant.[209]

We need convictions but not just 'any ole' convictions will do; we need specifically Christian convictions to leaven the lump of political philosophy. This will never happen if Christians are not convinced of the reality of Christian political concepts. On this point, Third Wayists are on to a winner. This is why we should reject Third Wayism as the search for the 'different' while endorsing it as the search for the 'Christian'. We may not be looking for a specifically 'third' way, but we are definitely on the prowl for the Christian way.

12

'The Christians Are Coming!'

Christian participation in politics is not universally welcome. The prospect of waves of beady-eyed fundamentalists descending on the country's ballot boxes triggers one primal response: fear.

Note, for instance, the reaction of an English reporter covering 'Pat' Robertson's 1986 announcement of his willingness to run for the presidency. She commented, 'The evening lasted for three hours and was a combination of song, dance and prayer. No one has ever declared in this way before.... I had found it a terrifying experience.'[210] Or consider the words of the rabbi who said, 'When I hear the words "Christian America" I see barbed wire.'[211]

The 'man in the street' is no less afraid. The *Wall Street Journal* conducted a survey to discover the ordinary voter's view of Robertson's 1988 presidential bid. The response of a fifty-eight-year-old real-estate broker, a Bush supporter, was not untypical: 'I'm scared to death of someone who thinks they have the one way.'[212]

Fear! Fear! Fear! Why?

Some of this is simply due to good, old-fashioned bigotry; to a popular prejudice against a perceived cultural type: the fundamentalist. Journalist Christopher Hitchens hits the right note when he writes:

Try a free association test of the Woody Allen sort. Close your eyes and brood upon the words 'southern fundamentalist'. The image that rises to the interior eye is one of fat-faced, loud-mouthed hypocrisy. The filling of the tent with the credulous, the parting of the credulous from their humble dollars, the gruesome insinuations about the sexual fervour of blacks and the heretical conspiracy of the Jews. All your reading of Eudora Welty and Flannery O'Connor and Sinclair Lewis has prepared you for the outcome, which is that of the demagogue exposed, with one hand on a flask of cheap spirit and the other thrust inexpertly up the skirt of a hopeless jade.[213]

But there is more than simple prejudice at work. People fear mixing religion with politics for several reasons, the first of which is that they associate politicised religion with repression.

Fear of repression

Pascal, himself a committed believer, observed: 'Men never do evil so completely and cheerfully as when they do it from religious conviction.' Twentieth-century opinion agrees. The fear is that the devout believer will be so committed to the eternal good he is effecting that he will blithely disregard the temporal bad he is inflicting.[214] He is so concerned about your eternal well-being that he does not mind ruining your present well-being.

This is why David Hume commented, 'Generally speaking, errors of religion are dangerous; those of philosophy only ridiculous.' The philosophical disposition is given to reflection and analysis (both its weakness and its strength), whereas the religious disposition is more prone to commitment and action. And that is exactly what people fear.

Fear of religiously motivated repression is not only to be found among secular left-wingers; conservative columnist R. Emmett Tyrell, Jr, has his doubts too:

> The pretensions of ordinary politicians are oppressive enough; the pretensions of the political divine would be intolerable...for he will be claiming the sanctions of God and the sanctions of Caesar.[215]

It is suspected that, in the name of righteousness, they will snuff out all our precious freedoms.

Now it must be admitted that 99 per cent of those who enter politics from Christian motivations do not speak the language of unlimited rights and unfettered freedoms. They want to clamp down on abortion, or pornography, or some social evil. But if Christians do not speak the language of absolute freedom, who does? Answer: no one. Why, then, should restraints advocated by

Christians be labelled 'repression' whereas secularist restraints pass as 'responsible government'?

Moreover, it would be grossly unfair to associate religion only with restraint. In fact, religion has played a leading role in the winning of freedom of conscience. The very country which, in the name of freedom, busily bans public manifestations of religion (the USA, which has outlawed school prayer, the displaying of the Ten Commandments, and so on) owes its tradition of individual freedom chiefly to the Christian religion. Dissenting Protestant groups fled to the New World to set up a society in which they could assure freedom for religion; today's lawmakers seem bent on ensuring freedom from religion. Religion is not antithetical to freedom.

If Christians in the West speak less of freedom today it is only because the pendulum has swung so far towards freedom as to make it less necessary. The battle for freedom of conscience has been won. The battle is now on for freedom 'for' conscience; the freedom for conscience and morality to speak in the public square, to enter as a player in the formation of public policy.

Christians must, if we are to assuage this prevailing fear of repression, publicly reaffirm our tradition of freedom and tolerance. It is not enough to speak out about the need for restraints in our national life while ignoring the need for individual liberty. We must be perfectly clear on this. If our sole note is the 'Thou shalt nots' is it any wonder that people begin to doubt our commitment to the 'Thou shalt be able tos'? We must not overreact to the 'rights mania' of modern society—with citizens claiming the right to kill foetuses, the right to have sex with children, and so on[216]—by denying wholesale the existence of rights. Overreaction is as damaging as inaction. Let us act with boldness but speak with care. Only thus can we do something to mollify the fears of those who see 'barbed wire' every time a believer enters the political arena.

Fear of rigidity

The next feature of the imagined fundamentalist/evangelical mind-set which strikes fear into the heart of the modern pagan is a rigid, absolutist mentality; a mentality impossible to reason with. This picture has entered our folk wisdom as a piece of general knowledge, one of the 'of courses' of our culture. So settled is it that Labour MP, Mr Jack Straw, while denouncing his own party's extreme left wing, felt he had scored a telling point against them when he succeeded in likening them to the proverbial 'bigotry of born-again Christians'. He said, 'They behave like born-again Christians who have read only the opening chapter of Genesis and then tell others that they know it all.'[217] So Straw has discovered the alarming fact that Christians firmly believe what they believe (unlike the eminently reasonable sceptic who doubts what he believes!), and then go on to tell others about it; a sure sign of bigotry!

Our age is not fond of absolutes. It has them but it shamefacedly prefers to keep them locked in the closet away from public view. Anyone who talks in terms of absolutes is seen as quirky, a 'bigot', a narrow-minded fool. In fact, it is almost a sign of brain damage and mental instability. 'Don't you realise no one believes in absolutes any more?' It is, frankly, a mental weakness. And can we afford to allow a person with such a mental weakness to get his hands on the levers of power?

Mr Edwards, a lawyer interviewed in the above-mentioned *Wall Street Journal*'s street survey, probably spoke for many when he said, 'I think the reason he's [Robertson] so frightening is that he does strike a real nerve...that thinks this is the one true way. I'm very afraid of that kind of thinking.'[218] So now it has come to this: if you believe in truth you are dangerous. Mr Edwards evidently thinks that convinced believers, like Robertson, have been struck with a severe case of 'rigiditis', a religious disease which cripples judgement and incapacitates the victim's ability to differentiate between matters demanding compromise and matters requiring an inflexible stand. If they are rigid in their private lives they will be rigid in their political lives; and, of course, believing in 'one true way' is an infallible sign of a rigid mind. What is overlooked here is that Christians believe in an absolute and revealed spirituality and not in a revealed and absolute political programme. Their one way refers to the path to heaven, not the path to a greater gross national product.

Politics is a process of compromises; the 'art of the possible'. Democracy, especially, is impossible without the spirit of 'give and take'. Citizens doubt that devout Christians, with their absolutist mentality, can enter easily into this process of compromise; they therefore doubt that Christians can enter wholeheartedly into the modern democratic experiment, or that they can make it work peacefully. Over twenty-five years ago Pulitzer Prize-winning author, Richard Hofstadter, wrote:

Characteristically, the political intelligence...accepts conflict as a central and enduring reality and understands human society as a form of equipoise based upon the continuing process of compromise. It shuns ultimate show-downs and looks upon the ideal of total partisan victory as unattainable, as merely another variety of threat to the kind of balance with which it is familiar. It is sensitive to nuances and sees things in degrees. It is essentially relativist and skeptical....

The fundamentalist mind will have nothing to do with all this: it is essentially Manichean; it looks upon the world as an arena for conflict between absolute good and evil, and accordingly it scorns compromises [who could compromise with Satan?] and can tolerate no ambiguities.... Whereas the distinctively political intelligence begins with the political world, and attempts to make an assessment of how far a given set of goals can in fact be realized in the face of a certain balance of opposing forces, the...fundamentalist mind begins with a definition of that which is absolutely right, and looks upon politics as an arena in which that right must be realized.... The issues of the actual world are hence transformed into a spiritual Armageddon, an ultimate reality....[219]

Unfortunately, this fear, although grossly exaggerated, is not completely unfounded. Christians have been political absolutists; we have identified secular programmes and goals as Christian goals. One Christian newsletter requested prayer for President Reagan in 1987, saying:

Pray that any arms treaty we make with the Soviets will not be disastrous. When good confronts evil, good always wins. However, when good makes a treaty with evil, evil always wins.[220]

The implication is that America should not really be making a treaty with the Soviets. Here America is too glibly identified with absolute good and the Soviets with absolute evil.

In a similar vein, *Christian Voice* issued, in the late 1970s, a morality 'report card' on how congressmen voted. The disturbing side to *Christian Voice*'s approach was that, along with school prayer and abortion, they included, as moral issues, economic sanctions against Rhodesia, the American defence treaty with Taiwan, and the creation of the Department of Education. (If you voted conservatively you were moral.) The ludicrous wrong-headedness of this approach was made plain from the fact that Senator Hatfield, who has been described by Senator Helms (his political opponent but Christian brother) as 'the most moral man in the

Senate', scored a paltry 23 per cent whereas a perfect 100 per cent was scored by Congressman Richard Kelly, who was later convicted of accepting a bribe in the Abscam scandal.

This is the kind of thinking we must renounce if we are ever to counteract a fear of fundamentalists and evangelicals as hopelessly rigid absolutists. We must be careful to stay within the bounds of the revealed absolutes of God's word. Everything else is relative, up for dialogue and compromise. Secular ideologies and nationalistic programmes must not be turned into moral crusades.

At the same time, the overwrought and morbid nature of the fear of absolutes must be exposed. Surely the lesson to be drawn from Neville Chamberlain's 1930s failed appeasement policy towards Hitler is that a determined and pig-headed stand for what is right is a better guarantee of peace than a polite, deferential giving away to the wishes of others. The politics of compromise needed to be replaced by the politics of conviction. The spineless relativist is no less a threat than the inflexible absolutist. At least the man with firm standards knows where he is going, whereas the easy-going relativist is lost in a fog of uncertainty.

Fear of raving lunacy

The third reason fear arises is because our technological, scientific world has a sneaky suspicion that anyone who believes in spiritual truth must be just a touch loony. It is not really those who simply take to religion who are suspect (a little bit can be quite a good thing: 'keeps Johnny off the streets'); it's those who take their religion seriously. They are the problem.

It's OK to believe in a vague God; it's not OK to believe specifically in Jesus. It's OK to search for God; it's not OK to find him. It's OK to believe in a God somewhere 'upstairs'; it's definitely not OK to believe that this God will speak to us down here, nor that he will respond to our prayers and intervene in our earthly events. In other words, a belief in God is acceptable as long as we do not let it affect the course of our practical lives. Those who do have to be watched.

How else can we explain veteran political commentator Gary Will's comments?

> ...the kook factor will do Robertson in.... Reagan believes in miracles.... But he never wrestled with a hurricane on television....

Robertson... has been captured on video showing all his Pentecostal fervor. The networks last week showed clips of him waving his arms as he spoke of curing hemorrhoids.... Bringing the Holy Ghost in on the cure of hemorrhoids seems, on the face of it, to disqualify the practitioner of such 'solutions' from sitting with the National Security Council in judgment of more complicated matters.[221]

So Robertson is a 'kook' because he takes Jesus seriously; he has the gall to believe in answered prayer. It is obvious to Wills that anybody so simple-minded, so naïvely gullible, would be a menace to national security and should never be allowed to hold any office higher than chief pencil sharpener.

Blitz magazine, a youth-oriented British journal, expressed a similar opinion when it mused, in an article on Robertson: 'Such a belief in supernatural intervention in human affairs may seem evidence of mental disorder to many of us in these rationalistic times, but for Robertson... this was perfectly normal.'[222] Does anybody want a mentally disordered lunatic in the White House?

Of course, despite these fears, belief in divine intervention and divine guidance has never been a hindrance to political ability in the past. American presidents have, in moments of national crisis, called for days of prayer and supplication. No one doubted their sanity for this.

When, with the British Expeditionary Force of 335,000 men trapped at Dunkirk before the advancing Germans, His Majesty King George VI requested Sunday 26 May 1940 as a National Day of Prayer, no one doubted his mental equilibrium. No, they prayed. And who can doubt that God answered? David Gardner reports:

While a storm of unprecedented fury broke over Flanders on Tuesday, 28 May, grounding the German Luftwaffe squadrons and enabling the British army formations... (now only ten miles away)... to move on up to the coast in the darkness of the storm and the violence of the rain, with scarcely any interruption from aircraft, which were unable to operate in such turbulent conditions.... Despite the storm in Flanders, a great calm—such as has been rarely experienced—settled over the English Channel during the days which followed, and its waters became as still as a mill-pond. It was this quite extraordinary calm which enabled a vast armada of little ships, big ships, warships, privately owned motor-cruisers... to ply back and forth in a desperate bid to rescue as many of our men as possible.... Mr Churchill... referred to what had happened as a 'miracle of deliverance'.[223]

And Gladstone, an astute and successful politician if ever there was one, was an ardent moralist who viewed his office as the vehicle for the expression of right versus wrong. He was also a firm believer in the reality of divine intervention. He prayed for guidance in his political decisions and actually believed he received answers.

If we worry about Robertson's biblical views on Armageddon influencing his politics, what about the Earl of Shaftesbury who, as MP for Woodstock, in 1839 urged his father-in-law, the British Foreign Secretary, Palmerston, to plump for a Jewish national home in Palestine on the basis that he believed the Bible prophesied a return to the Holy Land by the Jewish people?[224] But who can doubt that Shaftesbury was an extremely able politician who made a lasting contribution to the British political scene?

Belief in the supernatural is—despite *Blitz*, Wills and like-minded soul-mates—no disqualification for government office. Christians must never sacrifice their belief in the supernatural merely to win the favour of the sceptical. At the same time, a Christian politician must demonstrate an adeptness in the more ordinary skills of governing: diplomacy, the ability to engage in dialogue, the sense to know when the dialogue must stop and power-broking start. The Christian politician, in short, must walk both in the supernatural world and the natural world. Only then can we reassure our fellow citizens that we are not whackos set on blowing up the world in order to hasten the coming of our Lord.

Paradoxical commands of leadership

No, Christian participation in politics is not universally welcome. However, Christians do not enter the political arena because they are invited by their fellow human beings, but because they are commanded by God. In obeying God's commands to serve in this, the political arena, perhaps it would be helpful to remember what one preacher called 'the paradoxical commands of leadership'. Here they are:

1 People are illogical, unreasonable and self-centred. Love them anyway.
2 If you do good, people will accuse you of selfish, ulterior motives. Do good anyway.
3 If you are successful, you will win false friends and true enemies. Succeed anyway.

4 Give the world the best you have and you will get kicked in the teeth. Give it anyway.

After all, that's what Jesus did.

13

Models of Participation

When Jesus taught his disciples how to pray he did more than impart abstract principles and a wonderful philosophy of prayer; he gave them a concrete prayer to copy—the Lord's Prayer. In the same spirit, this chapter will give some concrete suggestions and real-life illustrations of how to apply this book's abstract principles.

Various models

God is a God of variety. God has led his people to address socio-political problems in a variety of ways. In looking at how Christians from different backgrounds and with differing skills have tackled community problems, we notice that not only have their goals varied but their tactics have differed as well. This should pose no problem for us. No one tactic is the definitively correct one. Tactics need to be flexible and fashioned according to the need of the hour.

From this it follows that the models I lay out are not exhaustive but simply suggestive. They are suggestive of the ways you might proceed in your own particular setting. Your own country will have its particular problems, styles and modes of political organisation which might differ markedly from the country in which my illustrations are set, yet the illustrations can still serve to embody general principles which are internationally applicable.

The first approach we want to look at is that of the Christian citizen acting on his own, outside of government and simply as a concerned individual.

Individual citizens

London's *Evening Standard*, in April 1991, reported the following story:

> A middle-aged secretary and mother of two has effectively changed the face of religious education in Great Britain and heralded a return to traditional Christian teachings.
>
> Mrs Denise Bell, 43, has fought a long campaign with her own money to ensure children everywhere will now be taught about Jesus Christ instead of the multi-ethnic approach ordered by Left-wing Labour councils.
>
> An elected parent governor of Acton High School, Mrs Bell was 'deeply offended' when she read a 22-page draft of Ealing Council's religious education syllabus, produced when the West London borough was run by Labour.
>
> Hearing 'somewhere or other' of the new syllabus, Mrs Bell wrote to the council asking for a copy. 'They sent me a copy and very proud they were of it too.
>
> 'But I was horrified, more than that, I was offended. There was no reference to God, the Bible or Jesus Christ.'
>
> Mrs Bell maintained that when Ealing Council left out references to God, the Bible and Jesus, it failed in its lawful public duty to abide by the conditions set out in the Education Reform Act, 1988.... The 1988 Act says that syllabuses adopted after 29 September, 1988, must 'reflect the fact that the religious traditions in Great Britain are in the main Christian'....
>
> Now, Education Secretary Kenneth Clarke has agreed with Mrs Bell and has written a private letter to Ealing Council offering his 'advice' that it should change the syllabus.
>
> This the new Tory leaders have readily agreed to do—but the implications will have a direct consequence on every other local authority throughout the land who now, deliberately or otherwise, omit references to Christianity in the religious education.
>
> In an unprecedented move, Ealing Council—won by the Tories in last year's local elections—is withdrawing its RE syllabus, used by 111 schools throughout the borough, in favour of a 'more Christian' approach.[225]

Here is one woman who took on the entire education establishment and won. She agitated, she wrote letters, she made phone calls. She drew so much attention to the issue that it could not be ignored. Instead, it was resolved.

Across the water, in America, we come across another Christian convinced his individual efforts could make a difference. The rap group 2 Live Crew made national news in America in 1990 with their hot-selling (1.7 million copies) double album *As Nasty As They Wanna Be*. The title was apt: the album was a nasty compilation of songs featuring 87 descriptions of oral sex, 116 mentions of male and female genitalia, and passages referring to male ejaculation and sodomy. This smut drew the attentions of authorities in Florida where, after a record dealer sold *Nasty* to an eleven-year-old girl, a Florida circuit court declared the album obscene and banned all sales in the state—the first such ruling against a musical group in the United States. Shortly thereafter, they were arrested for singing their obscene lyrics in a Hollywood, Florida, nightclub.

The telling point for us here is that the authorities were pushed, almost against their will, into prosecuting through the single-handed efforts of one dedicated citizen—Florida attorney Jack Thompson. It was Thompson who sent the transcripts of *Nasty* to Florida governor Bob Martinez, then on to every sheriff in Florida; it was Thompson who followed these letters up with a letter to prosecutors across the state appealing for action. Finally, prodded by Thompson, they did just that.

The *Los Angeles Times*, in doing a background story on Jack Thompson, found that he was a 'born again' Christian who 'wears a Batman watch. He drinks from a Batman mug. A large poster of the Caped Crusader is tacked to his refrigerator door.'[226] This is Jack Thompson's way of explaining his actions to the public. He says that 2 Live Crew is a group guilty of 'peddling obscenity to children' and his job is to help wake up government to do its job.[227]

> [The] 38-year-old Thompson...took on the obscenity problem in 1985 after he defended a woman, Ilena Foster, whose life was threatened by her husband because she refused to help him sexually abuse other children. Pornography, Thompson concluded, lay at the roots of sexual abuse and its attendant violence—'I found that one of the causes for it [sexual abuse] was obscenity, particularly obscenity that portrays people who are sexually abused as enjoying that abuse.... For me, that is the disturbing component of the 2 Live Crew album.'[228]

Thompson comments that *Nasty As They Wanna Be*, 'more than any other record...is "a clarion call to the sexual brutalization of women".'[229] For instance, on one track, the 2 Live Crew singer boasts about his sexual abilities as a woman in the background moans, 'No, no, no,' suggesting a rape.[230]

Professor Hubert Morken, formerly Professor of Government

at Oral Roberts University, presented a paper to the American
Political Science Association featuring the actions of Jack
Thompson. In it, Professor Morken wrote:

> Thompson has his own legal practice (his wife is a corporate attorney
> working in a large Miami firm) which gives him some financial indepen-
> dence even when he makes no money, as was the case for the...six
> months he pursued 2 Live Crew. Having some form of radical Christian
> commitment, yet thoroughly familiar with contemporary culture and
> legal advocacy, Thompson is not easily controlled by anyone, including
> more moderate Christians, the political process, or his chosen
> enemies.... Known for his independence, he has succeeded in carving
> out a niche for himself. Thompson said he made up his mind long ago to
> distance his campaign from other anti-pornographic forces within the
> Christian decency movement. He is not affiliated with any organization.
> No one else bears responsibility for what he does. His efforts are self-
> financed.

Here is an individual citizen, a political outsider, who is making
an impact. He has not opted to run for elected office, nor has he
joined a big organisation. He simply has put his private, professional skills to use to advance the public good. This is a simple
model that all can follow.

Often what begins as an individual effort broadens into a group
effort. Individual campaigners eventually attract others to them;
sympathetic outsiders are brought in through the galvanising effect
of a dynamic leader. An organisation is born. The use of organisations, where individuals pool their strengths and divide their tasks,
is also an important model for effective social and political action.

Citizen coalitions

The newsletter, *Empowerment*,[231] of the Free Congress Foundation, based in Washington, tells a fascinating story of two concerned mothers, Peg Luksik and Anne Zelnosky, who built up an
effective organisation. It prevailed on the tough issue of sex education over Pennsylvania's education bureaucracy. The article
begins:

> In 1987, the Pennsylvania Department of Education proposed a manda-
> tory AIDS education curriculum. In substance, it was nothing but the
> usual sex course which has been so controversial elsewhere. It gained
> political potency as a talisman against the AIDS epidemic.
> When Luksik and Zelnosky obtained a copy of the curriculum, they

discovered that it was far more graphic and far more offensive than they had imagined. In addition to introducing children in kindergarten to the details of sexual intercourse (including pictures), it contained sections extolling the virtues of incest, as well as such highly personal exercises as an 'anxiety inventory' in which students were asked whether they worried about the size of their genitals.

After reviewing the material, the two mothers began contacting state legislators and education officials about it. But legislators were unwilling to take on the bureaucracy, and the bureaucracy simply refused to pay attention to their concerns. It was clear that the Department of Education would not waver from its determination to impose this curriculum on every school district, and that legislators were not ready to do battle with the bureaucracy.

Luksik and Zelnosky realized that existing organizations in Pennsylvania were not positioned properly to defeat this program. It would be too easy for the opposition to frame the debate as a partisan issue, and dismiss critics as a fringe group.

Their first step, then, was to establish a new organization with no political baggage. They announced the formation of the Pennsylvania Parents' Commission, declaring that it would represent the concerns of parents on policy issues in the state. Their announcement did not allude to the specific issue which motivated the formation of the group; it was aimed simply at establishing the group's identity.

Three weeks later the newly-formed Commission publicly launched its attack on the curriculum mandate. During the interim period, the two women had laid the groundwork for their campaign.

'We wanted to deliver at least two letters to each member of the Legislature from people in their own districts, and to have them hit all on the same day,' explains Luksik. Beginning with no organization and no budget, both women contacted friends and allies throughout the state, one by one, to get those letters written.

'We did not cover every district, but we got almost all of them,' Luksik reported. Their grass roots contacts were instructed to prepare handwritten letters to their legislators and to send them, under separate cover, to the Commission. Then, two days before the Commission's news conference on the subject, all the letters were mailed at once: a letter from the Commission to each of the 202 state representatives and 50 state senators, plus at least two letters from constituents to almost the entire membership of both houses.

To heighten the impact of the letters from home, friendly legislators agreed to talk up the issue with their colleagues, mention that they had been receiving a lot of mail on the subject and ask their uncommitted colleagues whether the same concerns were felt in their districts. This focused the attention of legislators on the mail they were receiving and heightened their awareness to the concerns being expressed.

The news conference announcing the Parents' Commission's opposition to the mandated sex education curriculum was also designed to create a sense of grass roots concern. Instead of conducting just one event at the State Capitol, five news conferences were held simultaneously in key cities around the state. This generated more local publicity, and helped create the impression that a massive statewide movement had arisen.

Press kits were prepared that included copies of material from the curriculum guide. The strategy was to let the material speak for itself and to evoke responses from the reporters. The volunteer spokesmen for the Commission asked the reporters to review the curriculum materials and to decide for themselves whether this material was appropriate for small children. Because of the nature of the material, this unusual tactic worked. Normally stone-faced reporters began to verbalize their own shock at the material.

After the news conference, activists who had written to their legislators began to follow up those letters with telephone calls. Meanwhile, Luksik and Zelnosky identified thirty supportive state representatives, from both parties, who took on the task of keeping the talk going among their colleagues and raising tough questions with education department officials.

In little more than a month, the mandated curriculum controversy attained such a level of visibility and engendered so much public concern that the Department had to speak publicly on it. At first, they tried to deny the curriculum guide even existed but so many reporters and legislators had seen portions of it that this tactic simply increased the pressure.

The Department next defended the curriculum as good and argued that the materials the Parents' Commission had distributed were never meant to be used with children. This obvious lie damaged the Department's credibility further.

In response, a solid majority of the House of Representatives—114 members—signed onto a resolution called for an investigation into how the curriculum was developed, who authorized it, and what educational objectives were supposed to be served by the inclusion of the sensitive material.

Education Secretary Thomas Gilhool, now in full retreat, told a legislative committee that the information on the origin and development of the curriculum was 'lost in the sands of time.' But, he promised, 'You have my word: we won't mail any more out.' Of course, by this time, every school district in the state had received the curriculum with instructions from Gilhool to implement it.

The Parents' Commission had created a major issue. Luksik delivered a copy of the mandated curriculum to Governor Robert Casey. At the first press conference Casey held after receiving the material, he instructed Gilhool to destroy the curriculum, saying simply 'I'm a family man.' Within eight months, Secretary Gilhool resigned and with his resignation, the sex education curriculum died as a state mandate.

This victory, however, was a purely defensive one. The Parents' Commission had prevented a state mandate of the program, but the curriculum had been distributed to school districts and many proposed its local implementation. The highest priority, therefore, became defeating it at the local level.

Working with activists who had been recruited for the state-level battle, the Commission trained concerned parents, teaching them how to evaluate the curriculum and identify those elements that would best frame the issue, as well as how to talk to superintendents and school boards. They prepared packets of research material, drawn in part from current psychological literature, to give the parents a sound basis for challenging the course.

Parents were instructed to appear before local school boards not as experts, but as 'just a dumb parent,' to present the psychological evidence of harm to children from overly graphic and morally ambiguous courses, and then to ask the school officials what scientific evidence they could offer in favor of the program. It was an approach that not only put school officials at an intellectual disadvantage, but helped to build support among the uncommitted.

Another tactic the Commission proposed was 'opt-out' parties, where parents from a school district would meet and all sign the forms necessary to have their children exempted from the sex education program. 'Very few parents are willing to do that on their own,' said Luksik. 'They feel that they are the only ones in town who are doing it, and that their children might suffer retaliation. But the parties provided peer support, so parents felt confident enough to pull their children out of the classes.'

These efforts were widely successful in getting the curriculum rejected by school boards; the Parents' Commission won every local battle they engaged. These local successes also helped to build the support base for the Parents' Commission.

Starting with just two women and a few dozen contacts in late 1987, the Parents' Commission grew to over 20,000 active contacts and supporters in 1990. The Commission has become a major grass roots lobbying force in Pennsylvania and is now poised to launch a proactive agenda, pressing for positive legislation to promote the interests of children and families.

According to Luksik, the defensive battles are over: 'In 1991, we go on the offense—and we'll win.'

Again, as in our first model, we see ordinary citizens—citizens who have not left their ordinary callings for a life of professional politics—able to affect public life. Luksik and Zelnosky diverged from our first model in that, instead of the purely individual efforts of a Jack Thompson, they sought to mobilise and band together other ordinary citizens into a united effort. Through organising they could divide their tasks and multiply their effectiveness. Here is a model that can be fruitfully applied at either a local, regional or national level. Find the issue, find sympathetic supporters, find the right advisors and get to work.

Individual legislators

Yet another way to tackle the social issues plaguing our nations is to participate directly in the political process by actually becoming a politician. Instead of adopting the role of eternal gadfly[232] outside the system—the role, essentially, of our two previous models—the politician joins in the system, determined to use its machinery for good.

Consider the case of Representative Jean Dixon, State Representative of the 135th District, Missouri. Professor Morken writes:

Representative Dixon initiated the first mandatory labeling law[233] for record albums to be introduced in a state legislature, providing the model for the law recently passed in Louisiana and being considered in 20 or more state legislatures.

Dixon, a freshman[234] Republican legislator elected in the fall of 1988, determined to break the mold from the start. She decided to introduce legislation as soon as she arrived in Jefferson City to 'learn the process.' Told that she was to learn by watching and not by doing, she rejected this counsel and searched and prayed for an issue. Dixon considered picking up the creation/evolution question in the public school curriculum, but was not at ease with this choice. When a state highway patrolman brought her a video on rock music obscenity that had been produced by Tipper Gore's organization,[235] she grew incensed and joined the war.

The moment Rep. Jean Dixon introduced House Bill 931 requiring the labeling of X-rated albums in Missouri, not allowing the record industry to do what it pleased with volunteer labeling, Dixon's political education began. She travelled 10,000 miles in eight weeks; the local, state and national press descended on her; she appeared on national television; and she helped to conduct hearings. In the end, not surprisingly, the bill never got out of committee. Dixon is a woman, a freshman, a Republican, a conservative and religious activist: a combination not likely to appeal to the well-entrenched political establishment in Missouri.

In 1989 Dixon attended two conferences for state legislators, one totally secular and non-partisan, the other sponsored by an Evangelical organization. She was able to influence other legislators, encouraging them to pick up the issue. The Free Congress Foundation and other research organizations have given her help. Representative Ted Haik of Louisiana, who spearheaded the labeling legislation in Louisiana, worked closely with her in his effort. When the record industry's own proposal for voluntary labeling proved to be inadequate, she continued to press for mandatory labels over the objections of Tipper Gore and others who first raised the issue of obscenity in the record industry.

In 1988 before running for office the first time, Jean Dixon faced a personal decision: Should she start an art store specializing in picture frames or should she go into politics as her twenty-year-old son Bob advised? Married to a TWA pilot and the mother of five school age children, Jean opted for politics. She was born in Kansas City having lived on the east coast and attended a local Baptist church. Because Jean's roots lay outside of politics and home and church base keeps her financially, emotionally, and spiritually secure, she was able to release her considerable energy and talents without much concern for the consequences to her career or person. She had nothing to lose, unlike Tipper Gore,[236] by pressing the issues wherever they lead and in the face of considerable opposition from the entertainment industry.

Like Jack Thompson who reserves special scorn for weak public officials slow to enforce obscenity statutes, Jean feels obligated to put pressure on local authorities. . . .

Already labeled a cultural censor, by the fall of 1989, Jean chose to take on the local state university because it allowed an obscene play to be put on by its drama department. Dealing with homosexual themes, the play certainly offended local taste, but beyond that she felt the government had no business using tax dollars to subsidize trash. She asked the Southwestern Missouri State University President Dr. Marshall Gordon, a Baptist, to cancel the play, and when he refused, she appealed to the Board of Regents. All but one regent disagreed. She mobilized pastors, spoke on Christian radio and television, organized a rally of 1,500 people on campus, and gathered 7,000 petitions in five days, presenting it to President Gordon in his office before TV cameras. Jean was fully persuaded that she could win, that with enough prayer, pressure, and light on the issue, her faith and efforts would prevail. Even though she was up against the state education hierarchy, the press that labeled her a fascist, tyrant, and book-burner, the threat of a law suit and more, she was totally unprepared for the defeat that devastated her when it came. The play went on stage to a full house in October 1989.

For eight days, during the play's run, Dixon received police protection for her home. When the house of one of the play's participants mysteriously burned, all the principles in the controversy were given police protection. Ten days after the play ended and the police protection was removed, Dixon's home was substantially burned in a fire she is convinced was set by arsonists.

Dixon is a lightning rod for latent issues that are not being picked up by more established politicians. She is running for re-election, expanding her agenda of social issues, and feels that she is just finishing her legislative apprenticeship. What concerns her the most is the lack of support in state government for basic family and community concerns. Until there are more politicians who think as she does and are willing to push for community morals legislation, little can be accomplished by law.[237]

Here is an inexperienced housewife who gained experience fast. She is an amateur politician quickly becoming a professional. On the way, she has won some and lost some. The losses are surely discouraging; on the other hand, she is aware that you can lose some battles and still win the war. In her political optimism, her gritty determination and her willingness to take up political life, she is a model other Christians would do well to emulate.

However, not only do Christians need to enter the political process to use their individual gifts for the public good, they also need to join their gifts with those of sympathetic non-Christians.

Coalitions between Christians and non-Christians

In 1986, for the first and only time in Margaret Thatcher's eleven-year term as Prime Minister, a government-sponsored bill went crashing to defeat. Thatcher's move to deregulate and legalise Sunday trading was defeated by the Keep Sunday Special coalition.

Initially, this coalition consisted solely of committed Christians shocked at the suggested desecration of their holy day. These Christians realised, however, that it would be impossible to defeat the bill without mobilising wider support. They therefore looked beyond the narrow confines of the church and deliberately rallied support among those most affected by the proposed changes in the Sunday trading laws: retailers and shop-workers. Retailers realised that even if they did not want to work on Sunday they would be easily pressured into it; they would have to open their doors to keep up with their competition. Naturally, this would mean that shop-workers would also be pulled into working on Sundays. The small shops especially would be hit. Sunday would cease to be a day of rest.

In response, two groups were formed. A Pro-Sunday coalition, staffed solely by Christians, was set up with a brief to motivate and inform the Christian churches. At the same time, a Keep Sunday Special coalition was set up with the specific brief to elicit support from sympathetic non-Christians. This latter organisation, though staffed largely by Christians, deliberately avoided theological language and a churchy orientation. The tactic worked.

The end result was that the unexpected happened. A Conservative government saw its clear majority of 100 in the House of Commons whittled down until, on the day of the vote, the bill was defeated by fourteen votes. So great had been the public outcry at the proposed measure that MPs were aroused to stand in defiance of their Conservative Whip, thereby facing possible party discipline.[238] MPs changed their position and dug their heels in because of the energetic efforts of a coalition between Christians and concerned non-Christians.

Government officials are much more apt to listen to a viewpoint when it is backed by a broad-based group. They especially sit up and take notice when this broad-based group consists of those who do not normally work together. This very thing happened, for instance, in the 1989–90 session of Parliament. At this time, a number of Christian MPs joined with some well-known feminist MPs in standing against pornography.

These feminist MPs, in the light of the concrete harm that pornography has brought down on women, had begun to question the traditional libertarian assumptions about the desirability of allowing private, adult pornography. Behind the scenes, some Christians began to have dialogue with those feminist MPs. Their aim was first to understand the feminist position and second to see if it were possible to bring together these MPs with Christian MPs—with whom they were usually at loggerheads—over a common concern for pornography. Eventually, six MPs were found who, while agreeing to differ on other areas of family life, stood united in their opposition to porn.

These six MPs sponsored an Early Day Motion,[239] inviting other MPs to sign. Most Early Day Motions elicit only about ten to thirty signatures; a few manage to attract over 100 votes. This particular Early Day Motion generated 243 signatures, the most of any Early Day Motion presented during the 1989–90 Parliament (which saw over 1,000 such motions). It led to a parliamentary study of the effects of pornography; it also drew considerable media attention.

Pornography became an issue again. All this came about because some Christians decided to extend themselves in partnership with others who, though not sharing their ultimate convictions and worldview, still shared their values in a particular area.

Action and thought

Christians need to be active in the field of public policy. We can make a difference. But Christians should not only get stuck into action, they should get stuck into thinking.

Christian action needs to be based on Christian thought. Paul rebuked the Jews for their 'zeal...not based on knowledge' (Rom 10:2). Ignorance is not at a premium in the kingdom of God. Jesus nowhere coined the beatitude: 'Blessed are the stupid for they shall never be struck dumb—they're that already.' When Jesus admonished us to be 'childlike', he did not mean for us to be 'childish'. In fact, the apostle Paul specifically exhorts us to 'stop thinking like children.... in your thinking be adults' (1 Cor 14:20). Jesus reminded us that we were to 'love the Lord your God...with all your mind' (Mt 22:37). If God included, as part of the 'greatest commandment', a command to use our minds, then we can be assured that thinking is no frivolous pastime. God does not major on minors. He commands us to think because thinking is highly practical; because, in the words of Richard Weaver, 'ideas have consequences'.[240]

We looked briefly, in Chapter 11, at the impact of biblical thinking on Western culture, noting that the key features of Western civilisation—its valuing of the individual and its valuing of liberty—owe their existence to biblical roots.[241] The same can happen today in the West, East, North and South if contemporary Christian thinkers will but do as their forebears did: take the Bible seriously and apply it to all of life.

Taking the Bible seriously means more than giving it pride of place on the library shelf; it means taking it down and studying it. But studying it individually will not suffice either; after all, 'iron sharpens iron'. Christians ought to band together in Bible study groups devoted to determining what God has to say about current social themes—poverty, racism, unemployment, the elderly, pornography, sexual immorality, AIDS, abortion, government oppression. Christian think-tanks ought to multiply.

Studying our Bibles is only the first step. Second, we need to study the issues themselves. Take a social issue of concern to you and begin asking what is happening to whom and why. Until we know this we cannot apply the biblical analysis effectively. We need to combine heavenly wisdom with earthly information. Jesus did this when healing: natural knowledge often told him what was physically wrong (for instance, it was plain to see what ailed crippled beggars and faltering blind men); divine power provided the solution. Nehemiah, too, combined heavenly wisdom with naturally acquired information. Before attempting to carry out his divine commission, Nehemiah first went out to inspect carefully Jerusalem's walls (Neh 2:11–16). He held back from making any recommendations until he had first ascertained the extent of the damage and the specific trouble spots. Nehemiah knew that it was impossible to engage in effective problem solving without accurate problem identification. Revelation does not displace naturally acquired information; it complements it.

Christian think-tanks and Bible studies need to avoid the 'ivory tower syndrome'—the temptation to construct theories that are beautiful, logical, sophisticated...and unworkable. These are airtight theories that have much to recommend them save that they are totally divorced from reality. To avoid this we need to keep our ears to the ground. We must heed the contributions of those 'in the field', those actually involved in some form of social and political action.

Activists help theorists define what the real target is, what the real needs are, and where the real issues lie. Our approach should be no different from that of the physical scientist who mixes empirical studies with theoretical hypotheses. Theory needs action if it is to be fruitful; action needs theory if it is to be well-directed.

Moreover, biblical theorists need a healthy dose of the spirit of 'Ready! Fire! Aim!' Spend too long setting up our aim for the perfect shot and, by the time we are set, the target has moved. Doing something imperfectly is preferable to doing nothing perfectly. Imperfect help is better than no help.

'Imperfect help is better than no help' is true only when what we are offering is actually help. At this point in human history we should be well aware that some cures are worse than the problems they were meant to solve: Naziism was no solution to Germany's woes, Marxist-Leninism—with its gulags and secret police—was no remedy for czarist oppression. Germany and Russia would have been better off had Hitler and Lenin done nothing. They acted on falsehoods and lies; the result was havoc.

Our actions need to be based on truth. This is precisely why serious attention to our Bibles is so crucial. Truth is perceived only when we apply ourselves to its search: 'If you call out for insight and cry aloud for understanding, and if you look for it as for silver... then you will understand what is right and just and fair— every good path' (Prov 2:3, 4, 9). To apply ourselves means that we are to make efforts to observe, to take pains to think and to take trouble to pray; we have to observe and think about God's word, God's acts and God's world. (See, for instance, the writer's admonition in Proverbs 6:6 to 'go to the ant [and]... consider its ways', as well as the example of Solomon, in 1 Kings 4:33, who was given wisdom, not just about heavenly matters, but about God's world: 'He described plant life... animals and birds, reptiles and fish.')

Spirit-filled observation and biblically-informed thought are crucial. They are the first step in the Bible's three-step process: first, we seek truth; second, we find truth; third, this truth results in life and freedom. If we want the result, we have to apply the process. There is no short cut. It is Spirit-filled observation and biblically-informed thought that lead us to 'understand... every good path'. These good paths—whether in the arena of politics, economics or science—are the ones our society desperately needs to take. We are pursuing too many dead-ends, to our peril. O Christian, think!

What area of society are you concerned about? Find out what is going on in that area and discover what the Bible has to say about it. Next, ask what your particular spiritual gifts are. How can you actually help in your area of concern and how are you motivated to help? Then go on to find out what bite-sized piece of the problem you can take on and start there. We cannot wipe out poverty but there may be a poor family just down the street we can help. We cannot wipe away the blight of AIDS but there may be a hurting homosexual in our neighbourhood whom we can befriend and help. Jesus, when he came to save the world, did not start with a worldwide ministry; he started with one small country and eventually saw his message cover the entire globe. That was God's way then and that is God's way now.

The positive and the negative

It is imperative for Christians entering the socio-political sphere to remember that we have both a positive and a negative calling. Even as the prophet Jeremiah was called both to 'tear down' and to 'build' (Jer 1:10)—one without the other was only half his commission—so we are called to both.

Government itself has both a positive and a negative function. Its negative function is clearly portrayed by Paul's language in Romans 13:4, where we are informed of the government's responsibility to wield the 'sword'. Swords are scarcely positive; their special contribution is in the area of subtraction (heads and limbs) rather than addition.[242] Paul points out that, on one hand, God instituted government as 'an agent of wrath to bring punishment on the wrongdoer'; on the other hand, he meant it to 'commend' those who 'do what is right' (Rom 13:3–4). Government was set up to restrain evil, its negative orientation, and to encourage good, its positive goal. This has a clear implication for modern Christian crusaders: it is not enough to 'tear down' evil and to battle for legal constraints against evil actions—abortion, pornography, racism, and so on; Christian crusaders also need to 'build up' the good, to reach out in positive works of service—setting up homes for pregnant singles, providing work for the unemployed, supporting inner-city ministries to troubled minorities, and so on.

Colonel Doner, co-founder, in 1978, of *Christian Voice*, called by some the 'vanguard' of the Christian right in America, acknowledges that his movement failed to capture the hearts and minds of most Americans. He attributes this failure to one chief shortcoming: the Christian right's unbalanced approach to social action—they were long on denunciation but short on practical service. They were almost totally negative in their orientation. Millions of Americans were alienated by an apparently pharisaical, uncaring, 'holier-than-thou' group, more interested in imposing their values than in serving the community's needs.

Doner concludes that if the Christian right ever wants to influence the political course of events it first needs to serve. Service is the path to influence. Doner points to the example of Mother Teresa of Calcutta:

> I'm sure Mother Teresa could win any office she ran for.... The fact of the matter is that when a Mother Teresa, who has devoted her life to serving others, speaks out for the unborn in opposition to the inhu-

manity of abortion, almost everyone listens. They may not agree, but they listen. She has earned their respect. They know that she is truly concerned for others, that her 'agenda' is to serve others, not just to foist her 'morally superior' viewpoint on others less enlightened than she.[243]

Doner urges the Christian community to follow Mother Teresa's example. The result of this approach—which he terms 'the Samaritan Strategy'—will be that 'when Christians who have served their community ask their neighbors to join with them in an effort to restore justice and righteousness, people will follow'.[244]

Not surprisingly—after all, he was the originator of this approach—there was no better person to implement the 'Samaritan Strategy' than Christ himself. He did not rest content with denouncing evil. The Scriptures remind us that he did not come 'into the world to condemn the world, but to save the world' (Jn 3:17). He came, 'got his hands dirty', sought out and served evil people: 'I am among you as one who serves' (Lk 22:27), was here 'to seek and to save what was lost' (Lk 19:10). Jesus came to salvage, not to savage.

Jesus' reputation as 'the friend of sinners' (Mt 11:19) stemmed from his practice of compassionate service. This compassionate friendship was not reserved simply for the righteous, nor for the socially acceptable sinner; it extended to the disreputable as well. Jesus forgave 'even'[245] the hated tax collector, a practice which produced shock and dismay in some of his well-meaning admirers.[246] When, in the face of social evil, we are tempted to sound only the note of indignant denunciation and to ignore the softer note of caring concern, we must remember Jesus' friend-of-sinners approach. To neglect it is to misrepresent Jesus to the world.

Of course, overflowing compassion did not mean that Jesus pulled any punches in confronting sin. Although Jesus did not condemn the woman caught in adultery, he labelled her lifestyle sinful and ordered her, in no uncertain terms, to forsake it: 'Leave your life of sin' (Jn 8:11). And although Jesus was immediately ready to forgive the town slut who so offended righteous Simon, he was also determined to call a spade a spade, saying she indeed had 'sins' that desperately needed forgiving (Lk 7:48). Jesus was both the negative Prophet who denounced sin and the positive Redeemer who opened a way for sinners to escape sin. We must do the same.

Homosexuality

One area in which the church ought to operate according to this twofold biblical approach is the area of homosexuality. It is my conviction that Christians ought to agitate for criminal and civil sanctions against homosexual activity. Homosexual activity, even between consenting adults, is illegal in half the states of America and in a minority of European jurisdictions.[247] Those jurisdictions currently illegalising homosexual activity ought to continue to do so. Those jurisdictions currently legalising it—and holding out little prospect for a reversal in policy—ought at least to hold the line with civil sanctions.

Governments have for thousands of years regarded the prohibition of homosexual behaviour as within their jurisdiction. The 'privacy'[248] argument—that a man should be able to do as he pleases within the privacy of his own home—ought not to deter the illegalising of homosexuality, any more than it deters the illegalising of incest or racism. Racism's privacy does not protect it from the long arm of the law.

The state should also refuse to grant civil recognition to homosexual unions. By this I mean that it ought to deny access to those civil institutions formalising family status: marriage, adoption of children, health benefits available to family members, and so on. Professor of law, G. Sidney Buchanan, points out that there is a difference between 'toleration on the criminal side' and 'affirmative approval on the civil side'.[249] Affording civil recognition goes far beyond the mere toleration of a private activity; it puts the public seal of approval on such activity; it legitimises what the majority of the citizenry find repugnant. Even those who would want, in the name of tolerance, to decriminalise private homosexual activity might balk at publicly affirming it through our civil institutions. It is permissible to tolerate evil at times; it is never right to affirm it.

The homosexual movement is not content with private tolerance.[250] It is after much bigger game than that: it plans to co-opt the machinery of state into a 'means to publicly acknowledge their emotional bond'.[251] It wants to come out of the closet and it wants society to help it to do so. Such help we ought not offer.

The civil and penal responses urged above are part of the negative orientation of government; they are a legitimate aspect of the government's role in restraining undesirable and evil behaviour. This negative response, however, is only half the picture. The church must do more than condemn and restrain homosexuality; it must reach out to positively help the homosexual; it must minister to the homosexual even as Jesus did. How did Jesus minister? First, he brought truth ('leave your life of sin', Jn 8:11); second, he brought personal concern and involvement (Jesus did not minister by proxy, he went himself); third, he brought hope and the promise of eternal redemption; fourth, Jesus brought healing for temporal hurts.

Too often, the church has not reached out to the homosexual community with Jesus' love. It has brought truth without grace. Jeff Collins is the founder of Love and Action, a ministry to the AIDS-infected. After ministering in churches nationwide, Collins observes that the average church member's response to homosexual AIDS sufferers is a mixture of fear and anger; fear of close contact and self-righteous anger with those who sin in a different way than we do. This is worrisome when one considers that fear and anger were characteristics of the Pharisees in their response to 'sinners'. Fear and anger snuff out all motivation and ability to minister: we cannot reach out a helping hand when our real attitude is 'Jesus in me loves Jesus in you but I hate your guts.'

This curtailment of ministry is a tragedy for, with the onset of AIDS, Collins contends that the church faces an unprecedented opportunity to minister to homosexuals. They are open like never before. But, instead of hearing the gospel message of reconciliation and redemption, homosexuals are hearing the message that 'God hates queers'. We may not say that but, in preaching truth without grace, we are heard to be saying that. Homosexuals are presented with the option of the liberal church which offers love without hope, or the conservative church which has hope but does not offer it because it lacks love. Is it any wonder, then, that homosexuals opt for the gay-affirming liberal church? Better love without hope (of change) than no love and no hope.

McLean Bible Church outside of Washington, DC, was a church that saw its fear and anger changed to love.[252] A few years ago, if the McLean church members ever thought about AIDS, it was with fear and loathing. At any rate, this suburban church comfortably assumed that 'it could never happen here'.

All that began to change when the church pastor entered the waiting room of a garage where his car was being fixed. Across from him sat an emaciated lad of twenty-one who, suddenly, began to weep. The pastor went over to him, put his arm around him, saying, 'I am a pastor. Will you let me pray for you?'

The young man replied, 'You don't want to help me; I have AIDS.'

This encounter started a series of weekly meetings between the lad and the pastor that went on for three months. The pastor, however, felt his church would not readily understand or accept such close ministry to an AIDS victim. Therefore, he insisted on meeting the boy in his car in the church car park. There they had weekly prayer.

The boy needed more. He needed more of the life and fellowship of the church than the pastor could offer once a week in the car park. One day the boy disappeared. People went looking for him. Finally, he was found holed up in a motel, covered in his own vomit, dead.

This shook the pastor. He called his church together. The members began to re-evaluate their attitude to homosexuals and to AIDS victims. Then, one day, the disease that 'could not happen here' happened. A bright young man stood up one Sunday and confessed that he had once been a homosexual and that he was now dying of AIDS.

The church was rocked. This young man had at one time been a youth leader in their church, he had been the students' union president at Taylor University, he had been a full-time worker with Campus Crusade who had led others to Christ. All the while he had battled and succumbed to homosexual temptations.

The church, challenged now to act like Jesus, extended grace. Recipients of grace ought to extend grace. Spontaneously, through the course of the afternoon, church members went to the young man's house to embrace him and tell him of their care and concern.

Now the church began to change. Others began to confess sin, not just homosexual sin. The church became more real. The church also became more compassionate. They looked for others suffering from this dread disease. They found that, unknown to them, there were seven or eight others similarly stricken with AIDS in their congregation. They reached out beyond their church into the surrounding community. To date they have helped, both spiritually and physically, upwards of thirty AIDS sufferers. Instead of dying in despair covered in their own vomit, these AIDS victims can die with the hope of a better life, a better tomorrow.

That's the gracious ministry of Jesus; a ministry Christ handed to his church.

Conclusion

Christians ought to be busy about their Master's work, doing what Christ did. Christ's ministry was twofold. He is the Governor and Ruler of the universe: 'The kingdom of the world has become the kingdom of our Lord and of his Christ, and he will reign for ever and ever' (Rev 11:15). As such he restrains sin, promulgates and enforces law. In imitation of Christ, we Christians also need to be in the business of restraining sinful actions through government.

But Christ is more than the Ruler who restrains sin; he is the Saviour who regenerates from sin. He is not only the supreme Law-giver; he is also the pre-eminent Grace-giver. Here is the work of the church—bringing life and hope to a world in rebellion against God.

The ministry of restraining sin need not be opposed to the ministry of regenerating from sin. The apostle Paul upheld both grace and law. When he was accused of forsaking God's law in order to exalt God's grace, he responded, 'Do we, then, nullify the law by this faith? Not at all! Rather, we uphold the law' (Rom 3:31). He upheld both grace and law; he simply accorded to each separate spheres and separate functions. They were legitimate as long as they stayed within their spheres. This is exactly what Christians must do today: we must uphold both the law ministry of the government and the grace ministry of the church.

Without grace the church ossifies and the world dies. Without godly law the government languishes; it falls short of its intended function as 'God's servant to do you good' (Rom 13:4). God is determined to do the world good, both through government and the church. Let us co-operate with him as our callings and gifts permit, by giving ourselves to both.

Notes

[1] Quoted in Richard John Neuhaus, *The Naked Public Square* (Eerdmans: Grand Rapids, Michigan, 1984), p 10.

[2] Quoted in Richard John Neuhaus, 'What the Fundamentalists Want', in R.J. Neuhaus and M. Cromartie (eds), *Piety and Politics* (Ethics and Public Policy Center: Washington, DC, 1987), p 14.

[3] *The Guardian* (1 September 1986).

[4] *The Mail on Sunday* (27 July 1986), p 23.

[5] Doug Bandow, *Beyond Good Intentions* (Crossway: Westchester, Illinois, 1988), p 25.

[6] Mencken's biting description was simply a reworking of Thomas McCaulay's popular comment in 1825 that 'The Puritan hated bear-baiting, not because it gave pain to the bear, but because it gave pleasure to the spectators.' In this case, of course, the Puritans were right. One can tolerate pain but one cannot tolerate the degradation of a society which purposefully inflicts pain for pleasure and profit.

[7] George M. Marsden, *Fundamentalism and American Culture* (Oxford University Press: New York, 1982), p 187.

[8] *The Sunday Times* (18 April 1988), p 1.

[9] Quoted in Charles Colson, *Kingdoms in Conflict* (Morrow and Zondervan, 1987), p 140.

[10] Os Guinness, *The Gravedigger File* (Intervarsity Press: Downer's Grove, Illinois, 1983), p 51.

[11] Not only was the church a key force for continuity and survival in medieval life, it was also a key force for innovation. Historian Paul Johnson writes:

> In west, north-west and central Europe, the clearance of forest and the drainage of swamps were the prime economic facts of the entire Dark Ages. In a sense they determined the whole future history of

Europe: they were the foundations of its world primacy.... it was the monasteries which led the movement and for long sustained it.... In many cases the Church found that most efficient returns could be secured by settling manors with 'coloni', peasant tenant-farmers. In this way the Church led the move away from slavery, and hopelessly unproductive slave-farming.... We find them [the monks] pioneering the systematic and large-scale use of hedges, banks and ditches. And they founded towns...and developed markets for their surplus produce.... Bishops and abbots were the innovatory élite of society. But the situation did not last. The Church estates reached their peak in the mid ninth century, and thereafter tended to contract.

Johnson goes on to point out:

In the Dark Ages, the Church had stood for everything that was progressive, enlightened and humane in Europe; it had made...an enormous material contribution to the resurrection of civilization from the ashes.... Then, between 1150 and 1250, a fundamental change took place. Royal justice improved and manorial courts slipped into the background. Clerical sources of income came to be seen as exactions, and clerical privileges as abuses. The Church, as a hierarchical institution, ceased to be regarded with affection and respect; as a powerful phenomenon, it continued to inspire awe and fear, but the obedience it received was tinged with a growing element of hostility. Above all, the official Church began to be associated with financial exactions.

See Paul Johnson, *A History of Christianity* (Weidenfeld & Nicolson: London, 1977), pp 149, 150, 219, 220.

[12] Although it is true that 'secularisation is what makes modern life modern', it does not have to be this way. Surely we can have the modern gadgets without the modern gods. There is no reason why there cannot be modern technology and all the various breakthroughs of various fields while still keeping a supernatural, ie, non-secularised, worldview.

[13] Quoted in John Pollock, *Wilberforce* (Lion: Berkhamsted, 1978), p 38.

[14] John T. McNeil (ed), *The Library of Christian Classics* (Westminster Press: Philadelphia), vol XXI: John Calvin, *Institutes of the Christian Religion*, Book IV, ch XX, p 1487, n 7.

[15] *Ibid.*

[16] John A. Coleman, SJ, 'A Theological Link between Religious Liberty and Mediating Structures', in Jay Mechling (ed), *Church, State, and Public Policy* (American Enterprise Institute: Washington, DC, 1978), p 29.

[17] R.W. Southern, *Western Society and the Church in the Middle Ages* (Penguin: Middlesex, 1985), pp 91-169.

[18] Paul Johnson, *A History of Christianity* (Weidenfeld & Nicolson: London, 1976), p 105.

[19] *Ibid*, p 191.

[20] Southern, *op cit*, p 32.

[21] See Harold J. Berman, *Law and Revolution: The Formation of the Western Legal Tradition* (Harvard University Press: Cambridge, Massachusetts, 1983), p 51.

[22] See *ibid*, p 88.

[23] *Ibid*, p 277.

[24] *Ibid*, p 87.

[25] *Ibid*, p 209.

[26] Quoted in A. James Reichley, *Religion in American Public Life* (Brooking Institute: Washington, DC, 1985), p 285.

[27] McNeil, *op cit*, p 1495.

[28] See W. Fred Graham, *The Constructive Revolutionary: John Calvin & His Socio-Economic Impact* (Knox Press: Atlanta, 1978), p 110.

[29] *Ibid*, p 112.

[30] W. Fred Graham points out that in Geneva these sumptuary laws were not enforced

> as harshly as similar laws in France at the same period. The French *parlement* in 1559 had...more draconic means of enforcement: It denied to artisans the wearing of slashed hose and puffed taffeta on pain of being taken and strangled.

Graham, *op cit*, p 111.

[31] For instance, during the reign of Edward IV (1461–1483) a statute was passed prohibiting gentlemen from wearing shoes with high heels or platforms. Forrest McDonald informs us that 'during the reigns of Edward III (1327–1377), Edward IV (1461–1483), and Henry VIII (1509–1547), a multitude of sumptuary laws had accumulated in England'. See Forrest McDonald, *Novus Ordo Seclorum: The Intellectual Origins of the Constitution* (University Press of Kansas: Lawrence, Kansas, 1985), p 16.

[32] Will Durant notes:

> Fat men were a rarity in Lacedaemon [Sparta]; there was no law regulating the size of the stomach, but if a man's belly swelled indecently he might be publicly reproved by the government, or banished from Laconia.

Will Durant, *The Story of Civilization*, vol 2: *The Life of Greece* (Simon and Schuster: New York, 1966), p 85.

Pagan Rome had its sumptuary restrictions as well. James Kent, in his *Commentaries on the American Law*, commented:

> The sumptuary laws of ancient Rome had their origin in the twelve tables, which controlled the wastefulness of prodigals, and unnecessary expenditure at funerals. The appetite for luxury increased with dominion and riches, and sumptuary laws were from time to time enacted, from the 566th year of the city down to the time of the emperors, restraining, by severe checks, luxury and extravagance in dress, furniture and food. They were absurdly and idly renewed by the most extravagant and dissipated rulers.

J. Kent, *Commentaries on the American Law* (1830), pp 263-268.

[33] Quoted in Rousas Rushdoony, *The Institutes of Biblical Law* (Presbyterian and Reformed Publishing, 1973), p 791.

[34] Quoted in Reichley, *op cit*, p 67.

[35] Ewald M. Plass (ed), *What Luther Says* (Concordia: St Louis, 1986), p 575.

[36] Calvin, too, distinguished the spiritual government from the civil government. He differed with Luther not over the theory of 'two governments' but over the practical outworking of the theory, over the responsibilities given to each sphere.

[37] Quoted in Thomas Sanders, *Protestant Concepts of Church and State* (Peter Smith: Gloucester, Massachusetts, 1985), p 29.

[38] *Ibid*, pp 191-192.

[39] Quoted in Reichley, *op cit*, p 64.

[40] Quoted in Antonia Fraser, *Cromwell: Our Chief of Men* (Granada Publishing: London, 1981), p 403.

[41] Quoted in Reichley, *op cit*, p 56.

[42] *Ibid*.

[43] Although Williams was forced to leave the Massachusetts Bay Colony due to doctrinal differences, we also have to conclude that his dogged irascibility played its part too. Williams had the air of a man spoiling for a fight; tact was not high on his list of priorities.

This only became serious when, as an official minister of the Massachusetts Bay Colony (and therefore as an official spokesman), he

> started preaching that the King [of England] had no right to issue a charter to the Bay Colony, because the Indians (not the King) originally owned the land. He also charged the King with blasphemy for referring to Europe as Christendom.... by assertively attacking the King, he seemed bound and determined to jeopardize the Bay Colony's charter, and bring the full wrath of the Crown down on all of them. That was going too far. Now they [the Massachusetts Bay Colony leaders] strongly appealed to him to

cease making any further attacks on the King in regard to 'liberty of conscience.' But Williams replied with a treatise which he had prepared for publication, in which he denounced the King as a liar, and recommended that the Bay Colony either send the charter back to England as fraudulent—or return to England themselves!

Peter Marshall and David Manuel, *The Light and the Glory* (Fleming H. Revell: Old Tappan, New Jersey, 1977), p 195.

[44] Quoted in Reichley, *op cit*, p 66.

[45] This phrase, significantly, is found in Jefferson's letter of 1 January 1802 to the Danbury Baptist Association.

[46] Reichley, *op cit*, p 113.

Interestingly, these Methodists joined the Baptists in their whole-hearted support for Jefferson with his non-establishment-of-religion views. Reichley notes that 'Peter Cartwright, probably the most famous of the Methodist circuit riders, rivaled even John Leland in the warmth of his support for Jefferson'. Reichley, *op cit*, p 181.

[47] Although Calvin did not believe in civilly tolerating religious plural-ism—in this sense he was no friend of religious freedom—it would be unfair and untrue to hint that Reformed thinkers gave no value to freedom. Calvin wrote:

I freely admit that no kind of government is more happy than one where freedom is regulated with becoming moderation and is properly established on a durable basis.... Indeed, the magistrates ought to apply themselves with the highest diligence to prevent the freedom (whose guardians they have been appointed) from being in any respect diminished, far less be violated.

John T. McNeil (ed), *The Library of Christian Classics* (Westminster Press: Philadelphia), vol XXI: John Calvin, *Institutes of the Christian Religion*, book IV, ch. XX, p 1494.

In commenting upon a passage in Genesis Calvin wrote that 'Nothing is more desirable than liberty.' Quoted in *ibid*. Calvin valued freedom, he simply narrowed its scope more than we would today.

[48] Quoted in Paul Johnson, *A History of Christianity* (Weidenfeld & Nicolson: London, 1976), p 116.

[49] *Ibid*, p 117.

The same macabre, surreally sane tone is used in a discussion of torture by Francis Pegna, the leading Inquisition commentator, when he calmly wrote:

But if, having been tortured reasonably...he will not confess the truth, set other sorts of torments before him, saying that he must pass through all these unless he will confess the truth. If even this fails, a second or third day may be appointed to him, either *in terrorem* or even in truth, for the continuation (not repetition) of torture; for tortures may not be repeated unless fresh evidence emerges against him; then, indeed, they may, for against continuation there is no prohibition.

Pegna went on to forbid the torture of pregnant women, saying, 'We must wait until she is delivered of her child,' and to grant that children below the age of puberty and old people should be less severely tortured. See Johnson, *op cit*, p 254.

50 Quoted in R.W. Southern, *Western Society and the Church in the Middle Ages* (Penguin: Middlesex, 1985), p 17.

The 1930s saw the resurgence of Thomism. One of those swept up in this movement was Mortimer Adler. At that time Adler echoed Aquinas' view that heretics should be liquidated! He reasoned that (1) we do not tolerate disease germs that kill our bodies, (2) our souls are far more important than our bodies, (3) therefore it is unreasonable to tolerate the circulation of errors that destroy men's souls. See Sidney Hook, *Out of Step*, pp 338-339, where he recollects a Mortimer Adler lecture.

51 Quoted in Johnson, *op cit*, p 290.

52 John Courtney Murray, SJ, *We Hold These Truths* (Sheed & Ward: New York, 1960), p 23.

53 John Calvin, *Institutes of the Christian Religion*, translated by Ford Lewis Battles (Eerdmans: Grand Rapids, Michigan, 1975), p 207.

54 Ewald M. Plass (ed), *What Luther Says* (Concordia: St Louis, 1986), p 591.

55 Calvin, *op cit*, p 225.

56 Harold J. Laski, introduction to *A Defence of Liberty Against Tyrants* (Peter Smith: Gloucester, Massachusetts, 1963), p 27.

57 *Ibid*, p 54.

58 Rousas J. Rushdoony, *The Institutes of Biblical Law* (Presbyterian and Reformed), p 9.

Rousas J. Rushdoony can be regarded as the grandfather of the Reconstructionist movement. His *Institutes* book is the theological foundation of the movement. Notice the similarity between the titles of Rushdoony's work and Calvin's own magisterial work: *Institutes of the Christian Religion*.

59 Gary North carries on the old Reformation battle against the Anabaptists. He continues to misrepresent this movement as 'mass murderers' (see D. Chilton's *Productive Christians in an Age of Guilt Manipulators* ([Institute for Christian Economics: Tyler, Texas, 1982], p 15) because of the misdeeds in Munster of some fanatics claiming Anabaptist leanings. These fanatics were no more Anabaptists than Jim Jones (of the Guyana massacre) was an evangelical.

60 Dennis Peacocke, *Winning the Battle for the Minds of Men* (Alive & Free: Santa Rosa, California, 1987), p 67.

61 Chilton, *op cit*, p 48.

62 Rushdoony, *op cit*, p 2.

63 Gary North, *An Introduction to Christian Economics* (Craig Press, 1979), p 353.

64 Rushdoony, *op cit*, pp 679-680.

65 *Ibid*, p 399.

66 *Ibid*, p 235.

67 Quoted in Paul Johnson, *A History of Christianity* (Weidenfeld & Nicolson, 1976), p 309.

68 Rushdoony, *op cit*, pp 185-188.

69 *Ibid*, p 38.

70 *Ibid*, p 39.

71 *Ibid*, p 39.

72 *Ibid*, p 76.

73 *Ibid*, p 99.

74 Gary North's newsletter, *Christian Reconstruction* (November–December 1987), quoted in James McKeever's *End Times News Digest* (February 1988), pp 2-3.

75 Rousas Rushdoony, *The Institutes of Biblical Law* (Presbyterian and Reformed Publishing, 1973), p 4.

76 *Ibid*, p 23.

77 *Ibid*, p 732.

78 *Ibid*, p 733.

79 John W. Robbins, 'The Trouble With Conservatives', in Gary North (ed), *The Journal of Christian Reconstruction* (A Chalcedon Ministry, 1978), vol V, no 1, p 71.

80 Because of the Reconstructionist emphasis on the inability of the unconverted mind to perceive truth of any sort it is only natural that they should adopt presuppositional apologetics (versus 'evidential apologetics'—the attempt to present convincing evidence to the unconverted) as one of 'Christian Reconstructionism's five central points'. See Gary DeMar and Peter Leihart, *The Reduction of Christianity* (Dominion Press: Fort Worth, Texas, 1988), foreward by Gary North, p xxxi.

Reconstructionists adopt the 'Vantillian' mode of presuppositional apologetics—named after the Calvinist theologian Cornelius Van Til. Van Til objected to an approach which sought, for instance, to convince an unbeliever of the factuality of Christ's resurrection by marshalling evidence which could be rationally discussed and debated. Van Til taught that that approach assumed that the fallen unbeliever can perceive truth and implied that his mind was not, in fact, fallen. Van Til urged, as the correct Christian approach, that the main attention of Christian apologists (anyone seeking to give reasons for his faith) should be given to challenging the unbeliever's presuppositions (those fundamental ideas which undergird all his thinking, ideas he takes to be 'obvious' and self-evidently true). The unbeliever should be challenged to believe God's presuppositions solely on the basis that God is God. The non-Christian should be told to repent, to let God be God, to believe God's word simply because it is God's word and not because there is evidence to support it. Bow before God's sovereignty.

Van Til was convinced that fallen man would hopelessly twist all evidence presented to him. That route, therefore, was hopeless. The apologist should focus not on presenting evidence but on challenging the ungodly person's starting points, his anti-God presuppositions.

Van Til objects that 'traditional apologetics starts with the natural man.... Believers and non-believers have nothing in common...sinners look through coloured glasses.... Shall we who wish to prove that nothing can be explained without God...admit that man can interpret anything correctly without God?' For Van Til the complete fallenness of human reason and the total sovereignty of God override every other biblical truth.

Lutheran apologist John Warwick Montgomery takes a very different approach. He says that it is useless to challenge people to change their beliefs, their presuppositions, without giving a reason for doing so. Otherwise, he says, we are only arguing in a circle: 'Believe the Gospel. Why? Because it's God's word. How do I know it's God's word? Because he says so in the Bible.' But if the issue in doubt is whether the Bible is indeed God's word, it does not help the unbeliever to appeal to the Bible as authoritative proof. We need to present evidence showing why it makes sense to trust in Christ. Jesus did.

John Warwick Montgomery wrote *Faith Founded on Fact* in which he proposed his 'evidential approach' to apologetics. 'Evidently, my dear Watson' is his watchword. Montgomery is sure that it is no waste of time to present evidence to the fallen mind of unbelievers because he believes in 'common grace' which God gives even to unbelievers to enable them to function in the world. He believes that the human mind is faulty but functional.

81 Rex Downie, 'Natural Law and God's Law: An Antithesis', *The Journal of Christian Reconstructionism* vol V, no 1, p 79.

82 John T. McNeil (ed), *The Library of Christian Classics* (Westminster Press: Philadelphia), vol XXI: John Calvin, *Institutes of the Christian Religion*, Book IV, ch XX, p 1504.

83 *Ibid*, p 1502.

Calvin's seventeenth-century followers continued to propound his view of the valid place of reason, natural law and natural understanding. Samuel Rutherford, Scottish theologian and author of the widely respected political tract *Lex Rex*, wrote in 1644: 'Who can deny the law of nature to be a divine law?' He also wrote that the necessity of

NOTES 193

government was founded not only on 'the law of nature' but 'by the dictate of natural light in a community'. People had God-given 'natural light' which led them to certain truths. Samuel Rutherford, *Lex Rex* (Sprinkle Publications: Harrisonburg, Virginia, 1980), pp 1, 3.

Far from being anti-rational, Calvin and his followers are accused of just the opposite. Andrew C. McLaughlin, Professor Emeritus of History at the University of Chicago in the 1930s, speaks of the 'extreme rationalistic character' of the Puritans, Calvin's English disciples, who 'repudiated mysticism or any process of reaching truth save by intellectual attention to the law as laid down in the scriptures. . . . the Puritan leaders . . . detested mysticism or the awful idea that God spake in His own voice to the searching soul.' Andrew C. McLaughlin, *The Foundations of American Constitutionalism* (New York University Press: New York, 1932), pp 74-75.

The typical Calvinist view was that there 'is now no voice from heaven, no immediately inspired prophets such as Samuel and Elisha'. Rutherford, *op cit*, p 8. In their eagerness to refute Catholic mysticism and to elevate the Reformation principle of *sola scriptura* (the Scriptures alone as an authoritative guide to truth—as opposed to the Catholic emphasis on tradition and church councils), the Reformers went too far. One thing is clear, however; they certainly did not denigrate human reason nor doubt its important and useful role.

84 Some might object that, as Huram was half Jewish, this episode is not really an instance of God using unregenerate minds for his work. But it seems fairly clear that Huram was not one of God's people and that he identified more with his pagan father's side than with his mother's Jewish side. We can infer this from the very fact that he lived in Tyre. He threw in his lot with Israel's northern neighbour. His father's ruling influence can also be seen in the fact that he followed his father's trade: 'a man of Tyre and a craftsman in bronze' (1 Kings 7:14). King Hiram of Tyre had a trade agreement with Solomon by which he supplied men and materials to Israel (1 Kings 5:6–9). This and this alone seems to have been Huram's motivation for going to Israel to build their Temple.

85 David Chilton, *Productive Christians in an Age of Guilt-Manipulators* (Institute for Christian Economics: Tyler, Texas, 1981), p 204.

86 Quoted in Gary DeMar, *Ruler of the Nations* (Dominion Press: Fort Worth, Texas, 1987), pp 265, 266.

87 *Ibid*, p 6.

88 Rushdoony, *op cit*, p 39.

89 William Ebenstein, 'St. Thomas Aquinas', in William Ebenstein (ed), *Great Political Thinkers* (Holt, Rhinehart & Winston: New York, 1969), p 221.

90 DeMar, *op cit*, p 47.

91 Allowing a little bit of anything bad—whether it is a germ, a poison or

pagan influence—can be a dangerous thing. That is why Reconstructionists say, 'Tolerating an admixture of pagan influence eventually leads to outright apostasy.' DeMar, *op cit*, p 47. The Reconstructionists would nip all such potential problems in the bud by suppressing even a little bit of pagan influence.

92 Democracy is not a religious dogma but it is a fine thing nevertheless. The words of C.S. Lewis are well worth remembering on this point:

> A great deal of democratic enthusiasm descends from the ideas of people like Rousseau, who believed in democracy because they thought mankind so wise and good that everyone deserved a share in government.... The real reason for democracy is just the reverse. Mankind is so fallen that no man can be trusted with unchecked power over his fellows.... I am a democrat because I believe in the Fall of man.

93 Reconstructionists know that 'Leviticus 26 makes clear the curse which rests upon the land which despises God's law; if the people will not cleanse the land of evil, God will cleanse the land of its people'. Rushdoony, *op cit*, p 78.

94 Exodus 22:1, 4:

> If a man steals an ox or a sheep and slaughters it or sells it, he must pay back five head of cattle for the ox and four sheep for the sheep.... If the stolen animal is found alive in his possession— whether ox or donkey or sheep—he must pay back double.

95 To be specific, Chesterton said:

> The truth is that exploration and enlargement make the world smaller. The telegraph and the steamboat make the world smaller. The telescope makes the world smaller; it is only the microscope that makes it larger. Before long the world will be cloven with a war between the telescopists and the microscopists. The first study large things and live in a small world; the second study small things and live in a large world.

David Dooley (ed), *The Collected Works of G.K. Chesterton,* vol 1: *On Mr. Rudyard Kipling* (Ignatius Press: San Francisco, 1986), p 61.

Chesterton's point was that the seemingly large world and large ideas of the well travelled internationalist were only another variety of 'splendid parochialism', a parochialism hidden under international garb. My point is that every ardent libertarian is in fact a closet moralist; that inside every freewheeling libertarian chanting 'Freedom! Freedom!' at the merest hint of an 'imposed morality' lies the heart of a moralist straining to be let out—but not so eager to let his presence be known.

96   See William Dannemeyer, *Shadow in the Land* (Ignatius Press: San Francisco, 1989), p 15.

97   Gore Vidal, 'The State of the Union' in *Matters of Fact and Fiction* (Granada Publishing: London, 1978), pp 311-312.

98   H.L.A. Hart, *Law, Liberty and Morality* (Oxford University Press: Oxford, 1986), p 27.

99   Noel Malcolm, 'The Reason Why the Conservative Party Needs Lesbian Street Theatres', *The Spectator* (17 October 1987), p 6.

100 Quoted in Patrick Devlin, *The Enforcement of Morals* (Oxford University Press: Oxford, 1987), p 103.

101 *Ibid*, pp 2-3.

102 *Ibid*, pp 9-11.

103 A curious example of this is found in America's Civil War. In executing this war, fought to establish freedom for black slaves, Lincoln found it necessary to limit other citizens' freedoms. He called for the suspension of the rights of habeas corpus (now Americans could be thrown into prison on the virtual whim of a government official!). Americans' freedom of speech and freedom of association were limited in the cause of freedom!

104 John Pollock, *Wilberforce* (Lion Publishing: Berkhamsted, 1978), p 283.

105 *Evening Standard* (9 June 1988), p 3.

106 James Madison, *A Memorial and Remonstrance* in Marvin Meyers (ed), *The Mind of the Founder* (University Press of New England: Hanover, 1981), p 7.

107 John Calvin (translated by Beveridge) *Institutes of the Christian Religion* (Eerdmans: Grand Rapids, Michigan, 1981), Book 1, ch 2, para 1, at 40; as quoted in Gary Amos, 'Biblical Principles of Government: America a Case Study, 1987', p 107, Regent University, Virginia Beach.

108 Stanley N. Katz, introduction to William Blackstone, *Commentaries on the Laws of England*, vol 1 (University of Chicago Press: Chicago, 1979), p iii.

109 William Blackstone, *op cit*, pp 38-39.

110 See the order of redemption at work in Matthew 16:17 (where Peter comes to understand Christ's redemptive nature through personal revelation from his Father in heaven) and Luke 7:36ff (where a sinful woman finds redemption in the only way possible—through grace and forgiveness).

111 Quoted in William Buckley, Jr, 'Did You Ever See a Dream Walking?' in William Buckley, Jr, and C.R. Walker (eds), *Keeping the Tablets* (Harper & Row: New York, 1988), p 25.

112 Not all political libertarians are moral relativists. Some hold tightly to

moral absolutes in personal morality but believe it is not the place of government to impose these on the populace. So, for instance, when Jimmy Carter was US President, he personally opposed abortion as evil but equally opposed imposing this standard on his fellow Americans.

113 Quoted in Devlin, *op cit*, p 107.
114 H.L. Mencken, 'The Believer', in *A Mencken Chrestomathy* (Vintage Books: New York, 1982), p 11.
115 Hart, *op cit*, p 82.

It is clear that Hart's two moral principles—avoiding human misery and maximising freedom—are by and large Western society's accepted moral code today; the code which guides our political endeavours. The Labour Party and the Conservative Party may disagree on particular policies but they are agreed on these two fundamental principles.

Just consider the terms used during the 1988 debate on Clause 28, a local government bill wherein Parliament sought to stop the promotion of homosexuality by councils and schools. Michael Howard, the Conservative Minister of State for the Environment, said that it was no part of the government's intention to affect the civil rights of anybody. He said the clause was designed to prevent 'discrimination—discrimination in favour of a particular purpose, the promotion of homosexuality'. The minister here performs mental and verbal gymnastics in order to appear on the right side of freedom. He desperately lays hold of those two key buzz words, 'rights' and 'discrimination', and twists them to his purposes (the bill clearly had little to do with discrimination and everything to do with teaching the children what was right and wrong). He, by all means, does not want to appear to be restricting human freedom, when, of course, that is exactly what his legislation is advocating. Laws by their very nature have to discriminate against what is wrong and harmful.

One cannot criticise the minister for his gymnastics—given our present political climate it was probably a very tactful move—but one can rue an impoverished political discourse that knows nothing but the language of rights, has lost the concept of moral duties, and must force everything into the language of freedom.

Surely Isaiah Berlin's strictures are apropos here:

> Nothing is gained by a confusion of terms. To avoid glaring inequalities or widespread misery I am ready to sacrifice some or all of my freedom; I may do so willingly and freely; but it is freedom that I am giving up for the sake of justice or equality or the love of my fellow men.... Everything is what it is; liberty is liberty, not equality or fairness or justice or human happiness or a quiet conscience.

Quoted in Ferdinand Mount, 'Small mind and less Logic', *The Spectator* (14 July 1990), p 24.

[116] Vidal, 'The Top Ten Best Sellers' in *op cit*, p 30.

[117] Quoted in Devlin, *op cit*, p 12.

[118] Willmoore Kendall, *The Conservative Affirmation* (Henry Regnery: Chicago, 1963), p 116.

[119] Quoted in Charles Colson, *Kingdoms in Conflict* (William Morrow and Zondervan, 1987), p 101.

[120] Swedish Information Service, *The Anti-spanking Law: Text of the Law Background* (Swedish Consulate General: New York), p 3.

[121] David Dooley (ed), *The Collected Works of G.K. Chesterton*, vol 1: *Orthodoxy* (Ignatius Press: San Francisco, 1986), p 310.

[122] Quoted in Irving Bernstein, 'Patrician Conservatism: Mr. Justice Holmes' in Cushing Strout (ed), *Intellectual History in America*, vol II (Harper & Row: New York, 1968), p 90.

[123] *Ibid*.

[124]   Whereas the late King James the Second, by the assistance of divers evil counsellors...did endeavour to subvert and extirpate the protestant religion, and the laws and liberties of this kingdom....   cruel   punishments   inflicted....   The   prince   of Orange...the glorious instrument of delivering this kingdom from popery and arbitrary power.

See the 'Bill of Rights' in Richard L. Perry (ed), *Sources of Our Liberties* (American Bar Foundation: Chicago, 1978), pp 245-246.

[125] The declaration states:

If it was possible for men, who exercise their reason to believe, that the divine Author of our existence intended a part of the human race to hold an absolute property in, and an unbounded power over others, marked out by his infinite goodness and wisdom, as the objects of a legal domination never rightfully resistible, however severe and oppressive, the inhabitants of these colonies might at least require from the parliament of Great-Britain some evidence, that this dreadful authority over them, has been granted to that body. But a reverence for our great Creator, principles of humanity, and the dictates of common sense, must convince all those who reflect upon the subject, that government was instituted to promote the welfare of mankind, and ought to be administered for the attainment of that end. The legislature of Great-Britain, however, stimulated by an inordinate passion for a power not only unjustifiable, but which they know to be peculiarly reprobated by the very constitution of that kingdom, and desparate [sic] of success in any mode of contest, where regard should be had to truth, law, right have at length, deserting those, attempted to effect their cruel and impolitic purose of enslaving these colonies by violence, and have thereby rendered it necessary for us to close with their last appeal from reason to arms.

See 'Declaration of the Causes and Necessity of Taking Up Arms' in Perry, *op cit*, p 295.

126 Daniel J. Boorstin, *Mysterious Science of the Law* (Boston, 1958), p ii, as quoted in Gertrude Himmelfarb, 'Bentham Versus Blackstone' in *Marriage and Morals Among the Victorians* (Vintage Books: New York, 1987), p 110.

127 Himmelfarb, *op cit*, p 108.

128 Blackstone, *op cit*, pp 41-42.

129 'Declaration of Independence' in Perry, *op cit*, p 319.

130 Quoted in Himmelfarb, *op cit*, p 103.

131 Jeremy Bentham, 'Principles of Morals and Legislation', in William Ebenstein (ed), *Great Political Thinkers* (Holt, Rhinehart & Winston: New York, 1969), p 516.

132 See William Ebenstein, 'Bentham', in *Great Political Thinkers*, p 509.

133 *Ibid*.

134 See Himmelfarb, *op cit*, p 103.

135 George Will, *The Morning After* (The Free Press: New York, 1986), pp 178-179.

136 Michael Novak, *Free Persons and the Common Good* (Madison Books: New York, 1989), p 23.

137 This does not, I would argue, mean that biblical knowledge is irrelevant to agricultural development. Rather, it means that its relevance is of a broader sort. The Bible, although not a farmer's almanac, did contribute to agricultural development by setting the scene for its development. In giving manual work a value it did not have in ancient cultures and in establishing a worldview where natural cause-and-effect relationships prevailed, the Bible gave the needed stimulus to a scientific and technological revolution which gives us in the twentieth century the capacity to feed the world several times over.

138 Albert M. Wolters, *Creation Regained* (Eerdmans: Grand Rapids, Michigan, 1985), p 28.

139 Demos Shakarian, *The Happiest People on Earth* (Hodder & Stoughton: London), pp 162-163.

140 Os Guinness, *The Gravedigger File* (Inter-Varsity Press: Downer's Grove, Illinois, 1983), p 35.

141 Norman Vincent Peale, *The Positive Power of Jesus Christ* (Hodder & Stoughton: London, 1985), pp 42-45.

142 John Pollock, *Shaftesbury: The Poor Man's Earl* (Hodder & Stoughton: London, 1985), p 137.

143 John Pollock, *Shaftesbury: The Poor Man's Earl* (Hodder & Stoughton: London, 1985), p 113.

[144] Charles Colson, *Who Speaks for God?* (Crossway Books: Westchester, Illinois, 1985), pp 55-56.

[145] Charles Colson, *Kingdoms in Conflict* (William Morrow and Zondervan, 1987), p 283.

[146] Quoted in William F. Buckley, Jr, and Charles R. Kesler (eds), *Keeping the Tablets* (Harper & Row: New York, 1988), p 10.

[147] Quoted in A. James Reichley, *Religion in American Public Life* (Washington, DC, 1985), p 105.

[148] Quoted in Michael Novak, *Free Persons and the Common Good* (Madison Books: New York, 1989), p 50.

[149] The Victorians repealed the Test Act preventing Catholic and Protestant non-conformists from holding state or municipal office. They also opened the universities to men of all creeds. Prior to 1871, Catholics, for instance, were not allowed into either Oxford or Cambridge.

[150] Gertrude Himmelfarb, *Victorian Values* (Centre for Policy Studies: London, 1987), pp 14-15.

[151] Quoted in Garth Lean, *Strangely Warmed* (Tyndale House: Wheaton, Illinois, 1979), p 100.

[152] *Ibid*.

[153] Quoted in George F. Will, *The Morning After* (Free Press: New York, 1986), p 367.

[154] Daniel Bell, *The Cultural Contradictions of Capitalism* (Heinemann: London, 1979), p 15.

[155] *Ibid*, pp 28-30.

[156] Quoted in Charles Colson, *Kingdoms in Conflict* (Morrow and Zondervan, 1987), p 221.

[157] Paul Johnson, *Modern Times* (Harper & Row: New York, 1983), p 296.

Commandant Hess of Auschwitz has been described in the following terms:

> Among his most outstanding characteristics were a strict attention to detail, unselfishness, love of Nature, sentimentality, even a certain helpfulness and kindliness, simplicity, and finally a marked hankering after morality.

Quoted in Peter Vanstittart's introduction to John Buchan, *These For Remembrance* (Buchan & Enright: London, 1987). He had a morality, just the wrong one.

[158] Anthony Daniels, 'Born Again Guerillas', *The Spectator* (30 April 1988), p 19.

[159] *Ibid*.

[160] Johnson, *op cit*, p 168.

161 Gertrude Himmelfarb, *Marriage and Morals Among the Victorians* (Vintage Books: New York, 1987), pp 34, 36.

162 *Ibid*, p 28.

163 *Ibid*.

164 Herbert Schlossberg, *Idols For Destruction* (Nelson: New York, 1983), p 10.

It should be noted that, although Schlossberg here urges a third way, in a more recent letter to the author he wrote, 'I used this language [re the 'third way'] once in *Idols For Destruction*, but have since become disabused with the idea.'

165 Andrew Walker, *Enemy Territory* (Hodder & Stoughton: London, 1987), p 251.

166 Harry Blamires, *The Christian Mind* (Servant Books: Ann Arbor, Michigan, 1978), p 3.

167 Blamires writes, 'We have no Christian vocabulary to match the complexities of contemporary political, social, and industrial life. How should we have? A language is nurtured on usage, not on silence, however high-principled.' See Blamires, *op cit*, p 27.

168 *Ibid*, p 130.

169 *Ibid*, p 125.

170 *Ibid*, p 156.

171 Gary North, *An Introduction to Christian Economics* (Craig Press: Nutley, New Jersey, 1979), p ix.

172 Paul Marshall, *Thine Is The Kingdom* (Marshall, Morgan & Scott: Basingstoke, 1984), p 5.

173 *Ibid*, p 76.

174 Albert M. Wolters, *Creation Regained* (Eerdmans: Grand Rapids, Michigan, 1985), p 49.

175 Noel Malcolm, 'Playing happy families with the next manifesto', *The Spectator* (14 July 1990), p 6.

176 Blamires, *op cit*, p 3.

177 Karl Marx, 'The Communist Manifesto' in William Ebenstein (ed), *Great Political Thinkers* (Holt, Rhinehart & Winston: New York, 1969), p 730.

178 Jacques Ellul, *The Betrayal of the West* (Seabury Press: New York, 1978), p 17.

Ellul, Professor of Law and History at the University of Bordeaux, writes:

The essential, central, undeniable fact is that the West was the first civilization in history to focus attention on the individual and on freedom.... After all, we find justice, equality, and peace everywhere. Every civilization that has attained a certain level has claimed to be a civilization of justice and peace. But which of them has ever spoken of the individual? Which of them [save the West] has been reflectively conscious of freedom as a value? (*Ibid*, pp 17, 30.)

Ellul is far from being a chauvinistic champion of all things Western, a champion unwilling to see any of the West's faults and sins. His point is merely that the very real sins should not blind us to the very real contributions. He writes:

> If the world is everywhere rising up and accusing the West, if movements of liberation are everywhere under way, what accounts for this?... Today men point the finger of outrage at slavery and torture. Where did that kind of indignation originate? What civilization or culture cried out that slavery was unacceptable and torture scandalous? Not Islam or Buddhism, or Confucius, or Zen, or the religious and moral codes of Africa and India. The West alone has defended the inalienable rights of the human person (*Ibid*, pp 17-18).

[179] Michael Novak paints a scarifying picture of a pagan society—the Incan empire—possessed of a very firm concept of the rule of law-as-order. He writes:

> Every aspect of every Incan life was controlled from the top. Everyone reported to someone. Privacy was forbidden. To facilitate supervision, doors of peasant cottages had to be kept open even during the eating of meals. All land and utensils belonged to the state. Private property was forbidden. Each person received two cloaks, of color identical for all within the same region. Neither money nor trade was permitted. Private initiative was wholly eliminated and private life was regulated in minutest details. Marriage was by official decree, on scheduled occasions, between spouses chosen by the ruling Incas. The state distributed concubines.... The cardinal principle was uniformity. Citizens lived in identical houses on identical blocks, wore identical clothing, used identical utensils, walked identical roads, and worked in identical public buildings. The impression was of an awesome prison.

See Michael Novak, *Will It Liberate?* (Paulist Press: New York, 1986), p 185.

[180] In Deuteronomy 17:18–20 Jehovah lays down, as a perpetual rule for the kings of Israel, that:

> When he takes the throne of his kingdom, he is to write for himself on a scroll a copy of this law, taken from that of the priests, who are Levites. It is to be with him, and he is to read it all the days of

his life so that he may learn to revere the Lord his God and follow carefully all the words of this law and these decrees and not consider himself better than his brothers and turn from the law to the right or to the left. Then he and his descendants will reign a long time over his kingdom in Israel.

181 Aristotle, 'Politics', in Ebenstein, *op cit*, p 100.
    The fuller context of the quote is this:

> If, however, there be some one person, or more than one, although not enough to make up the full complement of a state, whose virtue is so preeminent that the virtues or the political capacity of all the rest admit of no comparison with his or theirs, he or they can be no longer regarded as part of a state; for justice will not be done to the superior, if he is reckoned only as the equal of those who are so far inferior to him in virtue and in political capacity. Such an one may truly be deemed a God among men. Hence we see that legislation is necessarily concerned only with those who are equal in birth and in capacity; and that for men of preeminent virtue there is no law.

182 Richard Tuck, *Natural Rights Theories* (Cambridge University Press: Cambridge, 1979), p 35.
183 This is Richard Strauss' view:

> It is reasonable to assume that Cicero's seemingly unqualified acceptance of the Stoic natural law teaching has the same motivation as Atticus...in order not to present his real views too openly.... It is then misleading to call Cicero an adherent of the Stoic natural law teaching.

See Richard Strauss, *Natural Right and History* (University of Chicago Press: Chicago, 1953), pp 154-156.
    And certainly the Renaissance humanists did not consider Cicero a proponent of natural law thinking. Tuck writes:

> Humanist lawyers found it virtually impossible to talk about natural rights, and extremely difficult to talk about rights *tout court*. What was important to them was not natural law but humanly constructed law; not natural rights but civil remedies.... The *locus classicus* for the picture of the natural life of man which was to become a commonplace for the early sixteenth-century juridical humanists was the first pages of Cicero's *De Inventione*.

See Tuck, *op cit*, p 33.

[184] J. Rufus Fears (ed), *Selected Writings of Lord Acton*, vol 1: *Essays in the History of Liberty* (Liberty Classics: Indianapolis, 1986), p 28. Lord Acton said:

> When Christ said, 'Render unto Caesar...' those words...were the repudiation of absolutism and the inauguration of freedom.... The new law, the new spirit, the new authority, gave to liberty a meaning and a value it had not possessed in the philosophy or in the constitution of Greece or Rome before the knowledge of the truth that makes us free.

[185] *Ibid*, vol 3, *Essays in Religion, Politics, and Morality* (Liberty Classics: Indianapolis, 1988), p 522.

[186] William Ebenstein, *John of Salisbury* in Ebenstein, *op cit*, p 190. Writing in the same vein, John Courtney Murray, SJ, comments:

> It is an historical commonplace to say that the essential political effect of Christianity was to destroy the classical view of society as a single homogenous structure, within which the political power stood forth as the representative of society both in its religious and in its political aspects.

John Courtney Murray, SJ, *We Hold These Truths* (Sheed and Ward: New York, 1960), p 202. Would that this was an historical commonplace. Many of us do not know our own Christian heritage and just how it has contributed to the positive development of Western civilisation.

[187] M.I. Finley, *Democracy Ancient and Modern* (Hogarth Press: London, 1985), p 115.

[188] Thomas Collett Sanders, introduction to Thomas Collett Sanders (ed), *The Institutes of Justinian* (Greenwood Press: Westport, Connecticut, 1970), p x.

This Roman marriage between 'church and state' (we use the term loosely as, quite obviously, there was no church before the birth of Christ) can be seen, for instance, in the political climb of Julius Caesar. Plutarch reports:

> Metellus the high priest, died, and Catallus and Isauricus, persons...who had great influence in the senate, were competitors for the office, yet Caesar would not give way to them, but presented himself to the people as a candidate [for the high priesthood] against them.

To Caesar and the rest of the Romans, religion was but a subset of state life; it was merely another expression of political life. By the way,

Caesar won the election. See Plutarch (translated by John Dryden), *Plutarch's Lives* (Modern Library), p 85.

189 Numa Denis Fustel de Coulanges, *The Ancient City: A Study on the Religion, Laws, and Institutions of Greece and Rome* (Doubleday: New York), pp 219, 220, 222.

190 Gelasius I wrote to the Byzantine emperor Anastasius I in AD 494: 'Two there are, august Emperor, by which this world is ruled on title of original and sovereign right—the consecrated authority of the priesthood and the royal power.' Quoted in Murray, *op cit*, p 202.

191 Harold J. Berman, *Law and Revolution: The Formation of the Western Legal Tradition* (Harvard University Press: Cambridge, Massachusetts, 1983).

Berman contends that 'the Western legal tradition has been transformed in the course of its history by six great revolutions...the Russian...the French...the American...the English...the Protestant Reformation...the Papal Revolution'. *Ibid*, pp 18-19.

192 Elisha Williams, 'The Essential Rights and Liberties of Protestants', in Ellis Sandoz (ed), *Political Sermons of the American Founding Era: 1730–1805* (Liberty Press: Indianapolis, 1991), p 55.

193 Laski, introduction to *op cit*, p 27.

194 King Ine was a famous warrior, ecclesiastical benefactor and legislator who, the Venerable Bede tells us, retired at the end of his life to Rome in order to better prepare himself 'for a more friendly reception in heaven'. See *Encyclopedia Americana*, 1988 ed, sv 'Ine'; William Smith and Henry Wace (eds), vol III, *A Dictionary of Christian Biography* (Kraus Reprint Co: Millwood, New York, 1974), sv 'Ine', pp 236-240.

King Alfred was another king combining both military prowess and a deep devotional life. He defeated the Danish king Guthrum who, afterwards, became so impressed with Alfred's faith that he himself freely underwent baptism. King Alfred constructed a code of law after studying King Ine's codes and after studying the principle of lawgiving in the Book of Exodus. See *The New Encyclopaedia Britannica*, vol 1 Miropaedia, 1986 ed, sv 'Alfred'.

195 Historian G.M. Trevelyan focuses on the archbishop's key role, saying:

> Stephen Langton was an enlightened guide to his baronial allies.... The Barons in arms who extorted it [Magna Carta] from King John at Runnymede were none of them, so far as we know, remarkable men, but their ally, the Archbishop Stephen Langton, had both moral and intellectual greatness. He was all the greater man because his support to the constitutional cause was contrary to the wishes of the great Pope Innocent III.

See G.M. Trevelyan, *A Shortened History of England* (Penguin: London, 1988), p 146.

Langton seems to have been like the Kings Ine and Alfred in his combination of both political insight and devotional depth. His contributions were more than just political. He was an outstanding professor of theology at the University of Paris for twenty-five years. Langton is also known as the man who first had the Vulgate Old Testament divided into chapters, a system which was subsequently applied to the Greek New Testament and Septuagint as well. See *Collier's Encyclopedia*, 1986 ed, sv 'Langton, Stephen'.

[196] The Franciscans, of course, as followers of St Francis of Assisi, weighed in on the anti-property side, saying that there was no natural right of private property. We could have right of use without there being any actual right of ownership. The Dominicans followed Thomas Aquinas who said there was such a right.

The legal influence of theology in the medieval era is understandable given the fact that the medieval 'Church as a whole...became not so much a divine society as a legal one'. See Paul Johnson, *A History of Christianity* (Weidenfeld & Nicolson, 1977), p 206. Historian R.W. Southern points out the intriguing fact that 'every notable pope from 1159 to 1303 was a lawyer', and goes on to state that the 'fundamental order of medieval, and to a large extent of modern, society owes a great debt to these popes'. See R.W. Southern, *The Middle Ages* (Penguin: Middlesex, 1985), pp 131-132.

[197] Calvinists, facing government-sponsored persecution, began to develop resistance theories that built on the less developed contract theories of some of the earlier Catholic theologians. The concept of covenant was absolutely central to these Calvinist thinkers. Two of the best known works on Calvinist resistance theories were France's *Vindiciae contra tyrannos* (1579) and Samuel Rutherford's *Lex Rex* (1644), both of which looked to scriptures such as 1 Chronicles 11:3 and 2 Kings 11:17 to establish that government was founded on a twofold covenant: the one between people and the sovereign, the other between the people together with the sovereign and God. The point for the resisters was that any contract being substantially breached released the subjects from their obligations.

[198] Paul Johnson, *Modern Times* (Harper & Row: New York, 1983), p 177. Johnson also writes:

> Until 1945 it [Japan] had no system of fixed law. It had maxims, behavioural codes, concepts of justice expressed in ideograms.... But it had no proper penal code; no system of statutory law.... The relationship between authority and those subject to it was hidden, often on important points.... It [the constitution] did not impose a definite system of rights and duties.... The law was not sovereign (*Ibid*, p 177).

Along these lines we note the anecdote Dutch scholar Ian Buruma tells of an incident in Japan where he was knocking about as the only foreigner in a Japanese theatre group. He got along with the troupe famously until one night, after

> the usual drunken party ended in bloodshed, as the producer, Kara Juro, banged a sake bottle against the nose of a film actor, then hurled a heavy glass ashtray at his Korean wife. At this point [I]...shouted at the producer, 'Don't throw things at women.'... Kara never forgave me. I had betrayed his expectations. By breaking the code of expected behaviour, by challenging the leader to his face, by standing up, however absurdly, as an individual, by claiming to speak out for higher principles, by suddenly behaving like a Westerner, I had betrayed Kara, betrayed the group.

Quoted in Richard West, review of Ian Buruma, *God's Dust: A Modern Asian Journey*, *The Spectator* (11 November 1989): p 54.

199 Karl Marx, 'The Communist Manifesto', in Ebenstein, *op cit*, p 732.

Marx thought that there was no connection between civil law and eternal, divine (or natural) law:

> Your very ideas are but the outgrowth of the conditions of your bourgeois production and bourgeois property, just as your jurisprudence is but the will of your class made into a law for all, a will whose essential character and direction are determined by the economic conditions of existence of your class (*Ibid*, p 732).

Ideas don't have consequences; ideas are consequences!

200 *Ibid*.

201 Soviet historians Mikhail Heller and Aleksandr Nekrich write:

> Arrests...were based on regional and district quotas. Planning applied to this area, too. Vladimir Petrov...recalls the text of some telegrams sent out at the time: 'Funze. NKVD. You are charged with exterminating 10,000 enemies of the people. Report results by signal. Ezhov.'

Mikhail Heller and Aleksandr M. Nekrich, *Utopia in Power* (Summit Books: New York, 1986), p 303.

202 Quoted in Heller and Nekrich, *op cit*, p 626.

203 Edward Hallett Carr, former deputy editor of *The Times*, characterised his own political stance as one of 'realism'.

> 'Realism' meant that in evaluating history's handiwork one must set aside one's moral scruples and repeat, with Hegel, that 'what-

ever is real, is rational.' In 1939, Carr's 'realistic' acceptance of German hegemony led him to endorse the Munich Agreement of 1938, calling it 'the nearest approach in recent years to the settlement of a major issue by a procedure of peaceful change.'

See Joseph Shattan, review of Leopold Labedz, *The Use and Abuse of Sovietology*, *American Spectator* (October 1988), p 44.

[204] *Congressional Record*, 15 November 1989, H 8633.

[205] Jean Francois Revel, 'The Two Kinds of Memory', in Franky Schaeffer (ed), *Is Capitalism Christian?* (Crossway: Westchester, Illinois, 1985), p 143.

Of course, with the benefit of 20-20 hindsight, it is easy now to pillory Chancellor Schmidt. As someone commented, 'Revolutions are declared impossible before they happen and inevitable afterwards.'

[206] William F. Buckley, Jr, 'The Week', *National Review* (19 November 1990), p 17.

[207] Quoted in William F. Buckley, Jr, *On The Firing Line* (Random House: New York, 1989), p 128.

[208] One journalist puts a mischievous twist to Clausewitz's aphorism when describing Nelson Mandela's 1990 grand tour through the United States as 'the continuation of show business by other means'. See 'A Man, Not An Icon', *The Spectator* (7 July 1990), p 5.

[209] Richard John Neuhaus, *The Naked Public Square* (Eerdmans: Grand Rapids, Michigan, 1984), p 146.

[210] Emma Gilbey, 'God On His Ticket', *The Spectator* (4 October 1986): p 14.

[211] Quoted by Richard John Neuhaus, 'What the Fundamentalists Want', in Richard John Neuhaus and Michael Cromartie (eds), *Piety and Politics* (Ethics and Public Policy Center: Washington, DC, 1987), p 6.

[212] *Wall Street Journal* (4 March 1988), pp 1, 17.

[213] Christopher Hitchens, 'Voting For The Millennium', *The Spectator* (7 June 1986), p 14.

It is an unfortunate that, when attempting to dispel such stereotypes, one has to note that Hitchen's comments were printed *before* the misproprieties of TV preachers Swaggart and Bakker came to light. It is difficult to dispel prejudices while simultaneously living up to them.

[214] Modern people's fear of religious repression is exaggerated but, unfortunately, not baseless. Indeed, staunch Protestant Oliver Cromwell's slaughter of 2,000 to 4,000 Irish Catholics at Drogheda was a textbook example of Pascal's dictum. Cromwell, upon completing the massacre, soothed himself with these reflections:

This is a righteous judgement of God upon these barbarous wretches, who have imbued their hands in so much innocent blood... it will tend to prevent the effusion of blood for the future, which are satisfactory grounds to such actions, which otherwise cannot but work remorse and grief.

215 Quoted in Antonia Fraser, *Cromwell: Our Chief of Men* (Granada Publishing: London, 1981), p 326.

215 R. Emmett Tyrell, Jr, 'Swaggart's Sweat', *The American Spectator* (April 1988), p 10.

216 For instance, the paedophile magazine *Minor Problems* editorialises in favour of the 'rights of children to have sex with adults'; a clever way of saying 'the right of adults to have sex with infants'. See Maurice Chittenden and Rosie Waterhouse, 'Porn group tries to link up with child charity', *The Sunday Times* (29 November 1987).

217 Quentin Cowdry, 'Straw attacks "far-Left bigots" ', *The Daily Telegraph* (2 July 1988).

218 *Wall Street Journal* (4 March 1988), pp 1, 17.

219 Richard Hofstadter, *Anti-Intellectualism in American Life* (Vintage Books: New York, 1963), pp 134-135.

220 'For Your Prayer Time', The McKeever Prayer letter (April 1987).

221 *Time* (22 February 1988), p 28.

222 Martin Roe, 'Prime Time President', *Blitz* (August 1987), p 77.

223 David E. Gardner, *The Trumpet Sounds For Britain*, vol 2 (Christian Foundation Publications: Altrincham, Cheshire, 1983), pp 49-52.

224 The source of this information is John Pollock, *Shaftesbury* (Hodder & Stoughton: London, 1985), p 54.

225 Dick Murray, 'Mother wins fight to put God in school', *Evening Standard* (3 April 1991).

226 Quoted from Hubert Morken, preliminary draft of paper, 'Religious Lobbying at the State Level: Case Studies in a Continuing Role for the New Religious Right', presented at the American Political Science Association Annual Meeting, San Francisco, September 1990, p 3 (see Appendix).

227 *Ibid*, pp 3-4.

228 *Ibid*.

229 Quoted in James LeMoyne, 'Three Men Who Took Aim at Rap Group', *New York Times* (12 June 1990): A14.

230 The *New York Times*, in reporting on 2 Live Crew's obscenity trial, summed up the contents of the album in these words:

> The album consists almost solely of relentlessly coarse accounts of the singer's lusts and sexual adventures. Typically the singer brags about the physical power of his penis, refers to a woman in terms of her genitalia and commands the woman—usually addressed as 'bitch'—to gratify his various sexual desires.

Sara Rimer, 'Rap Band Members Found Not Guilty In Obscenity Trial', *New York Times* (21 October 1990): A30.

[231] Michael Schwartz, 'Parent Power', *Empowerment* (January 1991), pp 4-6.

[232] Perhaps Flaubert's salutary warning concerning the risks inherent in the role of perpetual gadfly should be remembered: 'By dint of railing at idiots, one runs the risk of become idiotic oneself.'

[233] The labelling law required record producers to put a warning on album covers notifying the purchaser, or parent, that the contents contained so-called adult lyrics.

[234] This is an American term referring to novice legislators in their first term of office.

[235] Tipper Gore is the wife of the Democratic Senator from Tennessee, Albert Gore. She is the president of Parents' Music Resource Center (PMRC). PMRC advocated voluntary labelling by record companies; they would have nothing to do with state mandated labelling.

[236] Tipper Gore is the wife of Albert Gore, considered by some to be a presidential hopeful in 1992.

[237] Morken, *op cit*, pp 5-8.

[238] On government-sponsored bills the party Whip tells his party how to vote. Party members are expected to follow suit. On Private Members' bills, the MPs can simply vote their conscience.

[239] An Early Day Motion is not a formal bill proposing the passage of law. Rather, it is an expression of an opinion and a call to action.

[240] This was the title of a book published in 1948 by Richard Weaver, Professor of English at the University of Chicago.

[241] Alexis de Tocqueville once pointed out Christianity's unique contribution to Western civilisation, saying:

> The most profound and capacious minds of Rome and Greece were never able to reach the idea, at once so general and so simple, of the common likeness of men and of the common birthright of each to freedom; they tried to prove that slavery was in the order of nature.... the advent of Jesus Christ upon earth was required to teach that all the members of the human race are by nature equal and alike.

Alexis de Tocqueville, *Democracy in America* (Alfred A. Knopf: New York, 1976), vol II, p 15.

Pagan Greece and Rome may have given much to Western culture, but on the matter of liberty and individuality—the very elements which make Western political models so admired and emulated by other, non-Western cultures—they had little to offer.

Some might wonder just how the 'advent of Jesus Christ upon earth' had an effect upon social and political structures. After all, Jesus came preaching a spiritual kingdom, not a political kingdom. Perhaps a snapshot of an eighteenth-century encounter between gospel preaching and the prejudices of the day will help us here. The Duchess of Buckingham, illegitimate daughter of James II, once wrote to Lady Huntingdon, ardent supporter of the Methodists, saying:

> I thank Your Ladyship for the information concerning the Methodist preachers: their doctrines are most repulsive, strongly tinctured with Impertinence and Disrespect towards their Superiors, in perpetually endeavouring to level all Ranks, and do away with all Distinctions. It is monstrous to be told that you have a heart as *sinful* as the Common Wretches that crawl on Earth. This is highly offensive and insulting; and I can not but wonder that Your Ladyship should relish any Sentiment so much at variance with High Rank and Good Breeding.

Quoted in Garth Lean, *Strangely Warmed* (Tyndale House: Wheaton, Illinois, 1979), p 84.

In the Duchess' aristocratic view of the world, some were natural inferiors and others were natural superiors. The gospel, on the other hand, depicted all people as equals—equally created by God and equally sinners. Although this was primarily a spiritual message, it had clear social implications—implications which the Duchess of Buckingham immediately recognised and instantly resented. She knew that if she was the equal of other sinners in a matter so fundamental as salvation then she was fundamentally equal to the common herd; the pretence of inherent superiority would have to be dropped.

Western society was transformed as past Christian thinkers explored and applied the political and social implications of the biblical worldview.

242 Raymond Johnston, former Director of England's Care Campaigns, helpfully points out that even God's negatives (be the negatives government restraints or the divine restraints of Scripture—the 'Thou shalt nots' of the Ten Commandments) have, in fact, a positive orientation. He writes:

> Yet a negative is merely the reverse side of a positive. The Commandments protect good and beautiful things. One can rephrase them. 'Thou shalt not murder' can be rephrased as 'Thou shalt respect and regard as holy the image of God in the life of every other man'—life is a sacred thing. 'Thou shalt not commit adultery' becomes 'Thou shalt respect thy neighbour's marriage'— marriage as God gave it us is a bond between husband and wife which is meant to exclude all others. Every one of God's positives has a negative which protects it.

Raymond Johnston, *Caring and Campaigning* (William Collins Sons & Co: London, 1990), pp 44-45.

[243] Colonel V. Doner, *The Samaritan Strategy* (Wolgemuth & Hyatt: Brentwood, Tennessee, 1988), pp 42, 219.

[244] *Ibid*, p 214.

[245] When Jesus wanted to emphasise the lowest spiritual standard possible he reached for the tax collectors, saying, 'even tax collectors do that' (when teaching on loving the unlovely, Matthew 5:46) or 'even the tax collectors... acknowledged that God's way was right' (Lk 7:29). Yet it was these tax collectors, considered low-lifes and scum by the general populace, to whom Jesus ministered. See Luke 19:1-10; Matthew 11:19; 9:9-12.

[246] In Luke 19 we read of a sympathetic crowd of Jerichoites streaming out of their town to welcome Jesus as he came to teach and minister to them. The mood quickly turned ugly, however, when Jesus showed special interest in Zacchaeus, that tax-collecting traitorous friend of the oppressive Romans. Zacchaeus was not just unpopular with the Pharisees, he was resented and hated by 'the people'. But Jesus had not come to minister to certain popular or widely acceptable forms of sin; he had come to minister to all sins, no matter how socially disreputable.

[247] The Department of Gay and Lesbian Studies, University of Utrecht, reports: 'Laws against all gay sex... still apply in Ireland, Jersey, the Isle of Man, Gibraltar, Vatican City, and Cyprus, as well as in four parts of Yugoslavia, in the 15 republics of the Soviet Union, and in Rumania.' Kees Waaldijk, *Tip of an Iceberg: Anti-Lesbian and Anti-Gay Discrimination in Europe 1980-1990* (International Lesbian and Gay Association: Utrecht, 1990).

[248] The two arguments used most frequently by gay rights advocates are the privacy argument (that a man ought to be able to do what he wants in private) and the harm argument (that a man ought to do what he wants as long as he causes no harm). These arguments carry weight before justices in Europe as well as in America. *Bowers v Hardwick* (1986), an American Supreme Court case, was argued on these points as was the *Dudgeon case* (European Court HR, Series A no 45, 1981), a case in which the European Court of Human Rights held that Northern Ireland's law criminalising homosexual acts violated the European Convention of Human Rights—specifically, the Convention's Article 8 which stipulates that there 'shall be no interference by a public authority of this right... the right to respect for his private and family life....' The *Dudgeon case* was won on the argument that Mr Dudgeon, the homosexual being prosecuted, 'has suffered... an unjustified interference with his right to the respect for his *private* life' and that this interference lacked 'sufficient justification provided by the risk of *harm*' (*Dudgeon case*, para 60, 63; emphasis added).

Both the privacy arguments, as applied to homosexual acts, are attractive but ultimately unconvincing.

Yale University law professor Alexander Bickel used to pose a hypothetical question to Robert Bork: 'Suppose...that on an offshore island there lived a man who raised puppies entirely for the pleasure of torturing them to death. The rest of us are not required to witness the torture, nor can we hear the screams of the animals.' It is a private island; there is no public harm. Can we legislate? Of course we can, we do and we will continue to do so. Bickel comments: 'Moral outrage is a sufficient ground for prohibitory legislation.' Robert H. Bork, *The Tempting of America: the Political Seduction of the Law* (Free Press: New York, 1990), p 124. This is true even for acts done in private.

The harm argument is equally unpersuasive. Private homosexual acts do cause harm; they cause moral harm to the actors. One does not need evidence or proof for this; it is true by definition. By definition, any immoral act causes moral harm. Why should moral harm be considered less of a harm than physical harm? If moral harm is real then the harm perpetrated by immoral acts, even when in private, is real.

Consider, additionally, that immorality eventuates invariably in physical harm. This is immediately apparent in sexually transmitted diseases such as syphilis and AIDS. It is less immediately apparent in other cases. This lack of apparent, immediate harm is the root of professor at law Louis B. Schwartz's dismissal of morals legislation. He writes, concerning Amsterdam:

> No such [harmful] results impend from the commission of 'morals offenses.' One has only to stroll along certain streets in Amsterdam to see that prostitution may be permitted to flourish openly without impairing personal security, economic prosperity, or indeed the general moral tone of a most respected nation in the Western world.

Louis B. Schwartz, 'Morals Offenses and the Model Penal Code', in *Morality and the Law*, Richard A. Wasserstrom (ed), (Wadsworth Publishing: Belmont, California, 1971), p 87.

As I lived in Amsterdam for two years, I can speak with some knowledge on Schwartz's claim. All I can say is that it is evident that Professor Schwartz wrote his article in 1963, not in 1973. The Red Light district to which he refers became the cesspool of crime and degradation that is common to all such haunts. It is now a centre for drugs, muggings and police raids. One does not 'stroll along its streets', one marches warily watching one's back once night descends. Its sleazy atmosphere is the shame of all decent people in Holland, and so it ought to be.

249 G. Sidney Buchanan, 'Same-Sex Marriage: The Linchpin Issue', *University of Dayton Law Review* 10:3 (1985), p 560.

250 Homosexuals want more than mere toleration. The right to practise their personal lifestyles privately is not nearly enough. At a 1987 rally of homosexuals in Washington, DC, one speaker put it clearly:

> But our agenda is becoming broader than that: we are no longer seeking just a right to privacy and a protection from wrong. We also have a right...to see government and society affirm our lives.... [U]ntil our relationships are recognized in the law...we will not have achieved equality in American society.

Quoted in William Dannemeyer, *Shadow in the Land* (Ignatius Press: San Francisco, 1989), p 86.

251 Peter N. Fowler, 'Adult Adoption: A "New" Legal Tool for Lesbians and Gay Men', *Golden Gate University Law Review* 14 (1984), p 699.

252 The following details are from a phone conversation with Jeffrey Collins.

Caring For The Carers

by Christine Ledger

Caring means energy. It is not surprising, therefore, that long-term caring can become a physical and emotional assault-course for even the most compassionate person.

We can help those who look after others on a non-professional basis. Here some of them tell their own stories, before Christine Ledger—a carer herself both professionally and at home—goes on to suggest simple, realistic ways in which support and encouragement can be given to the unsung heroes of our society.

'An excellent, moving, practical, down-to-earth resource book for all those who are in the front line caring for family or friends, and for those who support them.'

DR PATRICK DIXON
Specialist in care of the dying and
Director, AIDS Care Education and Training

'A book that ought to be on every minister's shelves and in the home of any person who might one day find herself or himself at the point when caring passes into that area where they feel alone and forgotten.'
From the Foreword by **DR GEORGE CAREY**
Archbishop of Canterbury

This is part of a series of books published in association with CARE Trust, addressing the issues that call for political action and compassionate involvement and care.

 Kingsway Publications

False Images

by Nigel Williams

'Pornography is a false image of the true nature of men and women as God created us. Let us celebrate the positive and campaign against the negative with all our might.'

Nigel Williams challenges the glamorous profile awarded to so much pornography today, and reveals the truth behind the images that attract so many, especially men.

Whether it is television or video, newspapers or magazines, or other media now being exploited by pornographers, you can do more than shake your head in dismay or disapproval. Here are practical steps that can be taken in the fight against pornography.

'Nigel Williams has powerfully strengthened the hands of those seeking to put more muscle into our legal controls on pornography.'

—MICHAEL ALISON MP

NIGEL WILLIAMS is Campaigns Director of CARE (Christian Action Research and Education).

This is part of a series of books published in association with CARE Trust, addressing the issues that call for political action and compassionate involvement and care.

 Kingsway Publications

Schizophrenia: Voices In The Dark

by Mary Moate & Dr David Enoch

Schizophrenia is everyone's concern. It affects 1 in 100 people in their lifetime. Every year there are 6,000 new cases in Britain alone. This disease does not discriminate between sexes, cultures, societies, faiths or professions.

This book is for those who care for the mentally ill in families, churches and a wider community.

Mrs Mary Moate is the mother of Philip, a schizophrenic child whose story is so movingly told here. A member of the Salvation Army, she is a voluntary community worker.

Dr David Enoch is a leading Consultant Psychiatrist and Special Advisor to Mersey Regional Health Authority. He is author of *Healing the Hurt Mind*.

Revd Dr Nigel M de S Cameron, Care Series Editor, is Theological Research Consultant to CARE, Warden of Rutherford House in Edinburgh, and Editor of *Ethics and Medicine*. He travels internationally to speak on theology and ethics.

This is part of a series of books published in association with CARE Trust, addressing the issues that call for political action and compassionate involvement and care.

Kingsway Publications